In Her Prime

In Her Prime

New Views of Middle-Aged Women

Second Edition

Edited by

Virginia Kerns and Judith K. Brown

University of Illinois Press
Urbana and Chicago

© 1992 by the Board of Trustees of the University of Illinois
Manufactured in the United States of America
1 2 3 4 5 C P 5 4 3 2 1

This book is printed on acid-free paper.

Library of Congress Cataloging-in-Publication Data

In her prime : new views of middle-aged women / edited by Virginia
Kerns and Judith K. Brown. — 2nd ed.
        p.   cm.
    Includes bibliographical references and index.
    ISBN 0-252-01839-7 (cl). — ISBN 0-252-06204-3 (pbk.)
    1. Middle aged women—Cross-cultural studies. I. Kerns,
Virginia, 1948– . II. Brown, Judith K.
GN479.7.I5 1992
305.4—dc20   91-9246
                                                        CIP

To
Pauline Kolenda
colleague, mentor, and friend

and
in memory of Nancy Datan
whose work illuminated women's lives

Contents

Foreword   ix
   Beatrice Blyth Whiting

1 Introduction: New Views of Middle-Aged Women   1
   Karen Brodkin Sacks
2 An Evolutionary Perspective on Menopause   7
   Jane B. Lancaster
   Barbara J. King
3 Lives of Middle-Aged Women   17
   Judith K. Brown

   PART 1   SMALL–SCALE TRADITIONAL SOCIETIES   31

4 Work, Sexuality, and Aging among !Kung Women   35
   Richard B. Lee
5 Middle-Aged Women in Bakgalagadi Society (Botswana)   49
   Jacqueline S. Solway
6 *Tamparonga:* "The Big Women" of Kaliai
   (Papua New Guinea)   61
   Dorothy Ayers Counts

   PART 2   INTERMEDIATE SOCIETIES   75

7 Motherhood and Other Careers in Mayotte (Comoro Islands)   77
   Michael Lambek

8 Female Control of Sexuality: Garífuna Women at Middle Age 95
Virginia Kerns

9 A Study in Pride and Prejudice: Maori Women at Midlife 113
Karen P. Sinclair

PART 3   COMPLEX SOCIETIES   139

10 Bucking the Agnatic System:
Status and Strategies in Rural Northern Sudan 141
Janice Boddy

11 Sexuality and the Middle-Aged Woman in South Asia 155
Sylvia Vatuk

12 A Diminished Dichotomy:
Kelantan Malay and Traditional Chinese Perspectives 173
Douglas Raybeck

PART 4   INDUSTRIALIZED SOCIETIES   191

13 Tradition, Modernity, and Transitions
in Five Israeli Subcultures 193
Nancy Datan
Aaron Antonovsky
Benjamin Maoz

14 "What Are Women For?": Cultural Constructions
of Menopausal Women in Japan and Canada 201
Patricia A. Kaufert
Margaret Lock

15 Beyond Nurture:
Developmental Perspectives on the Vital Older Woman 221
David Gutmann

Notes on Contributors   235
Index   239

Foreword

Beatrice Blyth Whiting

The ethnographic data presented in this volume will enable social scientists to assess the similarities and differences in the experiences of middle-aged women in a variety of societies. Judith K. Brown and Virginia Kerns are to be complimented for stimulating cross-cultural research on the development of women. Kerns's pioneering studies of older women (1979, 1980, 1983) are well known. Judith Brown's earlier research on rituals at menarche (1963, 1981) has stimulated detailed analyses of female transition ceremonies (e.g., Paige and Paige 1981). Her recent article in *Current Anthropology* (Brown 1982) was the impetus for the writing of the chapters collected in this volume. Tracing themes suggested in the article, they describe the status of women, their rights and privileges, and their daily routines during their middle years, a period of life that until recently has been neglected. In the popular media in the United States "middle age" has often been characterized as a period of depression and aimlessness, concerned with the loss of children, beauty, and sexual pleasure. This volume presents a welcomed new perspective.

Anthropologists during the last decades have contributed greatly to our understanding of human development over the life course. The work of primatologists and biological and psychological anthropologists has broadened our perspective on the similarities and differences in the human experience across time and geographic areas. Without comparative data psychologists and other social scientists have no way of assessing the relative contribution of nature and culture to the cognitive, emotional, and social behavior of individuals growing up in the United States or western Europe. It is from populations in these countries that the majority of generalizations about human development are drawn. If we are to be sure that the generalizations will hold true they must be subjected to the widest possible spectrum of conditions.

There are promising indications that theories that hold across all societies can be developed. The recent research of anthropologists and cross-cultural psychologists indicates that universal and testable theories of human development are possible. Similarity has been found across a variety of cultures in the cognitive abilities of children as they mature during the first years of their lives. Piagetian theories of cognitive development during the preadolescent years have been tested in many parts of the world and, although the rate of development varies between societies, it progresses in a similar way (for review articles see Kagan 1981; Price-Williams 1971; Cole and Scribner 1974; Cole et al. 1971). Continuing research on the development of infants promises new insights into the relative impact of neurophysiology and socialization on infant growth and development (Chisholm 1983; Howrigan 1984; Kagan 1981; Super 1981; Super and Harkness 1982). Through collaboration among researchers the definition of the important variables has been agreed upon and viable techniques of measurement designed. As a result, comparable studies of infants have been made or are in progress in many parts of the world.

Progress in the development of a science of human development is only possible when researchers are willing to include the same variables in their studies and use techniques of measurement that produce comparable data. They must be willing to replicate studies, attempting to adapt the design to local cultural conditions to the best of their ability. Without this comparable data collected in a wide variety of societies, the progress toward a social and developmental science is impossible.

Anthropologists collect the data on which comparative studies can be based. Very often, however, when researchers attempt to use ethnographies, they find that the data they need to test their theories are not available. This is inevitable. No ethnography can anticipate all the information that is required. Describing in detail all the aspects of the culture and social behavior of a society is a monumental task, one that few modern anthropologists would venture to try. The sense of emergency that motivated anthropologists in the early decades of the century to attempt to record the culture of isolated, unknown communities has been replaced by more focused problem-oriented studies. Collaborative research in societies allows for a variety of these detailed studies. The testing of social science theories depends on these types of study, especially those that are so designed and described as to make replication in other environments possible.

The problems selected for focused study change with the intellectual climate and the preoccupations of social scientists. Most recently, the feminist movement has instigated detailed studies of the lives of women. Anthropologists motivated by recurrent interest in the relative power of nature and culture to shape the development of men and women have focused on the lives of women in the non-Western societies where they have studied.

One of the most important contributions of this volume is the documenting of the need for a transcultural definition of "middle age." It is clear that etic and emic definitions are required, the former based on identifiable physiological changes in a woman's body, the latter a sociocultural definition with its associated role specifications. In this volume, Virginia Kerns (pp. 95–96) and Janice Boddy (p. 142) suggest definitions that are most clearly of the first type, linking the loss of fertility to the entry into middle age. All of the authors give their judgments as to whether middle age is identified as a discrete age grade in the societies they studied and how it is defined. The chapters also discuss the sociocultural environments that are associated with the emic definitions.

The ethnographic material that Virginia Kerns and Judith K. Brown have assembled is drawn from societies throughout the world that vary in complexity, in subsistence activities, and in their ideologies as to the role of men and women. The focal interests of the authors and their research methods ensure that a wide variety of cultural conditions are described. The contributions of primatologists, medical anthropologists, and developmental psychologists add breadth to the presentations. However, despite this variety, there is a commitment among the authors to comment on Judith Brown's conclusion in the *Current Anthropology* article, that there are similar changes in the lives of women. They present their data with reference to the transcultural variables identified in her article. This enables the authors, as well as the readers of this volume, to evaluate the possibility of developing a universal and coherent theory of the developmental changes in women's lives in the middle years and the way in which these changes are channeled by the physical and social environment.

I commend this volume as an example of how one should initiate cross-cultural studies: defining the problem to be explored, reviewing the data that are available for comparison, identifying cultural domains that need to be detailed, and developing and exploring the validity of hypotheses concerning the contextual conditions that may illuminate similarities and differences in the cultural patterns that are being explored. It is fortunate that *In Her Prime* is published and that a wider audience can benefit by learning about the structure of women's lives in diverse cultural environments during middle age: the period that is defined by the universal physiological changes that occur at the beginning of the onset of menopause and end when women have perceptible physical deterioration.

REFERENCES

Brown, Judith K.

    1963   A Cross-cultural Study of Female Initiation Rites. American Anthropologist 65:837–53.

    1981   Cross-cultural Perspectives on the Female Life Cycle. *In* Handbook of Cross-cultural Human Development. R. H. Munroe, R. L. Munroe, and B. B. Whiting, eds. pp. 581–610. New York: Garland STPM Press.

    1982   Cross-cultural Perspectives on Middle-Aged Women. Current Anthropology 23(2):143–56.

Chisholm, J.

    1983   An Ethological Study of Child Development. New York: Aldine Press.

Cole, M., J. Gay, J. A. Glick, and D. W. Sharp

    1971   The Cultural Context of Learning and Thinking. New York: Basic Books.

Cole, M., and S. Scribner

    1974   Culture and Thought. New York: John Wiley.

Howrigan, G. A.

    1984   Making Mothers from Adolescents: Context and Experience in Maternal Behavior in Yucatan. Thesis presented to the Harvard Graduate School of Education.

Kagan, J.

    1981   Universals in Human Development *In* Handbook of Cross-cultural Human Development. R. H. Munroe, R. L. Munroe, and B. B. Whiting, eds. pp. 53–63. New York: Garland STPM Press.

Kerns, Virginia

    1979   Social Transition at Menopause. Paper presented at the Annual Meeting of the American Anthropological Association. Cincinnati.

    1980   Aging and Mutual Support. Relations among the Black Carib. *In* Aging in Culture and Society. C. Fry, ed. pp. 112–25. New York: Praeger/Bergin and Garvey.

    1983   Women and the Ancestors: Black Carib Kinship and Ritual. Urbana: University of Illinois Press.

Paige, K. E., and J. W. Paige

    1981   The Politics of Reproductive Ritual. Berkeley: University of California Press.

Price-Williams, D.

    1975   Explorations in Cross-cultural Psychology. San Francisco: Chandler and Sharp.

Super, C. M.

    1981   Behavioral Development in Infancy. *In* Handbook of Cross-cultural Human Development. R. H. Munroe, R. L. Munroe, and B. B. Whiting, eds. pp. 181–271. New York: Garland STPM Press.

Super, C. M., and S. Harkness

    1982   The Infant's Niche in Rural Kenya and Metropolitan America. *In* Cross-cultural Research at Issue. L. L. Adler, ed. pp. 47–55. New York: Academic Press.

In Her Prime

Janice Boddy

Margaret Lock

Michael Lambek

1 Introduction: New Views of Middle-Aged Women

Karen Brodkin Sacks

Writing of the Mpondo in the 1930s, Monica Hunter (1936: 208) found it worthy of note that "a woman of 40, no matter how wrinkled, is not too old to have her lovers." When I first read this in my twenties, it barely registered. On rereading it ten years later, it struck me that Hunter's description of funky forty-year-old women explicitly accepted but implicitly challenged the universality of Western notions about women and aging. Middle-aged women have been minor actors in the ethnographic literature—walk-ons, occasional comic relief, terrorizers of daughters-in-law—but seldom subjects in their own right. Likewise, discussions of the lives of women tend to be discussions about young women's lives. Age bias combined with male bias has left women little space between youth and uselessness.

There has been an interaction between feminist scholarship and changing attitudes about middle age in our society that is beginning to create a body of work that deals not only with gendered subjects but with age-specific ones as well. *In Her Prime* challenges the conventional wisdom about women and aging in the anthropological literature and in our own society. In so doing, it addresses the relation of biology and society in age and gender. Judith K. Brown and Virginia Kerns have put together anthropology's first collection to focus on "dirty old ladies," as Brown has informally termed them—women "no longer young, but not yet old." *In Her Prime* is a cross-cultural work whose theme is that middle-age does not have to be the way they say it is in our own society. Jane B. Lancaster's and Barbara J. King's "An Evolutionary Perspective on Menopause" takes an even longer evolutionary view, suggesting that menopause itself may be a relatively recent human creation, as women ceased to spend most of their reproductive years nursing without menstruating and instead spent most of them having regular menstrual cycles. The rest of the book focuses on social explanations for cross-cultural similarities in the developmental patterns of women's lives in middle age.

Judith K. Brown and Virginia Kerns are among the pioneers in anthropological studies of older women, Kerns in fieldwork with Garífuna women and Brown in developing theoretical perspectives through cross-cultural studies of women's lives and transitions. Here, they have given us a wonderful collection of essays on the lives of middle-aged women in twelve cultures, ranging from small-scale relatively egalitarian societies to Asian and Western industrial states, as well as an essay on the evolution of menopause.

In Her Prime is the first book-length anthropological treatment of middle-aged women as subjects worthy of analysis in their own right. One of its strengths is that it takes an implicit life-course perspective, which avoids the error of substituting an image of middle-aged women for one of young women as "essential woman."

As Beatrice Blyth Whiting points out in the Foreword, each of the contributors speaks to the issues raised by Brown's (1982) influential article "Cross-cultural Perspectives on Middle-Aged Women." As a result, this book has much more unity than is usual for a volume of case studies. Brown's chapter and the introductions to each of the sections systematically highlight the major themes. Each of the essays examines women's lives and their changing social relations from girlhood to old age and locates middle age in a shared developmental framework that also acknowledges cultural variation.

The subjects of this book are "women who have adult offspring and who are not yet frail or dependent" (Brown, p. 18), women who have made "a central transition in the female life course . . . from the childbearing to a nonchildbearing stage of life" (Kerns, p. 95). This working definition creates a cross-cultural category for comparative analysis, as well as allowing comparison with men's lives. The developmental perspective, focusing as it does on women's changing life circumstances, allows room for cultural variation, including the frequently made observation that middle age is not always a marked life stage.

Brown's chapter highlights cross-cultural patterns in the lives of middle-aged women that up-end conventional wisdom. First and foremost, this is the time in which a woman enjoys her greatest power, status, and autonomy. In some cultures this increase in power and status is gradual; in others, there is a sharp break with earlier requirements for women's seclusion and deferential behavior. Second, both in societies that sharply oppress young women and those that have egalitarian gender ideologies, the freedom, prestige, and authority of women increases at middle age and comes closer to that of men than it did in earlier years. So, whether it is seen in relation to a woman's own life or in relation to the lives of men of her culture and generation, middle age is a woman's prime.

Brown suggests three axes of social organization that contribute to women's heightened mobility, power and authority, and prestige in middle age. First, many of the restrictions that surround younger women are removed at middle age. Middle-aged women no longer have to defer to husbands, mothers-in-law, or others of a senior generation. In societies with patrilocal residence and patrilineal resource ownership and inheritance, by raising adult children women are "finally considered above disloyalty" to the husband's kin group. Thus, the middle-aged Bakgalagadi women of Botswana, discussed by Jacqueline S. Solway, develop claims on the resources of their husbands' kin group, as well as control over their own agricultural produce through their children's membership in that agnatic group. At middle age they manage their own compounds. Their ability to delegate chores allows them to travel more widely, to engage in exchanges and some political affairs.

Too, restrictions on women's behavior that stem from the powers of menstrual blood or fertility are also ended or diminished, as is described in Karen P. Sinclair's chapter "A Study in Pride in Prejudice: Maori Women at Midlife," Sylvia Vatuk's "Sexuality and the Middle-Aged Woman in South Asia," and Virginia Kerns's "Female Control of Sexuality: Garífuna Women at Middle Age." As a result, such women may extend their social and geographical spheres, even where there are sharper boundaries between the genders in their younger years. This appears to be the case among Kelantan Malays described in Douglas Raybeck's "A Diminished Dichotomy: Kelantan Malay and Traditional Chinese Perspectives," where women did most of the vending and where older women were more mobile than younger women, and sometimes their men. Related to but not identical with diminished fertility, middle-aged women are often a great deal bawdier than their younger sisters, as Richard B. Lee's description of !Kung women and Virginia Kerns's accounts both attest.

Second, at middle age women gain a great deal of social and economic authority in heightened control over people. They have the right to command labor for themselves from younger kin and to determine the organization of larger work projects. They also tend to be the authorities in determining or arranging marriages, and hence in shaping social relations among the next generation, as well as exerting power through sons and sometimes aging husbands. These themes emerge in Solway's analysis and in Dorothy Ayers Counts's chapter "*Tamparonga:* 'The Big Women' of Kaliai (Papua New Guinea)."

Third, and related, middle-aged women are often able to aspire to age-

or age/gender-related positions, ranging from midwives to religious and political statuses. Karen P. Sinclair describes the political centrality of women among New Zealand's Maori, who have become "a cultural minority in the land of their ancestors" (p. 123). Middle-aged women are at the center of Maramatanga, a religious movement in the Maori prophetic tradition of coping with white domination. Through this movement, women make use of their traditional cooperative networks and have become significant political leaders and mediators between Maori and the colonial culture. They have been prominent as well in the recent Maori cultural renaissance and political movement for economic justice. In a similar way, Michael Lambek's beautifully written essay "Motherhood and Other Careers in Mayotte (Comoro Islands)" describes alternative routes to authority available to women. Each rests on a particular set of strategies in building a network of ties, to a husband, affines, children, foster children and their parents, and so on. In Mayotte, middle-aged women's leadership includes that of women's age-group organization, participation in national political parties, spirit possession, curing, and midwifery.

These findings contrast sharply with received wisdom about middle-aged women in our own society, where there are no deference or menstrual restrictions, where grown children move away from their parents, and where valued older women's statuses do not exist. However, the chapters in this volume that deal with Western societies also challenge conventional wisdom. They stress continuities more than they do contrasts with nonindustrial societies. The findings of Nancy Datan, Aaron Antonovsky, and Benjamin Maoz in their study "Tradition, Modernity, and Transitions in Five Israeli Subcultures" indicate greatest similarities in well-being among middle-aged women in the most "traditional" and the most "modern" subculture, as well as a rarity of clinical depression among women in all subcultures. Patricia A. Kaufert and Margaret Lock's chapter " 'What Are Women For?': Cultural Constructions of Menopausal Women in Japan and Canada" also challenges some aspects of this conventional wisdom. They demonstrate the diversity in middle-aged women's lives and suggest the emergence of women's political opposition to medical models and social scripts for "the menopausal woman" in Japan and Canada. And Raybeck discusses women's creative responses to the recent intensification of wage labor in Kelantan, Malaysia, and the influence of Western media and Islamic fundamentalism. Rather than accepting the subordination each of these forces encodes, middle-aged Kelantanese women have built upon their sociocultural heritage and seized opportunities to maintain their egalitarian relations with husbands and their status vis-à-vis younger women.

The materials in this volume raise at least as many questions as they answer, and the ways in which they do so make *In Her Prime* a particularly rich text, one that will stimulate discussion and further research. One of the virtues of a focus on women's middle age is that a woman's fertility is no longer so easily confused with her sexuality. Perhaps for this reason four of the chapters taken together provide some very intriguing suggestions about the varieties of relationships among sexuality, male control, and fertility. In some cultures menopause does not signal the end of a woman's sexual interest, as illustrated by the Lusi of Papua New Guinea, the Garífuna, and !Kung women. In these cultures middle age brings with it expanded freedom for women to joke about sexuality and to display sexual interest. In striking contrast, the South Asian women described by Sylvia Vatuk are expected to cease being sexual people at just the time they work free of many of the more onerous forms of male social control. Vatuk suggests that female sexuality is seen as a socially destructive force in India, so that it would be especially dangerous if women not under intense male authority were to exhibit sexual interest.

Clearly, different social constructions of female sexuality (positive and expressive in the first three instances, dangerous and destructive in the fourth) are involved. So too are different associations of female sexuality with fertility and with male control. In India, female sexuality is only socially safe when under heavy male control, while among the Garífuna especially, middle-aged women exert more control than men do and fertility seems much more problematic than sexuality. Are negative social constructions of women's sexuality related to material conditions of agrarian patriarchal peasantries, where both brides and mothers-in-law do indeed have enormous economically destructive potential were they ever to collude? How might such situations compare to views about sexuality among nonstate patrilineal households where mothers-in-laws are sometimes said to collude as well as to clash with their daughters-in-law? Are expressive constructions of women's sexuality related to minimal or non-patrilineal inheritance?

Several other studies indicate alternative trajectories within a culture and attendant and heightened risks in the lives of women at middle age. Raybeck points out that while middle age offers women greater authority and scope for achievements, failure to realize its potential can lead to problems: a particular kind of psychosomatic illness among Kelantan women and suicide among Chinese women. Janice Boddy strikes a similar theme in "Bucking the Agnatic System: Status and Strategies in Rural Northern Sudan." Here, middle age can be a time of greater freedom and influence for women who have male economic support, but it can also be a disastrous time for women without male kin who are cast out by their husbands. Hence it is approached "with ambivalence, if not with trepidation" (p. 151). David Gutmann's chapter "Beyond Nurture: Developmental Perspectives on the Vital Older Woman" gives this theme a psychodynamic dimension. He suggests that there is a culture-free, creative vitality that flowers in midlife that can be either culturally recognized or denied. The latter leads to psychological pathology and to a social science that takes a "denigrating view of the older woman as perpetual victim" (p. 231).

This perspective relates to another theme only hinted at, of the biopsychological dimensions underlying and contributing to middle-aged women's social standing. Gutmann believes that "the clear and obvious advance of most postparental women across the most varied social settings is a culture-free phenomenon" (p. 231), a statement with which Brown would concur: "for women there appears to be a period of florescence later in life, and this has been noted by theorists as varied as Meillassoux and Jung" (p. 22).

NOTE

Portions of this chapter appeared in a somewhat different form in *Reviews in Anthropology* 14, no. 2 (1987).

REFERENCES

Brown, Judith K.
    1982   Cross-cultural Perspectives on Middle-Aged Women. Current Anthropology 23(2):143–56.
Hunter, Monica
    1936   Reaction to Conquest. London: Oxford University Press.

2 An Evolutionary Perspective on Menopause

Jane B. Lancaster
Barbara J. King

Reproductive data from Western nations indicate that the median age at menopause is between forty-nine and fifty-one years (Gosden 1985). In nonindustrialized societies, median age appears to be lower, but little variation exists across all populations in mean age at last birth, thirty-nine to forty-one years (Bongaarts and Potter 1983), although last birth at thirty-five years is noted in some studies (e.g., Howell 1979). Thus, human females spend over one-third of their lives in a postreproductive phase, much of which can be characterized as menopausal.

An evolutionary perspective on menopause in the human female has led recent theorists to ask whether it represents an evolved pattern that actively promotes a nonreproductive phase in the life cycle or whether it is an accidental by-product of other processes that selected for good health during the reproductive years. Proponents of the position that menopause is an evolved phenomenon (Alexander 1974; Gaulin 1980; Mayer 1982; Trivers 1972) all present some version of a parental investment theory that begins with a "grandmother hypothesis." The suggestion here is that a woman maximizes her reproductive success if, in middle age, she ceases production of new children and concentrates on investing in her last born and in her grandchildren.

Mayer (1982), for example, analyzed data from four New England genealogies containing 1,890 women who lived in the seventeenth through nineteenth centuries and concluded that those who died postmenopausally had greater fertility and inclusive fitness than those who died before reaching menopause. (Fertility was the total number of children born regardless of postnatal survival; inclusive fitness was the number of children, siblings, and first cousins, and all descendants of these kin, that were born and remained alive during the subject's lifetime.) In a critique of the Mayer study, Hames (1984) points out that the next step in this kind of analysis would be to control for the effect of age at death on inclusive fitness. It would then be possible to test the adaptive value of menopause more directly, with a major prediction being that women who reached menopause at average age would have higher inclusive fitness than those who achieved it early or late.

A direct test of the grandmother hypothesis was carried out in a living population by Hawkes, O'Connell, and Jones (1989), who collected data on foraging behavior of the Hadza hunter-gatherers of Tanzania during 1985–86. The Hadza invest a greater amount of time in the food quest than was expected from information on other hunter-gatherer groups such as the !Kung. Postreproductive Hadza women (grandmothers) foraged significantly longer than women of childbearing age during certain times of the year, with little difference in acquisition rate compared with younger women. Higher foraging effort by postreproductive women was associated with collection of tubers, which are difficult to dig up. Hawkes, O'Connell, and Jones (1989:359) conclude that the data "are most consistent with the proposition that senior women reduce the energy costs of foraging to their younger female kin by acquiring extra tubers for them." Hadza grandmothers thus seem to target extraction of a resource that is both high in quality and difficult to process as a way to help increase the reproductive success of their younger female relatives.

Another version of the grandmother hypothesis suggests that senescence itself is actively selected so that parents will remove themselves from competition with their offspring (Williams 1957). In such an analysis, menopause is only an early step along the way to total withdrawal from competition.

Other theorists (Washburn 1981; Weiss 1981) reject the view that menopause is an evolved phenomenon and instead suggest that selection favored relatively long-lived, healthy, reproducing adults rather than a postreproductive phase per se. They argue that during most of human history, life expectancy was too short and women lived too briefly past menopause for a period of nonreproduction to be selected and that the maximum human life span has been unchanged for the last one hundred thousand years, but that many more of those born are now likely to reach maximum length of life. Evidence for maximum human life span is equivocal, however. Trinkhaus and Thompson (1987:128) discuss "the extreme rarity and possible absence of Neandertals greater than 40 to 45 years in the fossil record," indicating that these early *Homo sapiens* rarely survived into a postreproductive period and that either maximum length of life at least in these hominids may not have been very long or very few individuals survived to the maximum length of life, so that benefits of a long life were rarely selected. If the second view of menopause as presented here is correct, then the fact that nonreproductive middle-aged women now comprise a significant percentage of the human population is an artifact of recent improvements in the human condition or is a life-course program associated specifically with modern *Homo sapiens.*

Human Reproductive Restraint

The relative merit of these two perspectives can be evaluated by first asking why reproductive restraint in the middle years might evolve, resulting in the halting of production of children well before the development of other aspects of senescence such as reduced physical capacity. Lancaster (1989, in press; Lancaster and Lancaster 1987) has argued that the human pattern of parental investment represents a unique evolutionary adaptation that was both profound and critical in the evolution of the genus *Homo.* According to this hypothesis, the sexual division of labor and the feeding of juveniles by adults from the time of weaning until reproductive maturity distinguishes humans from other animals.

The Lancasters' (1987) survey of the literature for data on the demography of survivorship of juveniles among human hunter-gatherers and horticulturalists, and among populations of free-ranging primates that are either self-feeding or provisioned by people, suggests that humans living in simple economies enjoy a survivorship comparable to nonhuman primates in populations that are not food-limited. Improved survivorship through the juvenile period based on the feeding of juveniles by adults may have given evolving humans two significant advantages compared with their closest relatives, the great apes. The first was a more efficient production of offspring that survive to reproductive age because of a lower juvenile mortality rate from starvation and disease. Second, the freeing of human juveniles from the demands of the food quest provided them with leisure time that allowed large segments of their time-energy budgets to be devoted to play and the manipulation of objects. The improved feeding efficiency from the human division of labor between hunting and gathering, guided by human intelligence, permitted the nutritional dependency of multiple young of differing ages upon their parents. From this perspective, the human species represents an extreme evolutionary development of two linked behavioral patterns: intelligence based on learning and high levels of parental investment from both sexes, particularly during the juvenile period.

Two questions point to ways of testing the hypothesis proposed by the Lancasters: Is menopause unique to humans? Did human females regularly survive menopause in time past? Investigations that attempt to identify menopause in nonhuman primates (Cranfield et al. 1988; Gould,

Flint, and Graham 1981; Graham, Kling, and Steiner 1979; Hodgen et al. 1977; Jones 1975; Wolfe and Noyes 1981) reveal that primate models for human menopause exist in the sense that the end of the life course in female monkeys and apes may be marked by reduced fertility, irregular and lengthened menstrual cycles, reduced levels of estrogens, and in some species, complete cessation of ovulation. In all cases, the subfertile or postreproductive phase is at the very end of life (making up perhaps only one-tenth of the life span), and is usually associated with evidence of diminished physical capacity.

These studies are marked, however, by differing ways of testing for menopause and differing results, including (1) noninvasive observation of free-ranging monkeys with collection of data on estrous cycles and reproductive output, showing that fertility decreases with age but not owing to menopause (Wolfe and Noyes 1981; but see Gouzoules et al. 1984); (2) hormonal and behavioral analysis of apes in captivity, indicating menopause in some cases but also menstrual cycling and even pregnancy just before death at an advanced age (Gould, Flint, and Graham 1981); and (3) experimental work in a zoo, comparing hormonal values from elderly monkeys to values from younger conspecifics that were surgically castrated, resulting in some evidence for menopause and allowing for differentiation of menopause and secondary amenorrhea due to hypothalamic dysfunction (Cranfield et al. 1988).

To date, then, the only example of a relatively long postreproductive phase (one-third of the life span) outside of humans comes from one strain of mouse (Jones 1975), although, as Gosden (1985) notes, rodents cannot in the strict sense be said to show menopause because they do not have menstrual cycles. In any case, at present it seems that among primates a long postreproductive phase may be unique to humans.

An equally important question is whether women lived long enough in evolutionary history for a postreproductive phase to be selected. To test this, biologically relevant parameters must first be established. It is important to recognize that life expectancy at birth is an irrelevant, though often cited, statistic. Although compared to other species, humans are very successful in raising juveniles, in simple economies such as hunting and gathering only 50 percent of those born usually survive to reproduction. Such a loss of immatures greatly lowers life expectancy at birth. The significant measure is not life expectancy at birth but life expectancy at age fifteen or at the onset of reproductive life. Further, the relevant statistic for establishing the cessation of the reproductive phase is not the end of menstrual cycling but the birth of the last child. As mentioned above, this statistic varies little across populations, with the mean falling at thirty-nine to forty-one years; this fits well with other evidence taken from modern Western populations, which indicates that fertility declines markedly and the frequency of fetal abnormalities abruptly increases after age thirty-five (Washburn 1981).

Using these two markers, life expectancy at fifteen and last birth in the late thirties, we have examined data drawn from life tables of twenty-four hunting-gathering and horticultural populations in the archaeological and ethnographic record. Pooling these data shows that of those women who survived to age fifteen, about half—53 percent—could expect to reach age forty-five. This means that a good proportion of reproducing women could expect to live long enough past the birth of the last child to see that offspring through many of its juvenile years. If natural selection actively favored parental investment by mothers during their middle years in a last child and grandchildren, demographic constraints would not have prevented it.

Recent Historic Change

Regardless of whether menopause and a postreproductive phase of the life course were favored by natural selection during human history, an evolutionary historical perspective leads us to note that there have been major alterations in the life-course experiences of women caused by changes in activity patterns, diet, and health. Although the data are controversial (Bongaarts 1980; Flint 1978; Frisch 1978, 1982; Short 1976), there is some evidence that the length of the reproductive phase of the life course has expanded and contracted during various periods of history. In general, when women are healthy, fat, and not extremely active physically, they enter reproduction early and remain late. Current values for modern Western women are menarche at the age of twelve and menopause at fifty. Women who are less healthy or lean and very active may have their reproductive lives shortened by as much as five years at both ends of the fertile period. !Kung hunter-gatherer women are reported to have menarche at seventeen, first birth at nineteen, last birth at thirty-five, and menopause at forty (Howell 1979). Probably the norm for most of human history lies between these extremes, but it appears that recent developments have maximized the length of the reproductive period. In other words, menopausal women may be becoming progressively older, and the secular trend in the age of menarche is probably paralleled by a secular trend in the age of menopause.

The actual experience of menopause in modern society may be very different from that in time past because of recent changes in child-care practices. Unpleasant physiological symptoms such as hot flashes, profuse sweating, and atrophic vaginitis are more frequent and more extreme in modern societies, with 10 percent of U.S. women reporting some problems (Flint 1982). Other complaints, such as depression and irritability, are also frequently reported. Beyene's (1989) book using a cross-cultural perspective on menopause points out that this symptomatology may be culturally conditioned; as Flint (1982) puts it, whether menopause is viewed as reward or punishment may be critical to women's experience.

We would like to propose, however, that other factors may also contribute to the unpleasant experience of so many modern women. As Short (1976) has argued, lactational amenorrhea is the normal biological state for women once they begin their reproductive lives. He estimates that for most of human history, women spent over fifteen years in lactation and just under four years each in pregnancy and menstrual cycling. In contrast, with fewer pregnancies and a longer reproductive period, the average modern woman will be pregnant and lactating for a total of only two years, whereas she will spend nearly thirty-five years in menstrual cycling.

Abundant but scattered data from the ethnographic record attests to the fact that women in many tribal societies nurse their last child for a longer period than is typical for earlier-born children. Figures of three to five years are frequently mentioned, and isolated cases of eight to ten years are reported for !Kung, Native Americans, and tribal India (Stephens 1963). This means that for many women in time past menopause occurred within the hormonal context of lactation. Unpleasant symptoms caused by abrupt fluctuations in circulating hormones may have been masked or regulated by the continuous presence of prolactin and oxytocin. As Howell (1979) notes, !Kung women may never actually experience menopause. They simply nurse their last infant for a long period and then do not resume cycling when the child is weaned.

Thus, although the verdict is not yet in on whether menopause represents an actively evolved pattern in the life course of women to promote parental investment in their last child, it is clear that such a selected program cannot be ruled out on the basis of the demography of the past. Regardless of the evolutionary origins of menopause, its experience in the modern world is very different from that of former times. Women may be older at menopause than they used to be and they experience it without the modulation that was once available from the hormones of lactation. An evolutionary and historical perspective on menopause may help us to appreciate some of the problems particular to modern women by virtue of major changes in their reproductive lives.

NOTE

The revised version of this chapter was prepared by Barbara J. King.

REFERENCES

Alexander, Richard D.
  1974 The Evolution of Social Behavior. Annual Review of Ecology and Systematics 5:325–83.
Beyene, Yewoubdar
  1989 From Menarche to Menopause: Reproductive Lives of Peasant Women in Two Cultures. Albany: State University of New York Press.
Bongaarts, John
  1980 Does Malnutrition Affect Fecundity?: A Summary of Evidence. Science 208:564–69.
Bongaarts, John, and Robert G. Potter
  1983 Fertility, Biology and Behavior: An Analysis of the Proximate Determinants. New York: Academic Press.
Brown, Judith K.
  1982 Cross-cultural Perspectives on Middle-Aged Women. Current Anthropology 23 (2):143–56.
Cranfield, Michael R., et al.
  1988 Diagnosing Menopause in the Macaque Species using Serum Hormone Profiles (abstract). Proceedings of the Joint Conference of the American Association of Zoo Veterinarians and American Association of Wildlife Veterinarians, pp. 194–95.
Flint, Marcha
  1978 Is There a Secular Trend in Age of Menopause? Maturitas 1:133–39.
  1982 Male and Female Menopause: A Cultural Put-On. *In* Changing Perspectives on Menopause. A. Voda, M. Dinnerstein, and S. O'Donnell, eds. pp. 363–78. Austin: University of Texas Press.
Frisch, Rose E.
  1978 Population, Food Intake, and Fertility. Science 199:22–30.
  1982 Malnutrition and Fertility. Science 215:1272–73.
Gaulin, S. J. C.
  1980 Sexual Dimorphism in the Human Post-reproductive Life-Span: Possible Causes. Journal of Human Evolution 9:227–32.
Gosden, R. G.
  1985. Biology of Menopause: The Causes and Consequences of Ovarian Ageing. New York: Academic Press.
Gould, Kenneth G., Marcha Flint, and Charles E. Graham
  1981 Chimpanzee Reproductive Senescence: A Possible Model for Evolution of Menopause. Maturitas 3:157–66.

Gouzoules, Harold, et al.
  1984   Comments on Reproductive Senescence among Female Japanese
          Macaques. Journal of Mammalogy 65:341–42.
Graham, Charles E., O. R. Kling, and R. A. Steiner.
  1979   Reproductive Senescence in Female Nonhuman Primates. *In* Aging in
          Nonhuman Primates. D. Bowden, ed. pp. 183–202. New York: Van Nostrand
          Reinhold.
Hames, Raymond
  1984   On the Definition and Measure of Inclusive Fitness and the Evolution
          of Menopause. Human Ecology 12:87–91.
Hassan, Fekri A.
  1981   Demographic Archaeology. New York: Academic Press.
Hawkes, Kristen, James F. O'Connell, and Nicholas G. Blurton Jones
  1989   Hardworking Hadza Grandmothers. *In* Comparative Socioecology:
          The Behavioural Ecology of Humans and Other Mammals. V. Standen and
          R. A. Foley, eds. pp. 341–66. Oxford: Blackwell.
Hodgen, G. D., et al.
  1977   Menopause in Rhesus Monkeys: Model for Study of Disorders in the
          Human Climacteric. American Journal of Obstetrics and Gynecology
          127:581–84.
Howell, Nancy
  1979   Demography of the Dobe Area !Kung. New York: Academic Press.
Johnston, Timothy D.
  1982   Selective Costs and Benefits in the Evolution of Learning. Advances in
          the Study of Behavior 12:65–106.
Jones, E. C.
  1975   The Post-reproductive Phase in Mammals. *In* Frontiers of Hormone
          Research, vol. 3. P. van Keep and C. Lauritzen, eds. pp. 1–20. Basel: Karger.
Lancaster, Jane B.
  1989   Women in Biosocial Perspective. *In* Gender and Anthropology: Critical
          Reviews for Research and Teaching. S. Morgen, ed. pp. 98–117. Washington,
          D.C.: American Anthropological Association.
  In press Parental Investment and the Evolution of the Juvenile Phase of the
          Human Life Course. *In* The Origins of Humanness. A. Brooks, ed.
          Washington, D.C.: Smithsonian Institution Press.
Lancaster, Jane B., and Chet S. Lancaster
  1987   The Watershed: Change in Parental Investment and Family Formation
          Strategies in the Course of Human Evolution. *In* Parenting across the Life
          Span: Biosocial Dimensions. J. Lancaster et al., eds. pp. 107–205. Hawthorne,
          N.Y.: Aldine.
Lee, Richard B.
  1980   Lactation, Ovulation, Infanticide and Women's Work: A Study of
          Hunter-Gatherer Population Regulation. *In* Biosocial Mechanisms of Popu-
          lation Regulation. M. Cohen, R. Malpass, and H. Klein, eds. pp. 321–38.
          New Haven, Conn.: Yale University Press.

Mayer, Peter J.
  1982   Evolutionary Advantages of Menopause. Human Ecology 10 (4):477–94.
Short, R. V.
  1976   The Evolution of Human Reproduction. Proceedings, Royal Society of London, Series B. 195:3–24.
Stephens, William
  1963   The Family in Cross-cultural Perspective. New York: Holt, Rinehart, and Winston.
Trinkaus, Erik, and D. D. Thompson
  1987   Femoral Diaphyseal Histomorphometric Age Determinations for the Shanidar 3, 4, 5, and 6 Neandertals and Neandertal Longevity. American Journal of Physical Anthropology 72:123–29.
Trivers, Robert L.
  1972   Parental Investment and Sexual Selection. *In* Sexual Selection and the Descent of Man. B. Campbell, ed. pp. 136–79. Chicago: Aldine.
Washburn, Sherwood L.
  1981   Longevity in Primates. In Aging, Biology and Behavior. J. March and J. McGaugh, eds. pp. 11–29. New York: Academic Press.
Weiss, K. M.
  1981   Evolutionary Perspectives on Human Aging. *In* Other Ways of Growing Old. P. Amoss and S. Harrell, eds. pp. 25–58. Stanford, Calif.: Stanford University Press.
Williams, G. C.
  1957   Pleiotrophy, Natural Selection and the Evolution of Senescence. Evolution 11:398–411.
Wolfe, Linda D., and M. J. Sabra Noyes
  1981   Reproductive Senescence among Female Japanese Macaques (*Macaca fuscata fuscata*). Journal of Mammalogy 62:698–705.

3   Lives of Middle-Aged Women

Judith K. Brown

During the past two decades there has been a strong interest in an anthropology of women. The development of an anthropology of aging is still more recent. The chapters that follow combine these contemporary trends, providing a new look at the worlds of middle-aged women, from developmental and cross-cultural perspectives.

There have been earlier studies of older women, but the pioneering cross-cultural research by Bart (1969), Griffen (1977), Kaufert (1979), and Kerns (1979, 1980) of necessity tended toward inclusiveness. Grandmotherhood, menopause, the status of the aged, and a whole variety of topics were considered, simply because *any* relevant data were difficult to find. For example, Bart surveyed information from the more than seven hundred societies in the Human Relations Area Files, but she found appropriate entries for a cross-cultural sample of only thirty societies. Today there is more information and the research has become more focused. An entire literature has developed on menopause including a special issue of *Maturitas,* edited by Flint in 1982, the book of readings *Changing Perspectives on Menopause* (Voda, Dinnerstein, and O'Donnell 1982), the ethnographic studies that focus on Israel (Datan, Antonovsky, and Maoz 1981) and on a fishing village in Newfoundland (Davis 1983), and a great variety of articles (e.g., Flint 1975; Dougherty 1978; Wright 1979; and Burgess 1982). A cross-cultural literature on aging is represented by Fry (1980) and Amoss and Harrell (1981), among others. And there is literature on the evolutionary significance of aging and the sex differences in the aging process, which includes the work of Alexander (1974), Gaulin (1980), and Mayer (1982). The present volume is part of this trend toward greater specialization. It deals with middle-aged women, but not with aged women, grandmotherhood, and widowhood; nor does it deal with middle-aged men.[1]

I have devised the following definition: middle-aged women (matrons) are women who have adult offspring and who are not yet frail or dependent. The lack of specificity about ages is appropriate for cross-cultural data, which are derived from many societies where the ages of adults are approximations because there are no birth records. Furthermore, since there are societies in which the end of childbearing and rearing is negotiable by means of adoption and fosterage, the end of childbearing does not provide a definition that can be applied cross-culturally. Middle age will be considered independently of menopause. Menopause is typically unmarked by ritual and therefore often remains unreported by ethnographers. Also the perimenopausal period in a woman's life tends to be briefer than middle age. Finally, although most traditional ethnographies have not noted menopause, older women are not absent from these descriptive accounts. The information about them is scattered under a variety of topics such as ritual, food distribution, and marriage arrangements. And so a social rather than a physiological definition seems in order here.

Researchers who conducted the early cross-cultural studies of older women expected to find variable conditions—some societies in which status improved with age and some in which it declined. But this is curiously not the case. The changes in a woman's life brought about by the onset of middle age appear to be somewhat positive in nonindustrialized societies. What does vary is the degree of discontinuity in women's lives. In some societies a younger woman is restricted and confined, and her life is one of subservience and toil, until she is middle-aged. Then she moves into a position of authority and relative leisure. In other societies, the life of young women is less onerous and does not differ so much from the life of older women.

As women reach middle age in nonindustrialized societies, three kinds of changes take place in their lives. First, they are often freed from cumbersome restrictions they had to observe when younger. Second, they are expected to exert authority over specified younger kin. This may involve the right to extract labor or it may be the right to make important decisions for the younger person. Third, the changes may include eligibility for special statuses, and thus for recognition beyond the confines of the household.

The Removal of Restrictions

In many societies, middle-aged women are freed from exhibiting the deferential and even demeaning behavior they had previously been expected to display to the senior generation or to the husband. Although some aged persons may still require expressions of respect, at middle age women have become the active senior generation and now receive the deference they once had to display. Furthermore, menstrual customs no longer apply in those societies that regard menstruating women as dangerous and defiling. In societies that demand great propriety in younger women, in which their conduct is narrowly prescribed, many rules are lifted. Older women may interact informally with men who are nonrelatives; they may be allowed to drink too much on ceremonial occasions; they may use foul language, dress immodestly, and even urinate in public.

One aspect of this major change is the greater geographic mobility that older women are often allowed. Child care has ceased or can be delegated, domestic chores are reduced, and so commercial opportunities, the hospitality of relatives living at a distance, and religious pilgrimages may provide an opportunity to venture forth from the village. In some societies, all younger women are restricted to the household because they are believed to be sexually voracious and in need of constant supervision. Here older women are the supervisors because they are believed to be beyond sexual escapades that would bring dishonor to the entire kinship group. In many societies in which the young bride must move into the household of her husband and his family, she is at first mistrusted. It is only as the mother of grown sons that she is viewed as assimilated into her kin group by marriage. She is finally considered above disloyalty. In societies where travel is dangerous and where young women need protection, older women may be granted a certain immunity and therefore some freedom of movement. Thus, once a woman is the mother of adult offspring, she is no longer encumbered with elaborate rules of conduct concerning menstrual custom, modesty, and display of respect; nor is she confined.

The Exercise of Authority

A second major change brought on by middle age is a woman's right to exert authority over specified younger kin. This authority is of two kinds. The first is the right to extract labor from younger family members. In matrilocal societies this pertains to daughters, married and unmarried, and to sons-in-law. In patrilocal societies, this pertains to unmarried daughters and daughters-in-law. In many societies, an older woman is expected to be leisured, and it reflects unfavorably on the entire family if she is not. The daughters and daughters-in-law will be reprimanded by the woman's sons and will be the object of disapprobation by the community.

The work of older women tends to be administrative: delegating subsistence activity tasks and making assignments to younger women (see Mary Jemison on the Iroquois [Seaver 1961], Richards [1956] on the Bemba, Murphy and Murphy [1974] on the Mundurucú). They administer the food production, processing, preparation, and preserving and they oversee food distribution. Within the household the matron may have absolute control over who eats what and when. A recalcitrant daughter-in-law can be starved into submission or even poisoned. In traditional societies, hospitality and the authority to distribute food to nonhousehold members have significant political and ritual implications. By providing or withholding food, older women can influence the celebration of a ceremony or the meeting of a political council (Hahn 1919; Brown 1970).

The authority of older women also finds expression in shaping important decisions for certain members of the junior generation: what a grandchild is to be named, who is ready to be initiated, and who is eligible to marry whom. In some societies, older women have specific responsibilities in the material exchanges that solemnify a marriage. In the societies that maintain very separate worlds for men and women, older women are the go-betweens. The mother of the groom may be the only member of his kin group who actually sees the potential bride and converses with her before formal negotiations take place (see Mernissi 1975). The report of the older woman is crucial to the arrangements, although the groom's father is officially in charge.

Perhaps most significant are reports by many ethnographers concerning the tremendous influence that mothers exercise over and through grown sons. Often a man's relationship to his mother supersedes that with his wife. In some societies the husband is typically very much older than his wife. Early in the marriage, the age discrepancy favors the husband, but as he grows aged and feeble, his middle-aged wife gains in power. This power is further enhanced when combined with the allegiance of grown sons, the old man's successors.

Eligibility for Special Status

A third major change brought on by middle age is the eligibility that older women have for special statuses and the possibility these provide for recognition beyond the household. Societies vary in the number of special positions that their female members can occupy. In some, such opportunities are restricted and there is only the vocation of midwife. In other societies, there are a variety of special offices: curer, leader of girls' initiation ceremonies, holy woman, guardian of the sacred hearth, matchmaker.[2] Such positions are typically not filled by younger women, sometimes because the exercise of spiritual power is considered harmful to a nursing child or to the baby a pregnant woman is carrying. Sometimes the incompatibility is the result of the great demands of child-care and subsistence activities, which when undelegated, allow neither time nor energy for ritual roles. Further, in many societies the belief that menstruation is defiling, disgusting to the spirits, or dangerous makes women ineligible for dealing with sacred matters until later in life. Even a midwife evokes more confidence if she has given birth to many children and has attended at the births of many more.

The American Matron

The circumstances of middle-aged women in industrial societies like our own differ from those suggested by the cross-cultural data. The "forty-year-old jitters" (Henry 1977) and the "empty nest syndrome" may have exaggerated the unenviable aspects of the lives of American middle-aged women (see Neugarten 1970). Or perhaps these descriptions were accurate for the women of a previous generation. Nevertheless there are reasons why middle age does not bring as many positive changes into the lives of women in our own society as it does into the lives of women elsewhere. First, middle age does not usher in a life of fewer restrictions because these are negligible in the first place. Second, although Philip Wylie's classic *Generation of Vipers* (1942) decried the power of "Mom" in an earlier generation, American middle-aged women have far less power over their younger kin than their counterparts in other societies. Adult offspring often live at great distances from their mothers, since the location of employment determines the place of residence. The support given by adult children, so central to the definition of middle-aged women cross-culturally and so crucial to their relatively privileged position, often consists merely of occasional telephone conversations, letters, and brief holiday visits. Younger kin may seek advice or may be manipulated covertly. The latter is seen as unbecoming intrusiveness and not as a maternal right. The control of food is also not the older woman's prerogative. Caterers, vending machines, restaurants, and fast-food emporiums have undermined the family meal, trivialized food, and reduced its political and religious implications. Third, our society does provide the possibility for recognition beyond the household, either through volunteer activities in the community or through a career,[3] but such opportunities are open to all women, regardless of age. Spiritual power, delivering babies, and curing are not associated with older women but with various specialists in our society, and the specialists are likely to be men. Although American middle-aged women are not as sinister or as pitiable as they have been portrayed, they do not share all the advantages enjoyed by matrons in nonindustrialized societies.

Toward a New View

These generalizations[4] will be explored and augmented in the chapters that follow—a unique collection of ethnographic accounts focusing on the lives of middle-aged women.[5] The chapters are arranged according to the societies' complexity and scale: from small-scale and traditional to intermediate (a designation used by Simić [1978])[6] to complex to industrialized. They also differ in type of setting, in means of livelihood, and in gender ideology. In these widely varied contexts, there is a consistent, basic theme: women experience a relatively enhanced position once middle-aged.

There is no such thing as "the status of women" in any particular society. Age modifies the position of women, just as gender modifies the position of the aged. Nor does having adult offspring usher in immediate frailty and dependence. For women there appears to be a period of florescence later in life, and this has been noted by theorists as varied as Meillassoux and Jung. Thus Meillassoux writes:

> Marx is therefore right to believe that women probably constituted the first exploited class. All the same, it is still necessary to distinguish different categories of women in terms of the function they fulfill according to age by which they are not in the same relations of exploitaton and subordination. . . . After menopause, and even more so as a grandmother, . . . socially she comes into her own. (1981:76, 78)

And from a psychoanalytic perspective Jung remarks:

> There are many women who only awaken to social responsibility and to social consciousness after their fortieth year. . . . One can observe women . . . who have developed in the second half of life an uncommonly masculine tough-mindedness which thrusts the feelings and the heart aside. . . . Intelligent and cultivated people live their lives without even knowing of the possibility of such transformations. Wholly unprepared, they embark upon the second half of life. (1960:398)

Fortunately the readers of this book will not chance "wholly unprepared" upon the phenomenon both authors describe. The chapters that follow provide full details of the "transformation" Jung merely intimates. As Meillassoux notes, the middle-aged woman is woman come into her own.

Addendum to the Second Edition

As noted in the opening paragraphs of this chapter in the first edition, the study of older women has moved from the general to the specific; first, because more data have become available, and second, because we are now in a position to ask more informed questions. What was subtitled in the introduction to the first edition as "The Exercise of Authority," now invites a more detailed examination, with a focus on the relationship of middle-aged women to their younger female kin. Cross-culturally this relationship is shaped by three variables. The first is the division of labor by sex in subsistence activities (what members of a society do to make a living, such as hunting, herding, horticulture). The second is the cultural rule for postmarital residence (where a married couple is expected to set up housekeeping, whether with the groom's family, the bride's family, or on their own). The third is the cultural rule for reckoning descent (whether the individual is viewed as descended from the father's paternal male ancestors, the mother's maternal female ancestors, a combination of these two lines, or from ancestors of both parents and both sexes).

Subsistence Activities

In some nonindustrialized societies, women are the major breadwinners. When the very survival of the group depends upon the output of female labor, older women dominate their younger female kin in the interest of productivity. The middle-aged woman's managerial role often is carried out so deftly that it goes unremarked by the ethnographer. However, Murphy and Murphy (1974) provide a full description for the Mundurucú of South America. Traditionally in this tribe the household of up to fifty people was under the undisputed direction of the oldest woman. She also organized the cultivation and processing of bitter manioc, the staple of the Mundurucú diet. The production of flour from bitter manioc is laborious and involves several sequential tasks that have to be coordinated and rotated among the women of the household. Also, the household's activities have to be coordinated with those of other households in the village. According to Murphy and Murphy, the women cooperated easily and with no friction, and the work was administered quite unobtrusively by the elder women.

The status inequality imposed by this division of labor by age contains the promise for its younger members that they will become administrators. In their years as laborers, the junior women have ample time to acquire the skills needed for the senior managerial positions. A woman gradually builds up her authority by creating obligations among her juniors (see Lambek, Sinclair, this volume). In a sense, she earns the right to delegate the tasks she formerly performed. Perhaps there is a lesson in this.

For a complex, industrialized society like the United States, it is difficult to generalize because American women's contribution to making a living varies from household to household. When older women exercise authority over younger women, it is typically over nonkin in the workplace. But unlike the Mundurucú, our society underutilizes the managerial capacity of older women.

In our own society, the alleged incompatibility between women's family responsibilities and their employment (see Ehrlich 1989; Fuchs 1988; Schwartz 1989), noted by numerous observers, casts its long shadow also across the lives of older women. If they interrupted their years of employment to raise children they are at a distinct disadvantage when reentering the labor force. If their employment is continuous they frequently encounter the "invisible ceiling" because they have been assigned to the "mommy track." The outcome? A recent article in *Business Week* reports: "Only about 2% of corporate officers at major public companies are women" (Ehrlich 1989).

Postmarital Residence

The relationship between a middle-aged woman and her younger female kin may be that of mother and daughter, mother-in-law and daughter-in-law, or senior wife and junior wife, among others. Although a single senior woman can fulfill numerous kinship roles simultaneously, only some of these relationships will be of actual importance in any one society. This is because societal rules concerning which relatives should share a household will bring certain relatives into close contact, while separating others.

When these rules dictate that a bride must move into the household of her husband's family at marriage (patrilocal residence), particularly if she must marry a man from a community other than her own (community exogamy), the mother-in-law/daughter-in-law relationship becomes emphasized, whereas the relationship between a mother and her married daughter becomes tenuous. Patrilocal residence makes it possible for the mother-in-law to provide supervision of her daughter-in-law. This monitoring is particularly significant for societies, such as those described below, in which men and women lead separated daily lives because custom dictates that men spend their time with men and women with women. (The demands of child-care and subsistence activities separate the sexes to a certain extent in all societies, yet in some, it is as if men and women inhabit two different worlds. See Whiting and Whiting 1975.)

In patrilocal societies, once women move into the family home of the husband at marriage they are "lost" to the family and household of their birth. As Freedman (1967) has noted for traditional Chinese society, a woman's allegiance to the family and household of her husband is questioned until she proves herself worthy of trust by producing sons, and thus has blood ties to her husband's family.

The lives of women in these societies are characterized by discontinuity. As a bride in the household of her husband and his family, she is in a position of servitude, separated from her own kin, living under the authority of her mother-in-law, and treated as an outsider even by her own husband. It is the birth of sons that raises her status. As these sons mature, she becomes the imposing and respected mother-in-law with authority over her daughters-in-law and with the power to exert strong influence upon and through her grown sons. The latter often are more deeply attached to her than to their young wives.

A full description of this metamorphosis is provided by Roy (1975), whose report is based upon the detailed life histories of some fifty upper-class Bengali women. The young bride, homesick for her village and family, restricted to life in purdah among strangers, compelled to demonstrate industriousness and respect for her husband's kin, eventually becomes the matron-mother. Mernissi (1975) gives a strikingly similar account for traditional Moroccan Muslim society. Living in the household of her husband's family, the young bride is tutored and protected by her mother-in-law, for whom she performs daily, prescribed deference rituals. When she becomes a mother-in-law, the submission of her daughters-in-law is required by modern law.

In societies that confine and restrict junior women, the bride often is wedded at an extremely young age, and the marriage actually may not be consummated until years later. The mother-in-law becomes a surrogate parent who completes the daughter-in-law's upbringing and she may even orchestrate the sex life of the recently married couple (see Vatuk, this volume). Although the older woman who imposes her authority on the daughter-in-law was once similarly subjugated by her own mother-in-law, this is not simply an example of "identification with the aggressor," rather, such behavior is motivated by the need to assure the legitimacy of a son's offspring.

When postmarital residence is other than patrilocal, the mother-in-law/daughter-in-law relationship is not emphasized. For example, when a married man is required to live in the home of his wife's family (matrilocal residence), a woman and her daughters share a household all their lives. Here the mother/daughter relationship predominates and her daughters-in-law reside elsewhere in the homes of their respective mothers. The mother's and the mother-in-law's authority is very much reduced in societies like our own, in which the married couple typically sets up a new home separate from both sets of parents (neolocal residence). This arrangement, relatively rare in the nonindustrialized world, provides younger women with a certain measure of autonomy.

Descent

Most nonindustrialized societies practice patrilocality and also patrilineal descent. This means that the individual is viewed as descended from the father and the father's paternal male kin and is allied with relatives who share these male links to the ancestors. Whereas patrilocal residence makes it possible for a mother-in-law to supervise and restrict her daughter-in-law, patrilineal descent provides the motivation for that monitoring.

When descent is patrilineal, a problem arises concerning the certainty of paternity, creating a special need, on the part of the patriline, to control and monopolize the sexual behavior of women. Thus Gaulin writes: "There is an inherent sex-bias in parental certainty: females will always know their offspring but males can only elevate their parental certainty by monitoring their mates" (1980:229). In some societies such "monitoring" requires the confinement of all women and girls of childbearing age, making them economically dependent and thus subservient to the patrilineage. For older women in patrilineal societies, only the children of their sons are culturally defined as their descendants. The offspring of their daughters are relinquished to the descent groups of the sons-in-law. Since her sons' children are her descendants, the older woman has a stake in ensuring their legitimacy, therefore she participates in the "monitoring" noted by Gaulin above, supervising and restricting the behavior of her daughters-in-law.

On the other hand, in societies practicing matrilineal descent (in which the individual is viewed as descended from the mother and her female maternal ancestors), the parental certainty of a woman's descendants is inevitably assured, since they are the children of her daughters and not those of her sons. And in societies practicing bilateral descent (such as our own, in which the individual is viewed as descended from both parents and their male and female ancestors), the concern with a daughter-in-law's virtue does pertain (see Kerns, this volume), yet it is less extreme, since the descendants of an older woman can include children of both sons and daughters.

In our own society, the coresident, multigeneration family is the exception. Often great distances separate an older woman from her daughters and daughters-in-law. This fact, and the negative valuation our society places on intrusiveness in the senior generation, vastly reduce the dominance American middle-aged women exert over their younger kin.

In our own society, being in charge, exerting authority, and assuming managerial responsibility are roles for middle-aged women that remain largely underutilized in the workplace and that are not esteemed within the family. Yet in certain nonindustrialized societies, such as the Iroquois (Brown 1975), matrons were expected to manage the cultivation of food and to exert political and domestic power. The cross-cultural evidence suggests that our society may be wasting the potential of its middle-aged women.

NOTES

1. Gilligan (1981) presents the rationale for a "sex-segregated" study of adulthood.

2. See Kerns (1983) for an unusually full description of ritual roles for older women among the Garífuna.

3. Barnett and Baruch stress the importance of considering the conditions and the status of American women's work, as these "appear to have a profound effect upon women's experiences particularly in the second half of the life span" (1978:192).

4. The foregoing generalizations are documented in detail in a previous article (Brown 1982).

5. All but one of the chapters in the first edition of this book were initially presented in two symposia dealing with middle-aged women at the 1982 annual meeting of the American Anthropological Association, held in Washington, D.C.

6. Simić (1978) uses this classification in introducing a collection of studies of aging. "Intermediate societies" are those in which modernization is occurring, yet many elements of traditional life persist.

REFERENCES

Amoss, Pamela, and Stevan Harrell, eds.
  1981   Other Ways of Growing Old: Anthropological Perspectives. Stanford, Calif.: Stanford University Press.
Alexander, Richard
  1974   The Evolution of Social Behavior. Annual Review of Ecology and Systematics 5:325–83.
Barnett, Rosalind C., and Grace K. Baruch
  1978   Women in the Middle Years: A Critique of Research and Theory. Psychology of Women Quarterly 3:187–97.
Bart, Pauline
  1969   Why Women's Status Changes in Middle Age: The Turn of the Social Ferris Wheel. Sociological Symposium 3:1–18.
Brown, Judith K.
  1970   Economic Organization and the Position of Women among the Iroquois. Ethnohistory 17:151–67.

1975   Iroquois Women: An Ethnohistoric Note. *In* Toward an Anthropology of Women. R. Reiter, ed. pp. 235–51. New York: Monthly Review Press.

1982   Cross-cultural Perspectives on Middle-Aged Women. Current Anthropology 23(2):143–56.

Burgess, Carolyn

1982   A Cultural View of Menopause. Paper presented at the Women and Mental Health Conference and Proceedings. Norman, Okla.

Datan, Nancy, Aaron Antonovsky, and Benjamin Maoz

1981   A Time to Reap: The Middle Age of Women in Five Israeli Subcultures. Baltimore: Johns Hopkins University Press.

Davis, Dona

1983   Blood and Nerves: An Ethnographic Focus on Menopause. St. John's: Memorial University of Newfoundland.

Dougherty, Molly

1978   An Anthropological Perspective on Aging and Women in the Middle Years. *In* The Anthropology of Health. E. E. Bauwens, ed. pp. 167–76. St. Louis: C. V. Mosby.

Ehrlich, Elizabeth

1989   The Mommy Track. Business Week 113:126–34.

Flint, Marcha

1975   The Menopause: Reward or Punishment? Psychosomatics 16:161–63.

Flint, Marcha, guest ed.

1982   Maturitas 4(3).

Freedman, Maurice

1967   Rites and Duties, or Chinese Marriage. London: London School of Economics and Political Science/G. Bell and Sons, Ltd.

Fry, Christine L., ed.

1980   Aging in Culture and Society: Comparative Viewpoints and Strategies. New York: Praeger/Bergin.

Fuchs, Victor

1988   Women's Quest for Economic Equality. Cambridge, Mass.: Harvard University Press.

Gaulin, S. J. C.

1980   Sexual Dimorphism in the Human Post-reproductive Life Span: Possible Causes. Journal of Human Evolution 9:227–32.

Gilligan, Carol

1981   Adult Development and Women's Development: Arrangements for a Marriage. *In* Women in the Middle Years: Current Knowledge and Directions for Research and Policy. J. Z. Giele, ed. pp. 89–114. New York: Wiley-Interscience.

Griffen, Joyce

1977   A Cross-cultural Investigation of Behavioral Changes at Menopause. Social Science Journal 14:49–55.

Hahn, Ida

1919   Dauernahrung und Frauenarbeit. Zeitschrift für Ethnologie 51:243–59.

Henry, Jules
   1977 [1966] Forty-year-old Jitters in Married Urban Women. *In* Annual
      Editions: Readings in Anthropology 77–78. D. Rosen et al., eds. pp. 262–
      68. Guilford, Conn.: Dushkin.
Jung, C. G.
   1960 [1931] The Structure and Dynamics of the Psyche. R. F. C. Hull, trans.
      Bollingen Series 20. New York: Pantheon.
Kaufert, Patricia
   1979 The Menopause as a Life Crisis Event. Paper presented at the Annual
      Meeting of the Society for Applied Anthropology. Philadelphia.
Kerns, Virginia
   1979 Social Transition at Menopause. Paper presented at the Annual Meeting
      of the American Anthropological Association. Cincinnati.
   1980 Menopause and the Post-reproductive Years. National Women's Anthro-
      pology Newsletter 4(2):15–16; 4(3):26–27.
   1983 Women and the Ancestors: Black Carib Kinship and Ritual. Urbana:
      University of Illinois Press.
Mayer, Peter J.
   1982 Evolutionary Advantage of the Menopause. Human Ecology 10(4):
      477–94.
Meillassoux, Claude
   1981 Maidens, Meal and Money: Capitalism and the Domestic Community.
      Felicity Edholm, trans. New York: Cambridge University Press.
Mernissi, Fatima
   1975 Beyond the Veil: Male-Female Dynamics in a Modern Muslim Society.
      Cambridge, Mass.: Schenkman.
Murphy, Yolanda, and Robert Murphy
   1974 Women of the Forest. New York: Columbia University Press.
Neugarten, Bernice
   1970 Dynamics of Transition of Middle Age to Old Age: Adaptation and the
      Life Cycle. Journal of Geriatric Psychiatry 4:71–87.
Richards, Audrey
   1956 Chisungu: A Girls' Initiation Ceremony among the Bemba of Northern
      Rhodesia. New York: Grove Press.
Roy, Manisha
   1975 Bengali Women. Chicago: University of Chicago Press.
Schwartz, Felice N.
   1989 Management Women and the New Facts of Life. Harvard Business
      Review 89:65–76.
Seaver, James E.
   1961 [1824] A Narrative of the Life of Mrs. Mary Jemison. New York:
      Corinth Books.
Simić, Andrei
   1978 Introduction: Aging and the Aged in Cultural Perspective. *In* Life's
      Career—Aging: Cultural Variations on Growing Old. B. Myerhoff and A.
      Simić, eds. pp. 9–22. Beverly Hills: Sage.

Voda, Ann, Myra Dinnerstein, and Sheryl O'Donnell, eds.
　　1982　Changing Perspectives on Menopause. Austin: University of Texas
　　　　Press.
Whiting, John, and Beatrice Whiting
　　1975　Aloofness and Intimacy of Husbands and Wives: A Cross-cultural
　　　　Study. Ethos 3:183–207.
Wright, Anne
　　1979　Roles and Cultural Interpretation of Menopause. Paper presented at the
　　　　Annual Meeting of the American Anthropological Association. Cincinnati.
Wylie, Philip
　　1942　Generation of Vipers. New York: Farrar and Rinehart.

PART 1

Small-Scale Traditional Societies

Although their settings and their subsistence activities differ, the !Kung, the Bakgalagadi, and the Lusi are small-scale traditional societies whose middle-aged women lead somewhat similar lives. The importance of "kin keeping" by older !Kung women is stressed by Richard B. Lee. This specialized knowledge gives them considerable influence over the lives of their juniors, since kinship information provides the basis for marriage arrangements. A similar theme appears in Jacqueline S. Solway's data for the Bakgalagadi, and Dorothy Ayers Counts reports that mothers are as involved as fathers in arranging marriages, although the Lusi claim it is a male prerogative.

Older women among the !Kung enjoy a relatively more leisured life, one that is physically less demanding than that of younger women. The middle-aged Bakgalagadi woman delegates the work she formerly performed to younger members of the household. In all three societies, older women become increasingly active in trade networks because they have more time to devote to such activities and because they enjoy increased geographic mobility and greater control over resources.

Both Counts and Solway introduce the theme of responsibility. (Also see the later chapter by Sinclair.) Mere longevity does not guarantee esteem for a woman who is judged foolish or improvident. Yet Lee notes a relaxation of inhibitions among older !Kung women. Their sexuality is no longer a source of conflict, and they are not expected or compelled to give up sexual relations. (This is also the case for Garífuna women, in contrast to middle-aged women in India. See the later chapters by Kerns and Vatuk.)

None of the accounts mentions a special status such as matchmaker or medicine woman for individual middle-aged women. The absence of such statuses may simply be due to the relative lack of specialists in such small-scale traditional societies. Middle-aged women enjoy the authority to contribute to important decisions, the right to extract labor from younger kin, and exemption from restrictions they had to observe earlier in life. It is particularly significant that Lee reports an enhanced position for older women among the !Kung, who have an egalitarian gender ideology. Changes in status at middle age are not limited only to societies in which young women are disadvantaged and powerless.

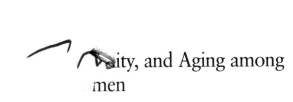

KUNG

4 ...ity, and Aging among ...men

...rd B. Lee

In many societies of sub-Saharan Africa and other areas discussed in this volume, we find older women playing leading roles on the stage of life. The !Kung San, a former gathering and hunting people of northwestern Botswana, are a case in point. The status of !Kung women, generally high, increases with age and reaches a peak in the decades after the child-rearing tasks are completed. The postmenopausal !Kung woman is a mover and shaker in !Kung society and is one of the main agents and sources of sexual joking. The high status of !Kung women has been noted by a number of observers. What has received less attention is the way in which this status waxes and wanes through the life cycle among the !Kung and in other societies as well.

The !Kung are a Khoisan people speaking a click language who live in Botswana and Namibia and number about fifteen thousand. Botswana, where I did my fieldwork from 1963 on, is an independent African nation. Before attaining independence in 1990, Namibia was a neocolony illegally occupied by South Africa. Until the early 1960s about 20 percent of all !Kung continued to live as relatively isolated full-time gatherer-hunters without agriculture and without domestic animals. More recently the pace of change has accelerated; the Botswana !Kung have become involved in stock raising, agriculture, and wage labor, while their Namibian neighbors have been settled on government stations for two decades. Beginning in 1975 and continuing into the 1980s (unfortunately), a number of Namibia !Kung worked full-time as trackers and soldiers for the South African occupation army. In this chapter, I will be referring to the !Kung in the Dobe area of Botswana between 1963 and 1969, the time of my main fieldwork.

The !Kung San are one of the best documented gatherer-hunter peoples in the world. Detailed studies of many aspects of !Kung life have been published (see Lee and DeVore 1976; L. Marshall 1976; Lee 1979; Howell 1979; Yellen 1977; Katz 1982). !Kung studies are particularly fortunate to have a rich corpus of data on !Kung women to draw upon. At least six anthropologists have worked on this topic since 1950. The work of Lorna Marshall (1976) is well known; Pat Draper has written about sex roles (1975) and gender aspects of child rearing (1976); Nancy Howell has done studies of !Kung demography (1979); Marjorie Shostak has collected life history materials (1981); Megan Biesele has worked on folklore (1976) and Pauline Wiessner on trade relations (1982); and others have also contributed. In particular, in addition to my own field data, I will be drawing on two important papers on !Kung aging, one by Biesele and Howell entitled "The Old People Give You Life" (1981) and the other by Shostak called "Being of Age among the !Kung San" (1980).

Demographics and Food Gathering

First we need to ask how many older !Kung there are. What proportion of the !Kung live to the ripe age of sixty? According to popular belief, which characterizes foraging peoples like the !Kung as worn out by the struggle to survive, the answer would be "not very many." The literature on foragers is full of impressionistic statements to the effect that men and women are old at thirty and dead at forty-five. Thus it may come as a surprise that a considerable proportion of !Kung—about 10 percent—are over the age of sixty, a proportion comparable to that of the North American population around the turn of the twentieth century. Infant mortality is high among the !Kung—about four hundred per one thousand live births (Howell 1979)—but those who do survive to age fifteen have a reasonable expectation of reaching sixty, and not a few !Kung live to be seventy or even eighty.

In the older age groups women heavily outnumber men. Table 1 shows the proportion of men and women in three age groups in three different censuses (1964, 1968, and 1973). This preponderance of older women has important consequences for rates of widowhood and remarriage.

Let us now look at women's work in the foraging context. Gathering of wild plant foods provides between 60 and 80 percent of the diet by weight, and women play a very important role in providing food for the group. Young women don't really start to gather seriously until the age of fifteen. But then for the bulk of their adult lives, the women produce the major proportion of all the food brought into camp, about 55 percent of the total. Men produce the other 45 percent, including almost all of the

Table 1. Age-Sex Composition of Dobe Population

Age	Males Number	Males Percentage	Females Number	Females Percentage	Total Number	Total Percentage
1964						
Old	14	8.1	23	11.2	37	9.8
Adult	112	64.7	123	59.7	235	62.0
Young	47	27.2	60	29.1	107	28.2
Total	173	100.0	206	100.0	379	100.0
1968						
Old	17	7.8	23	9.5	40	8.7
Adult	141	65.3	145	60.2	286	62.6
Young	58	26.9	73	30.3	131	28.7
Total	216	100.0	241	100.0	457	100.0
1973						
Old	19	9.1	30	12.1	49	10.7
Adult	125	60.1	140	56.2	265	58.0
Young	64	30.8	79	31.7	143	31.3
Total	208	100.0	249	100.0	457	100.0

Note: Old = 60+; Adult = 15–59; Young = 0–14 years.

meat that is eaten (about 30 percent of the total diet), and about 15–20 percent of the gathered food.

Women's economic importance is underscored by the fact that women produce more food than men but actually work shorter hours to do it: one study showed a 2.4-day work week for women and a 3.0-day work week for men (Lee 1979:260). If one breaks down women's work effort by age, a rather interesting point emerges: the highest work effort is among women in the age group twenty to thirty-nine, i.e., women who are raising young children. Not only are they producing more of the food and working longer hours, but they are also carrying their babies around on their backs. After age forty, a !Kung woman's work effort drops considerably (but see Lancaster and King, p. 8).

Women and Child Care

Now let us look at women's work in parenting. Menarche is late in the !Kung woman. According to Howell, it occurs at age 16.5, and age at first birth is even later—about 19.5 years (1976:144–45). Adolescent sterility is common, so if there are premarital affairs, they don't normally lead to pregnancies. Fertility is overall very low for the !Kung—Howell's data indicate 4.6 live births or 4.6 completed family size for postmenopausal women, a very low value for a noncontracepting population. There is a tremendous investment of labor in each individual child; the !Kung have few children, but their quality of child care is quite high. Birth spacing is three or four years and breast-feeding continues for two or three years. The !Kung must be among the world's most prodigious lactaters: twenty-four-hour breast-feeding on demand continues into the child's third year of life. Evidence now indicates that until recently lactation suppressed ovulation amongst the !Kung for at least the first twenty-four months of the child's life (cf. Lee 1979, 1980; Konner and Worthman 1980). !Kung women also carry the child on their back for the first twenty-four months of the child's life, and although overall work effort among the !Kung is moderate, a rather high proportion of that work effort falls on the parents with young children. With the growth of the children to maturity, of course, this high level of work effort declines.

Sexuality

Like her counterparts in other foraging societies, the !Kung child becomes familiar with sexuality early in life. The youngest children sleep under the same blankets with their parents and are under the blankets during their parents' lovemaking. From the age of eight or ten, children engage in sex play, which may include intercourse. Shostak, in her insightful biography of a !Kung woman, quotes Nisa as saying,

> At night, when a child lies beside her mother, in front, and her father lies down behind and her mother and father make love, the child watches. . . .
> Perhaps this is the way the child eventually learns, because as she gets older, she begins to understand that her mother and father are making love. At first she thinks, "So that's another thing people do with their genitals." Then if the child is a little boy, he'll take the little girl, or perhaps his sister, and do the same thing to her, he'll teach himself. He'll make believe he's having sex with her as he saw his mother and father do. And once he's learned it, he'll try to play that way with everyone. . . .
> That's what an older child does. He waits until he is with a little girl and lies down with her. He takes some saliva, rubs it on her genitals, gets on top and pokes around with his semi-erection, as though he were actually having intercourse, but he is not. Because even though young boys can get hard, they don't really enter little girls. Nor do they yet know about ejaculation. Only when a boy is almost a young man does he start to have sex like an adult.
> At first, girls refuse that kind of play—they say all that poking around hurts. But when they are a little older, they agree to it and eventually, even like it. (1981:111–12)

It will be clear from the above that the !Kung have no notion of virginity. I have never been able to come up with a concept or a sense of a word that would correspond to our word *virgin*. Given the early sex play, I will hazard a guess that there are few !Kung virgins, male or female, at puberty. (Puberty for girls is marked by a dramatic ritual which is still performed. In the Eland Dance, the menstruating girl is secluded for several days and nights while the women of the village dance naked before her. Men are excluded from the Eland Dance.)

As puberty approaches, however, a girl's sexuality, once a trifling matter, becomes an explosive issue for the !Kung. The existence of an unattached sexually attractive young woman in a group draws male suitors like moths to a flame, and many fights, some fatal, have broken out amongst rival suitors (Lee 1979:chap. 13). Therefore, the goal of parents is to betroth their daughters as young as possible and to marry them off early to minimize the chance of potential conflict. Before 1960, most !Kung girls were married between the ages of twelve and fifteen, well before reaching menarche. This eagerness to marry girls off at a young age sometimes reached absurd lengths. Concerning the Nyae Nyae !Kung, for example, people in other regions have a saying: "The girls of Nyae Nyae go from their mother's breast to their husband's bed on one day." In some of Lorna Marshall's photographs of brides, they look like they are nine or ten years old, and N!ai, the subject of a television documentary (J. Marshall 1980) was married at the age of eight. Thus the saying about the girls of Nyae Nyae, though not literally true, does have an element of truth in it.

Because the girls are so young, the first years of marriage are usually spent uxorilocally, with the wife's family. Husbands are usually seven to fifteen years older than wives at first marriage. Once married, a woman's sexual development, or we should say further sexual development, may be delayed, and a further stormy period follows as she adjusts to life with a much older man in an arranged marriage. We have a number of accounts of !Kung marriages being consummated only two or three years after the actual ceremony. About half of these arranged first marriages fail, and the divorce is almost always initiated by the wife. The woman may then take a series of lovers before settling down in a second match that usually lasts for many years.

Adult sexuality is an area about which we have a lot of fragments of information but no systematic study. Summing up observers' impressions, we can say the following: By Western standards, the !Kung have good sex lives. Sexuality is a topic of light, easy banter among groups of men and groups of women. It is regarded as a natural and positive area of life. There are few cases of reported sexual dysfunction. Women experience orgasm and have spoken about it at length with observers (e.g., Shostak

1981). The term *tain,* which is used for orgasm, is the same as the term describing the sublime sweetness of wild honey. A rather nice metaphor.

Do married !Kung have affairs? Some married people are generally acknowledged by the community to be strictly monogamous. For others, extramarital love affairs seem to play an important role in their lives. As Shostak's interviews revealed, love affairs, while not very frequent among the !Kung, do loom large in women's consciousness. But love affairs, while exciting, are also risky. Privacy is at a premium among the !Kung, and no matter how discreet they are, lovers are from time to to time discovered and exposed. Aggrieved spouses, both male and female, will frequently attack their spouse or rival, and other family members will get drawn in. Arguments, brawls, and even poison arrow fights have occurred over the question of adultery. I recorded about a dozen such fights without weapons during three years of fieldwork, and when I collected histories of homicide in the past, adultery was time and again mentioned as one of the precipitating causes. It is interesting to note, however, that the person who gets killed is often not a principal in the original conflict, but a bystander or third party who got drawn in.

The possibility of serious conflict over extramarital sex puts a certain damper on the activity. !Kung women in the active childbearing years, twenty to forty, go to great lengths not to flaunt their sexuality in a provocative way. The preferred behavior in public for a woman in this age group is a shy sweetness—they are supposed to cover their mouths when they laugh and they are supposed always to take care to smooth the pubic apron over the genitals when they seat themselves. There is a great deal of arranging of skirts and tucking in and fidgeting when a woman sits down; this is considered modest decorous behavior. If women in this age group do have affairs, they do so with the utmost discretion.

Life after Forty

After the age of forty, however, major changes occur in !Kung women's behavior, body language, dress code, and demeanor. They become more open about sexuality, more playful, more outspoken at public events, and more politically central. What is the basis for this change and how is it manifested?

First, the older !Kung women become central nodes in kinship networks. Kinship play, the manipulation of kin terms and behavior for fun, is a central theme of !Kung kinship. In their complex kin system, it is by no means clear what term of address is to be used in any given case. Older women are the experts who decide what is the appropriate kin term. They are referred to on a daily basis about how this or that person should be addressed. In a very real sense, they are in charge of kinship classification for the society.

Second, older women gain power and responsibility from their role in arranging marriages and gift exchange. The !Kung traditional *hxaro* network involves men and women with dozens of exchange partners throughout the Dobe area and beyond (Wiessner 1982). People in the forty to fifty-five age group have the peak number of *hxaro* partners and also are the age group with offspring of marriageable age.

Perhaps most striking are the changes in sexual behavior. An older woman may take a younger man as a lover and do this more openly. The reasons are not clear to me. There seems to be less danger attached to it, since husbands are often away for long periods or perhaps are less jealous. In a number of recorded cases, after divorce or widowhood a woman has married a man younger than herself, in some instances ten or twenty years younger. I know of one case in which a woman married a man thirty years younger than herself. At the /Xai/xai water hole, about 20 percent of all marriages are of older women and younger men.

The freedom of older women is graphically illustrated by changing dress codes. The height at which !Kung women wear their pubic apron on their abdomens is a very important marker in their presentation of self; it communicates something about status, marital situation, and age. The higher the position of the apron above the navel, the more chaste and modest is the woman's demeanor, while the lower positions, which can get very low indeed, can mean several different interesting things.

First of all it can refer to informality. When the !Kung are living in small groups in the bush instead of living in large groups at the permanent water holes, the women lower their pubic aprons two or three inches and wear them just above the pubic bone. The lowering of the apron is an index of familial intimacy; in a small camp with a dozen people who know each other well or are all related, the aprons indicate ease and familiarity but not sexual intimacy.

If the lowered pubic apron is worn in a larger group, however, it *can* indicate a sexual message. If a woman's husband is away, she may be communicating something about her sexual availability. On the other hand, women who are fighting with their husbands may wear the apron lower as a way of indicating their anger.

The lowering of the apron also seems to correlate with age. The apron gets lower and lower as the woman goes from fifty to sixty, and it continues to get even lower as the woman goes from sixty to seventy. One can actually see daylight between the apron and the pubes of some sixty-five-year-old women, a manner of dress that would be unthinkable for a younger woman. Thus what appears to be an inviolable dress code *is* violable; a sixty- or seventy-year-old woman feels no compunction about letting her genitals be partially displayed.

The !Kung use of the pubic apron as a marker of age or sexual status reminds me of Murphy's famous study of the Tuareg entitled "Social Distance and the Veil" (1964). Murphy described how the veil goes up in Tuareg men to cover the face in front of strangers and how it goes down in more intimate situations. On the whole question of the pubic apron and the exposure of the female genitals, I would refer the reader to Olson's fascinating discussion of the Northwest Coast "Some Trading Customs of the Chilkat" (1936). Olson relates how Bella Coola women traders would move inland, marry Carrier Indian men, and take them as trading partners to provide goods for the burgeoning Bella Coola potlatches. In some sense, one could talk of these women as being in a Big Woman's system. As the Bella Coola potlatches increased in scale and the demand for goods became greater and greater, the women used all sorts of tricks in their trading relations with the inland peoples. They would have enormous success during gambling sessions, for example, by lifting their genital apron while seated in the middle of a tense game. The men's concentration would be broken, and the women could win every hand and walk away with the whole pot.

The contemporary !Kung don't gamble, but the women do engage in provocative public displays that parallel the Chilkat practices. With male joking partners, for example, older women may engage in bawdy horseplay including grabbing the men's genitals and playfully mounting the man and pretending to have intercourse. We see this kind of grabbing as well among men, and also among women of the appropriate joking categories, but only women over fifty will engage in this kind of horseplay with the opposite sex. I well remember the day that five !Kung women aged fifty to sixty-five jumped a male co-worker, Richard Katz, and myself, with shouts of hilarity and tried to force us to have intercourse with them. However, our virtue was preserved by the timely intervention of a Herero neighbor and by the fact that we were all laughing too hard to continue. (Howell also tells a story of how she came into camp once and saw five females jumping rope, four girls from the age of ten to fifteen and one sixty-five-year-old woman, who was not only having a good time but was also very good at it.)

Discussion

The boldness and ease of public presentation of self coupled with the prominent social and economic role played by older !Kung women deserves some explanation. We know that menopause is a time of transition for women in all societies. Why among the !Kung—in common with other Third World women—do the women undergo a blossoming rather than a shrinking or contraction? First of all, there is the major drop in the work demands upon these older women. Their children are grown and doing their own foraging, and the flow of food from parents to children may reverse. Mothers who had fed children for years and years may now become net receivers, getting more food from their adult offspring than they are giving. Also, the labor of carrying children is no longer required. Clearly, one aspect of the "coming out" of older !Kung women has to do with taking a vacation from the world of work.

The second area of explanation focuses on the social and political centrality of the generations of people in the forty-five to sixty-five age group. These are the people, male and female, who are at the peak of their political powers. Collectively, they are the parents, the older siblings, or parents-in-law of the 75–90 percent of the population who are younger than they are. In !Kung kinship, age is a crucially important factor and all kin terms have an older/younger designation built in. To be the older member of a kinship dyad carries with it important prerogatives of respect and deference. Kin terms are assigned according to a complex set of rules derived from personal names. One of the mysteries of !Kung kinship is that from the point of view of the younger person the kinship term used for an older person often doesn't fit. The reason is that it is the older persons who generate the kin term and they decide what term to use according to their lights, whether or not it makes sense to the younger person (cf. Lee 1984:chap. 5). Yet once imposed, the kin term chosen by the older person begins to develop a logic of its own as it becomes transmitted in turn by the younger people to others even younger than they. In a real sense, therefore, the elders are legislating the classification structure of society.

One could argue that by the criterion of age it must be the very oldest people, those in their seventies and eighties, who are the most respected, because they have in effect classified all the people younger than themselves. But the eldest of the elders, the "old-dead" in !Kung terms, are well past their physical prime and they play an increasingly marginal role in !Kung society.

Rose (1968) took these same biological and social facts about age, political centrality, and power and applied them to the Australian Aborigines. He argued that these facts generated in Australia a gerontocracy in which elder males controlled the lives of women and younger males. A similar model has been developed for West African agricultural societies by Meillassoux (1964) and Dupré and Rey (1973), to mention just two studies. Among the !Kung, however, both women and men take the

hough the power of either sex is severely circumscribed by
alitarian social arrangements of the !Kung. (Woodburn has
overview of the nature of egalitarian societies [1981]. See
...o Silberbauer 1982.)

To the factors of easing of work demands and sociopolitical centrality must be added a third, which may turn out to be the most important: the changing evaluation of women's sexuality. From the age of fifteen to forty women's (and men's) sexuality was a potentially explosive issue, probably the most explosive issue the !Kung had to deal with. After a woman's menopause, however, the emotional level of this tension falls precipitously.

People rarely fought in the past over land or property, but we have over a dozen cases of men fighting over contested betrothals or adultery. Sexual matters were the main causes of fatal fighting among the !Kung (Lee 1979:chap. 13). One of the paradoxes of !Kung life is that despite the low development of property concepts, there is a high level of sexual jealousy: both men and women express a great deal of it and will attempt to hurt or kill a spouse or rival if they discover an act of adultery.

After a certain age, however, this situation changes dramatically. The angry jealous sexuality of the young gives way to a much more relaxed attitude. Affairs become more open and tolerated; although fights may still occur, they are less intense and less likely to escalate into bloody battles. A woman's (and a man's) sexuality can now be expressed without unleashing disruptive, destructive social forces.

To conclude, then, the !Kung San have been regarded as a society exhibiting one of the world's highest levels of sexual egalitarianism. We have seen how !Kung women behave as actors on the stage of their society's history and not just as spectators. The aging process enhances women's power instead of weakening it. For the older !Kung women the long-term cycles of work effort and family responsibility and rising social centrality converge to make the period of middle age a time of unparalleled influence in the affairs of the community. And it is also the period in which a woman's sexuality, which until then was a strictly private affair, becomes a subject for public display and celebration.

NOTE

This study, originally presented at the annual meetings of the Canadian Ethnology Society/Societé Canadienne d'Éthnologie, Ottawa, in March 1981, has been substantially revised for this volume.

REFERENCES

Biesele, Megan
    1976   Aspects of !Kung Folklore. *In* Kalahari Hunter-Gatherers. R. B. Lee
        and I. DeVore, eds. pp. 302–24. Cambridge, Mass.: Harvard University
        Press.
Biesele, Megan, and Nancy Howell
    1981   "The Old People Give You Life": Aging among !Kung Hunter-Gatherers.
        In Other Ways of Growing Old: Anthropological Perspectives. P. Amoss
        and S. Harrell, eds. pp. 77–98. Stanford, Calif.: Stanford University Press.
Draper, Patricia
    1975   !Kung Women: Contrasts in Sexual Egalitarianism in the Foraging and
        Sedentary Contexts. *In* Toward an Anthropology of Women. R. Reiter, ed.
        pp. 77–109. New York: Monthly Review Press.
    1976   Social and Economic Constraints on Child Life among the !Kung. *In*
        Kalahari Hunter-Gatherers. R. B. Lee and I. DeVore, eds. pp. 199–217.
        Cambridge, Mass.: Harvard University Press.
Dupré, G., and P. Rey
    1973   Reflections on the Relevance of a Theory of the History of Exchange.
        Economy and Society 2:131–63.
Howell, Nancy
    1976   The Population of the Dobe Area !Kung. *In* Kalahari Hunter-Gatherers.
        R. B. Lee and I. DeVore, eds. pp. 152–65. Cambridge, Mass.: Harvard
        University Press.
    1979   Demography of the Dobe Area !Kung. New York: Academic Press.
Katz, Richard
    1982   Boiling Energy: Healing among the Kalahari !Kung. Cambridge, Mass.:
        Harvard University Press.
Konner, M., and C. Worthman
    1980   Nursing Frequency, Gonadal Function, and Birth Spacing among !Kung
        Hunter-Gatherers. Science 207:788–91.
Lee, Richard B.
    1979   The !Kung San: Men, Women, and Work in a Foraging Society. New
        York: Cambridge University Press.
    1980   Lactation, Ovulation, Infanticide and Women's Work: A Study of
        Hunter-Gatherer Population Regulation. *In* Biosocial Mechanisms of Popu-
        lation Regulation. M. Cohen, R. Malpass, and H. Klein, eds. pp. 321–48.
        New Haven, Conn.: Yale University Press.
    1984   The Dobe !Kung. Case Studies in Anthropology. New York: Holt,
        Rinehart and Winston.
Lee, Richard B., and Irven DeVore, eds.
    1976   Kalahari Hunter-Gatherers: Studies of the !Kung San and Their Neighbors.
        Cambridge, Mass.: Harvard University Press.

Marshall, John
    1980   N!ai: The Story of a !Kung Woman. Watertown, Mass.: Center for
    Documentary Resources. (Film)
Marshall, Lorna
    1976   The !Kung of Nyae Nyae. Cambridge, Mass.: Harvard University Press.
Meillassoux, Claude
    1964   Anthropologie economique des gouro de côte d'lvoire. Paris: Mouton.
Murphy, Robert
    1964   Social Distance and the Veil. American Anthropologist 66(6):1257–74.
Olson, R. L.
    1936   Some Trading Customs of the Chilkat Tlingit. *In* Essays in Anthropol-
    ogy Presented to A. L. Kroeber, pp. 211–14. Berkeley: University of Califor-
    nia Press.
Rose, Frederick G. G.
    1968   Australian Marriage, Land-Owning Groups, and Initiations. *In* Man the
    Hunter. R. B. Lee and I. DeVore, eds. pp. 200–208. Chicago: Aldine.
Shostak, Marjorie
    1980   Being of Age among the !Kung San: Adulthood and Aging in a Gathering-
    Hunting Society. Paper presented at the Conference on Cultural Phenome-
    nology of Adulthood and Aging. Harvard University.
    1981   Nisa: The Life and Words of a !Kung Woman. Cambridge, Mass.:
    Harvard University Press.
Silberbauer, G. B.
    1982   Political Process in G/wi Bands. *In* Politics and History in Band Societies.
    E. Leacock and R. B. Lee, eds. pp. 23–36. New York: Cambridge University
    Press.
Wiessner, Pauline
    1982   Risk, Reciprocity and Social Influences on !Kung San Economics. *In*
    Politics and History in Band Societies. E. Leacock and R. B. Lee, eds. pp.
    61–84. New York: Cambridge University Press.
Woodburn, James
    1981   Egalitarian Societies. Man (n.s.) 17:431–51.
Yellen, John E.
    1977   Archaeological Approaches to the Present: Models for Reconstructing
    the Past. New York: Academic Press.

5 Middle-Aged Women in Bakgalagadi Society (Botswana)

Jacqueline S. Solway

Much of the anthropology of women has focused on women's status as compared to men's, and it has generally been found that women occupy a lower status than do men in most societies. Although arguments claiming that male dominance is necessarily universal or inevitable are unconvincing, the fact remains that some degree of male dominance strikes many of us as a cross-cultural reality in the contemporary world (Ortner 1974; Rosaldo and Lamphere 1974; Leacock 1981).

However, only posing questions evaluating the relative status of men and women probably obscures relevant issues instead of elucidating them. Status is not a unidimensional feature; rather, categories of people may have high status in one domain of social life but lower status in other domains (cf. Tiffany 1979; Quinn 1977; Whyte 1978). The determinants of status vary cross-culturally. And in any particular society, the individual's rights and obligations in relation to other sex-age groups will vary with progress through the life course.

Status is used here to indicate the general position of a member or a category of members in society. Among the Bakgalagadi high status is achieved when individuals attain greater degrees of autonomy in determining the course of their lives. No individual as a member of society is ever completely autonomous. However, given the constraints imposed by the values, norms, and rules of any society, autonomy relates to an individual's ability to make decisions about his or her activities, the use of his or her labor, and the fruits of this labor. It relates to an individual's capacity to make decisions concerning the activities of others, the respect with which these decisions and opinions are greeted by the community, and the general degree of deference the individual is afforded.

Ethnographic Background

The Bakgalagadi are a Sotho-speaking people in the Kalahari Desert. They are similar to the neighboring Batswana studied by Schapera (1950, 1967) but are less politically centralized and live in smaller, less concentrated, and more isolated villages. The economy is based on pastoralism supplemented by agriculture. Until rather recently, the Bakgalagadi also depended on earnings derived from migrant labor to the South African mines (Solway 1979a, 1979b, 1990).

The kinship system is largely patrilineal in that the majority of property is inherited patrilineally, political office is inherited patrilineally (and based on the principle of primogeniture), and the individual is identified with and comes under the jural authority of the patrilineage. However, like other Sotho-speaking peoples, the Bakgalagadi permit cousin marriages of all kinds, therefore allowing lineage endogamy. This element complicates the principle of unilineality by creating ambiguous and overlapping links (Schapera 1950:149–65; Comaroff 1980:639; Kuper 1970:468), thus weakening the patriline and lending a cognatic element to the system. Postmarital residence is initially patrilocal, and ideally local residential groups are formed by lineage segments. However, in practice less than two-thirds of local households reside according to the ideal of lineal-based local groups, and matrilateral links and other cooperative relations frequently influence residential decisions.

Among the Bakgalagadi local ideology recognizes men as being more important: their work is more highly valued,[1] they are considered to have greater skills at making and enforcing decisions about most matters, their opinions are taken more seriously, and at most stages of the life cycle, they have greater autonomy. In addition, deference behavior is more often displayed toward men. However, this is a very general view and does not account for the fact that status is a dynamic phenomenon, changing with age for both men and women. Also, the spheres of activity, the domains of social life in which people attain prestige and position, are different for men and women in Bakgalagadi society and are not necessarily comparable in all respects. Toward middle age there tends to be a blurring of sex-role distinctions, and for women in particular, there are more avenues open for the achievement of high status.

Middle age is not an age category marked or recognized as a particular phase of life; nor are middle-aged people recognized as a unit. Perhaps before the 1930s, when initiations and the associated age regiments were common and had more importance, certain regiments were "middle-aged." However, several age regiments (*mephato*) would fall simultaneously into the middle-aged category, and it is unlikely that the middle-aged regiments formed a coherent unit.

Thus "middle age" is a designation I impose upon a clustering of features that tend to occur simultaneously in a Bakgalagadi woman's life. The most important are becoming head of the compound and the attainment of young adult status by her elder children, a status usually indicated by marriage or employment. Unlike younger women, a middle-aged woman has greater control over her productive and reproductive powers, greater authority over junior relatives, and within the larger community, greater opportunity to participate in social life.

A similar pattern emerges from an examination of the position of Bakgalagadi women in the context of the three phases of the domestic cycle identified by Fortes (1958): expansion, dispersion, and replacement. A married woman's status reaches its highest point at the overlap of the expansion and dispersion stages (Solway 1981). This is when her children marry and her mother-in-law loses control over the domestic sphere in the extended family household.

Sex Roles

For most of their lives, men and women participate in different domains of social life. Women's domain is the domestic sphere and agriculture. Men's domain lies outside the domestic sphere in herding (the activity from which the major means of publicly recognized exchange is produced), in the public political arena, and for a period of their lives, in wage labor employment outside the village. Only on ritual occasions are the domains kept rigidly distinct. The separateness of the sexes' domains is most clearly expressed in funeral practices.[2] On a day-to-day basis, however, distinctions are less strict and some overlap in activities occurs. The extent to which sex-role boundaries are crossed depends largely on an individual's place in the life cycle. Middle-aged women, particularly widows, are least tied to their traditional female domains and most able to participate in a full complement of social activities.

In a previous study (Solway 1981), I described the transformations in women's status that culminate in middle age. To summarize, a young, adult, unmarried woman enjoys a short period of relatively high status. She resides in her parents' compound, where younger siblings and sisters-in-law assume many household responsibilities. She has some autonomy over her activities and is often afforded luxuries, such as education, by her parents. Upon marriage and assumption of patrilocal residence, a woman's status declines significantly. A young wife is under the constant scrutiny of her affines, particularly her mother-in-law, and the young wife is expected to work hard and to produce children. In fact, one of her few times of relief occurs when she returns to her mother's compound to give birth. She spends two months in postnatal seclusion, during which female relatives indulge her. A young wife has few rights in her affines' compound, and she has little autonomy.

As a woman approaches middle age her status improves. She is no longer under the tutelage of her mother-in-law and is normally in charge of her compound. She has adult children to support and assist her. As head of her compound, she can delegate chores and responsibilities to daughters and to daughters-in-law who have assumed residence in her household, thus allowing the middle-aged woman greater participation in activities outside the domestic sphere. All Bakgalagadi women participate in exchange networks throughout their lives. However, a middle-aged woman, by virtue of her control over agricultural harvests, participates more substantially in public exchanges through both gift giving and sales of agricultural produce.

In addition, as grandmothers—a role that begins in middle age and extends through old age—women exert some control over kinship networks (cf. Lee 1981; also see Lee, this volume). In the field, I asked people why they applied specific kinship terms to others. Often they explained the kinship relationship that indicated a particular term. However, in many cases people did not know their precise relationship to others and they explained that they used the term because their grandmothers had told them to do so. Grandmothers thus influence future generations' social relations by contributing to their grandchildren's socialization into the kinship system.

In Bakgalagadi society status improves for both men and women as they advance through the life cycle. While women become heads of their compounds and managers of agricultural activities, men become heads of households, herd managers, and active participants in the *kgotla* (central village meeting place and court). Women also participate in the *kgotla* but rarely to the extent that men do. Although multiple factors interact to improve the position of both sexes, an important factor for both is parenthood and the associated statuses of husband and wife. The Bakgalagadi have a proverb which translates "An impala without a baby impala is stupid. Cleverness of the impala comes from its young one." It is believed that the responsibilities of parenthood make one wise. While parenthood is clearly important for all Bakgalagadi, women's status is more dependent on the roles of wife and mother than the status of men is on the roles of father and husband. Status (here identified with levels of autonomy and decision-making power) increases not only with age, but with the respect acquired when rights and obligations are fulfilled responsibly. Women more than men fulfill their obligations through others.

Responsible behavior (also see Counts, this volume) must be demonstrated in a variety of ways, including participation in culturally prescribed exchanges and public participation in community matters at the *kgotla*. In both activities, men take a more visible and active role. *Kgotla* participation is expected of adult males, particularly household heads, as they reach middle age. While the role of household head occurs at a similar stage in the life cycle and contains parallels to the role of compound head, the former involves publicly representing the household in extradomestic matters and the disposal of household resources other than food and normally includes ultimate decision-making powers over household members' extradomestic activities (although all adult household members confer about most decisions). The role of compound head revolves around managing agricultural and domestic activities and the distribution of agricultural produce. In terms of production, the household head is responsible for herd production while the compound head is responsible for agricultural production. However, agricultural production depends upon herd production in that plow animals must be available for agricultural activities to commence.

Household headship is normally a male role, but the position is occupied by a woman if the household lacks a man of the appropriate age or level of responsibility. Those women who assume household headship do so when they are middle-aged or approaching middle age and are single as a result of divorce or widowhood or as a result of never marrying—an increasingly common option in Botswana (cf. Gulbrandsen 1982).[3] *Kgotla* participation is not limited to household heads but is open to all adults. Yet middle-aged people are most active because they have reached the stage of life when they are freed somewhat from routine activities. They are also considered wiser. However, all Bakgalagadi households should be represented, and household heads have the strongest voice. Thus women, while ideally able to participate in the *kgotla,* do so less than men and are never listed by the court clerk as officially making up the court. Women are most welcome in the *kgotla* when they represent their households.

Exchange Relationships

Mother's brother (*malome*) is an important position in Bakgalagadi society. Many rights and obligations accrue to mother's brother, and if carried out responsibly, they contribute to a person's elevated status. Women can never participate on the senior side of the mother's brother/ sister's child relationship. There is a specific kinship position for father's sister (*rakgadi*). However, it does not carry equivalent status, place the individual in a similar exchange network, or carry many of the rights and obligations inherent in the mother's brother position.

The mother's brother/sister's child relationship is marked by exchanges that occur throughout life. However, a particular linked set of exchanges is a fundamental part of the relationship. Sister's child initiates the exchange relationship by giving mother's brother a male animal, usually a bull, and the first item of importance acquired by sister's child. In the past this was usually the first animal successfully hunted. Today an individual's first paycheck often replaces or is given in addition to the first animal. Innovations occur in this category of gift, e.g., a child's mother's brother was presented a comb won in a Botswana Independence Day running race. Subsequent gifts include parts of animals hunted or slaughtered, small gifts of cash or other material items, and general types of assistance and support. Mother's brother is meant to return to sister's child a cow, thus contributing to herd accumulation on the part of the sister's child. In addition, mother's brother offers sister's child general aid and support.

On the junior side of the relationship, the kinship term for sister's child (*motgogolo*) is not sex specific. Thus ideally both sexes could participate equally. However, the socioeconomic circumstances of young men and women are different, a fact which is reflected in their differential participation in the exchange. Women rarely have the resources to allow them to independently give their mother's brother an appropriate gift. Men and women both inherit livestock but they do so at different stages of the life cycle. Men inherit as small boys; thus by the time they are young adults they have small herds from which an animal can be selected to give to mother's brother. Women inherit as young adults and thus have a reduced ability to accumulate a herd. In addition a woman's livestock are often turned over to her husband by her father, or they are secretly kept for her by her father or brother. Since they are the woman's secret security base, public exchanges are not made from them.

Employment opportunities for young women are extremely rare compared to those for men. Women can find employment as domestics, teachers, nurses, etc. Most of these options require education, and positions are limited in number. Young men work as herders, teachers, civil servants, etc., and virtually all able-bodied young men can find employment at the South African mines. Over 90 percent of the men but fewer than 10 percent of the women I interviewed had held wage employment outside the village. Wage employment inside the village is virtually nonexistent. Thus women are less likely to have a first paycheck to give to their mother's brother, and since women do not hunt, they cannot present their mother's brother with a hunted animal.

Women are said to have their obligations to their mother's brother fulfilled by their husbands upon marriage. A young man must give his wife's mother's brother an ox when he marries. This exchange is different and independent of bridewealth and is said to meet the obligations of the woman to her mother's brother. Women thus often depend on their husbands in fulfilling their obligations, and mother's brother is not under the same obligation to return a gift of a cow to sister's daughter when her obligation has been fulfilled by her husband. Women usually are excluded also from bridewealth, which is perhaps the most significant exchange in Bakgalagadi society. Although collected from a number of sources, bridewealth is given by a man, representing himself and his close agnatic kin, to his wife's father or brother. Rarely will a woman receive the bridewealth payment, and if she does so, it is in lieu of her son or some male relative who is either absent or too young to accept the bridewealth. The delivery of bridewealth cattle is a public event announced to the village by the ululating of the wife's relatives. Bridewealth exchange is marked by long and elaborate festivities sponsored by the wife's family. Payment of bridewealth occurs some years after the marriage has taken place, usually when the husband is approaching middle age. Providing much prestige to the parties paying, it is an avenue for status achievement virtually confined to men.[4]

Although women are restricted from participating in certain exchange relationships, they take part in others for which livestock are the medium of exchange. Middle-aged women are most likely to take part in these activities. A young wife has an insecure relationship to the means of production. In the household in which she is producing (her affines') she has little control over resources and produce. In addition, she is supposed to be home, helping her mother-in-law and producing children. The longer she is married, the more secure her position in her affines' home becomes. Once a woman's bridewealth has been paid, her children are legitimate members of their father's patrilineage, and thus the children are owners of property. This clarifies and substantiates the woman's claim to her affines' resources and her own produce. Thus it is in large part through her children's secure position in their lineage that a woman's position in her affines' lineage is strengthened.

Middle-aged women may sell agricultural produce, and it is common for women to send buckets or bags of grain as gifts. Women are more likely to be involved in livestock exchange during middle age than at any other stage of their life cycle. In fact, some of the larger livestock owners in the village are widows. Upon reaching middle age, the women become increasingly autonomous from their brothers-in-law and brothers and take part in selling and exchange of livestock like any head of household.

Thus, women generally achieve high status in the domestic sphere and in agriculture. But, in middle age a blurring of sex-role distinctions occurs, and women participate in a wider variety of activities. Nonetheless, women have fewer opportunities open to them for achieving high status, and unlike men, they are more dependent on their children and spouses for fulfilling obligations and gaining security. In Bakgalagadi society, status improves for both sexes with increasing age, yet the transformations of middle age are more marked for women. No longer controlled by and dependent on their affines, they manage their own compounds and gain the autonomy associated with being head of the compound. Middle-aged women manage the domestic sphere and agriculture and control agricultural produce. They can delegate chores and responsibilities, thus gaining greater freedom of movement to visit, travel, and actively engage in village and extravillage political affairs.

NOTES

My fieldwork in Botswana was carried out from October 1977 through July 1979 with the assistance of a University of Toronto Open Fellowship and an Ontario Graduate Scholarship. I would like to thank Michael Lambek and Judith K. Brown for their support and comments. In addition, I am indebted to the Bakgalagadi for their patience and help when I was in the field.

1. Contributing to social reproduction by rearing children and participating in subsistence activities is certainly important. However, other activities are important as well, such as those discussed in the chapter.

2. Women are buried in the compound whereas men are buried in the kraal. During the days of mourning following a funeral, other restrictions are applied to the sexes. For example, men and women eat different parts of the ritually sacrificed animals, and in the evenings men and women separate. Men meet and sleep at the kraal, women in the compound.

3. Women who assume household headship achieve high status, and indeed some women household heads are among the most influential and respected people in the village. However, the position often has negative aspects as well, as the combined responsibilities of household head and compound head can be quite formidable.

4. There are odd cases where a woman could pay bridewealth. While woman-woman marriage is not practiced among the Bakgalagadi with whom I worked, a woman could conceivably pay her widowed mother's bridewealth or pay for her deceased brother's wife. In such cases a woman would be paying bridewealth in the name of a deceased male relative.

REFERENCES

Comaroff, Jean
    1980   Healing and the Cultural Order: The Case of the Barolong Boo Ratshidi
    of Southern Africa. American Ethnologist 7:637–57.
Fortes, Meyer
    1958   Introduction. *In* The Developmental Cycle in Domestic Groups. J.
    Goody, ed. pp. 1–14. Cambridge: Cambridge University Press.
Gulbrandsen, Ø.
    1982   To Marry—Or Not to Marry. Department of Anthropology, University
    of Bergen, Norway. Unpublished manuscript.
Kuper, A.
    1970   The Kgalagari and the Jural Consequences of Marriage. Man 5:466–
    82.
Leacock, Eleanor
    1981   Myths of Male Dominance. New York: Monthly Review Press.
Lee, Richard B.
    1981   Social Transformation: The Lives of !Kung Women. Paper presented at
    the Annual Meeting of the Canadian Ethnology Society. Ottawa, Canada.
Ortner, Sherry
    1974   Is Female to Male as Nature Is to Culture? *In* Woman, Culture and
    Society. M. Z. Rosaldo and L. Lamphere, eds. pp. 67–87. Stanford, Calif.:
    Stanford University Press.
Quinn, Naomi
    1977   Anthropological Studies on Women's Status. *In* Annual Review of
    Anthropology 6. B. Siegel, A. Beals, and S. Tyler, eds. pp. 181–225. Palo
    Alto, Calif.: Annual Reviews.
Rosaldo, Michelle Z., and Louise Lamphere
    1974   Introduction. *In* Woman, Culture and Society. M. Z. Rosaldo and L.
    Lamphere, eds. pp. 1–15. Stanford, Calif.: Stanford University Press.
Schapera, Isaac
    1950   Kinship and Marriage among the Tswana. *In* African Systems of Kin-
    ship and Marriage. A. R. Radcliffe-Brown and D. Forde, eds. pp. 140–65.
    London: Oxford University Press.
    1967   The Political Organization of the Ngwato of Bechuanaland Protectorate.
    In African Political Systems. M. Fortes and E. E. Evans-Pritchard, eds. pp.
    56–82. London: Oxford University Press.
Solway, Jacqueline
    1979a   People, Cattle and Drought. Gaborone, Botswana: Ministry of Agri-
    culture.
    1979b   Socio-economic Effects of Labour Migration in Western Kweneng.
    Gaborone, Botswana: Central Statistics Office.
    1981   Women, Marriage and the Domestic Cycle in Bakgalagadi Society.
    Paper presented at the Annual Meetings of the Canadian Ethnology Society.
    Ottawa, Canada.

1990   Affines and Spouses, Friends and Lovers: The Passing of Polygyny in
       Botswana. Journal of Anthropological Research 46:41–66.
Tiffany, Sharon
    1979   Introduction. *In* Women and Society. S. Tiffany, ed. pp. 1–35. Montreal:
           Eden Press.
Whyte, Martin
    1978   The Status of Women in Preindustrial Societies. Princeton, N.J.: Princeton
           University Press.

6 Tamparonga: "The Big Women" of Kaliai (Papua New Guinea)

Dorothy Ayers Counts

For women in many societies, middle age and the end of childbearing bring about a radical change in their lives. Women, whose activities and options were limited when they were young and who were denied the opportunities and privileges enjoyed by their male peers (Ortner 1974; Friedl 1975; Reiter 1975; Kessler 1976), often find that their lives improve dramatically after menopause. They enjoy more opportunity for achievement and recognition, fewer restrictions, and more authority, sometimes even over their aging husbands and certainly over younger people of both sexes (Keith 1980; Brown 1982).

Various explanations for this phenomenon are discussed by Brown (1982), including the following:

1. Explanations that stress the importance of menopause and the end of a woman's reproductive life
2. Explanations that, while stressing menopause, focus on the end of a woman's ability to contaminate men by her menstrual blood
3. Explanations assuming that physical changes ending female reproductive capacity also end responsible parenthood—the care of dependent children
4. Hypotheses emphasizing the domestic, political, and economic authority that accrue to a woman in her middle and later years

Based on my research with the Lusi women of Kaliai, West New Britain Province, Papua New Guinea, I argue that attention should be focused on a component that is implicit but not emphasized in many of these explanations: the notion of responsibility (also see Solway, this volume). The increased prestige, authority, and autonomy of the Lusi *tamparonga*

tely, "elder," does not represent a radical
.e as a younger woman. Neither can it be
biological or social changes associated with
; asexuality, declining ability to contaminate,
.ng of small children. Instead, as I argue, the
..der status occur because, with the maturity of
..uecline of her parents, a woman becomes *responsible:*
. nerself, for her younger kin and affines, for the care of her
dep.. ..it parents, and for the maintenance of society.

The Lusi are an Austronesian-speaking people numbering about one thousand who live in five villages located along the coast of the Kaliai area. They are primarily swidden horticulturalists whose major cash income is from the sale of copra. They maintain an active traditional life that includes ceremonial celebrations of the initiation of children, marriage, and death. These ceremonies involve feasting and the distribution of shell money, pandanas mats, pigs, and other wealth items. The Lusi are also actively involved in a trading system that links New Britain's northwest coast with the Kaliai interior, the Vitu and Siassi islands, and the New Guinea mainland. Socially, the Lusi are normatively patrilineal and virilocal. Married people reside together in single-family dwellings that include separate houses for sleeping and cooking. It is common for a couple to have residing with them, usually sleeping in the cook house, an elderly woman whom one of them calls "mother."

Nevertheless, Lusi women who are in their late childbearing or postreproductive years enjoy considerable autonomy. Some neutralization of gender roles occurs for both Lusi men and women in extreme old age (Gutmann 1969, 1975; Counts and Counts 1982). This does not, however, significantly affect everyday life, and it is not a primary factor in the independence of Lusi women who are in their middle years. Instead, these women are very like younger Lusi women, only more so: in middle age the cultural themes that provide a counterpoint to the idea of male dominance reach culmination. There is a multiplicity of rules, to which both women and men subscribe. Some of these rules oppose or contradict one another. People must choose among alternatives when they formulate a course of action to explain behavior, and their choice is almost always contextually determined. For example, Lusi women are forbidden to enter the men's house, to see or touch certain sacred masks, or to remain in the village when especially dangerous spirits are released at a ceremonial climax. When I asked if these restrictions were ever lifted for old women, my consultants insisted that they were not. Later, during another discussion on a different topic, one of these same consultants recounted that when he was a boy an old woman was permitted to remain in the village when the spirits left the men's house. When he asked his father for an explanation, the older man had replied, "It's all right. She's an old woman. Her hair is white and she will die before long. She is just like us men. *Aia mali mao* [she has no contaminating essence]. She can stay." This remark led other people present to elucidate the circumstances and contexts under which specific old women might enter the men's house, handle sacred items, and remain in the village when dangerous spirits are abroad. The general rule then, is that as a category, old women must behave as do other women, but in specifically defined contexts, certain old women follow a different set of rules.

The Norms of Male Dominance

I have enumerated elsewhere (Counts 1980b:338–40) the ways in which male dominance is expressed in Lusi society. To sum up briefly,

1. Political leaders, both traditional and modern, are male. There is no female equivalent of the male term *maroni* (*bikman*), leader or "bigman," a title that must be earned and applies only to some men.
2. A woman derives her status from the older men with whom she is associated, especially her father and husband.
3. Men claim the right to control the sexuality of their female kin. Fathers, and to a lesser extent older brothers, arrange the marriages of their daughters and sisters, and husbands have exclusive rights over the sexuality of their wives.
4. Husbands have authority over wives, authority that is occasionally enforced by violence. Wife beating is not an everyday occurrence,[1] but it is not uncommon and falls within the boundaries of normal marital behavior.

Tamparonga

There is no Lusi term for middle age, but there are terms that translate as female and male elder. The terms of address *tamparonga,* "female elder," and *taparonga,* "male elder," are terms of respect used by younger to older persons. Women become elders (*tamparonga*) when they have grandchildren and when their own parents are either dependent or deceased. Although most are near the end of their childbearing years,[2] there is no special term for menopause and no special significance attached to it. Lusi women do not retire to menstrual huts, nor do they avoid cooking for their families or eating particular foods. Menstrual blood is considered to be *mali* ("contaminating"), and a menstruating woman must be careful not to get even a trace of it in food or water lest she or someone else become ill. Menstrual blood poisoning (also called *mali*) is the only form of poisoning that Lusi women are thought to do. Most fertile women, however, do not spend much of their lives in a state where their contaminating potential is a problem. As Lancaster and King (this volume) observe, women such as the Lusi-Kaliai, who lack effective birth-control methods and who customarily nurse their children for two years or longer, spend a relatively small portion of their reproductive years menstruating as compared with women in industrialized countries. If menopause is seen in this context, it is reasonable that a postmenopausal Lusi woman enjoys no special privileges and suffers no particular disadvantages not shared by younger women simply because she is no longer menstruating. The only change in their lives that older women note is the end of fertility, and the *tamparonga* who were my consultants said that women generally welcomed the end of pregnancy and childbearing. They attributed to menopause none of the symptoms of illness—depression, hot flashes, emotional instability—that are stereotypically associated with it by North Americans.

Sexuality

The end of the reproductive ability does not bring an end to either sexual activity or the responsibilities of parenthood. My consultants considered sexual behavior to be a private and personal matter, and opined that some people remain sexually active until very old age. As one consultant said, "Some old people 'itch for sex.' Others don't."

Because the Lusi consider the effluvia and odors of sexual intercourse to be contaminating (*mali*) and dangerous to newborns, ritually incised children, and the very ill (people who are in a liminal state), sexually active but postmenopausal women continue to have the potential to endanger others and are, therefore, still required to control their sexual essences.

Adults of both sexes and all ages are intensely interested in sexual activity, and adulterous affairs are common, even until midlife. Grandmothers are expected to be discreet in their adulterous affairs, however, and to choose partners who are near their own age. There was, in one village in 1981, a woman whose sexual appetite was considered to be insatiable and who continued having affairs with younger men even after she had several grandchildren. Her behavior was the subject of scandalized gossip, and she was nicknamed "The Frog" because she hopped from man to man. Both women and men were offended particularly by the fact that some of her partners were men who were younger than her own sons. Obviously, her husband did not effectively control her sexuality, and their neighbors speculated that he had given up trying.

Arranged Marriage

There are a number of factors that modify the ideal right of Lusi men to control the sexuality of their female kin.

1. Quinn makes a valid point when she observes that in societies where women are exchanged in marriage, both young people—the groom as well as the bride—lose their autonomy in selecting a mate (1977:209).

2. A right is only as effective as the holder's ability to enforce it. The Frog's husband could not enforce his rights over her sexuality, and fathers frequently have difficulty exercising their rights over the sexuality of their daughters. Young Lusi women regularly refuse to marry the husbands selected for them and choose their own lovers. Many a disgruntled father is left to collect bridewealth for a marriage that became an accomplished fact without his consultation. Personal histories demonstrate that this has been going on for years—at least since the present great-grandparental generation was young—frequently with the collusion of one or both mothers.

3. In spite of the official line that marriages are transacted between fathers, it seems that those marriages that are successfully arranged according to the ideal are the product of negotiation between both sets of parents—mothers as well as fathers—at the request of at least one of the young people involved. If everyone is agreeable, or at least acquiescent, the proceedings go forward. A successful arrangement is not one that is imposed on anyone.

Affinal Relationships

In some societies, the mother-in-law/daughter-in-law relationship is marked by the authority and control of the older woman over a young wife (see Brown 1982:145 for discussion and examples). This characterization does not describe the interaction between Lusi mothers- and daughters-in-law. Lusi affines avoid one another, but avoidance rules are relaxed between affines of the same sex. Ideally, the relationship between mother-in-law and daughter-in-law is one of friendly cooperation, courtesy, and mutual respect. A young wife is expected to be respectful and obedient to her husband's mother because she is a senior affine. This does not necessarily impose a burden on the daughter-in-law because often the two women are fond of each other and enjoy each other's company— especially if the two mothers were involved in arranging the marriage. A woman is expected to give her daughter-in-law help and direction. Cordial relations are especially important between the two women if the young wife has settled virilocally and is living far from her own kin. In this case, the older woman should not take advantage of her vulnerable daughter-in-law. Instead, she should treat the younger woman with respect and courtesy. The Kaliai myth of Akro and Gagandewa contains an object lesson in the potential disaster that awaits the woman, and society as well, should she abuse her son's wife. In the myth, the wife, who is a foreigner, commits suicide as a result of verbal abuse by her husband's mother. Consequently, the older woman is murdered by her grieving son, and war is declared on the husband's village by the offended wife's kin (see Dorothy Counts 1980a for a detailed analysis of the myth).

This rule is normally followed in everyday life, and Lusi mothers-in-law are urged to behave with restraint, even when provoked. One of my consultants told me of a crisis that had occurred when her son, Peter, and his wife had quarreled, and the wife had ambushed Peter outside his mother's house, knocking him unconscious with a club. For a few minutes Peter's family believed him to be dead, and his mother turned on the wife and began cursing her in Lusi. The wife, who was an outsider, asked people standing by what her mother-in-law was saying as she could not understand the local language. "Nothing," she was told. "She's just upset because she thinks her son is dead." At the same time the distraught mother's friends were urging her to be quiet and not say anything in Tok Pisin, which the wife did understand. "They told me," she said, "that his wife was an outsider here, and that if she understood what I was saying she might be ashamed and kill herself. I really did want to kill her, but I couldn't even say what I thought."

A woman does become an elder when her children marry, but clearly she does not derive any significant degree of power from having a daughter-in-law at her mercy.

Motherhood

The end of a Lusi woman's childbearing ability does not necessarily mean the end of motherhood because parenthood, especially motherhood, is based on nurturance rather than biology, and people continue to nurture and adopt young children until late in life. Elders seek to adopt young kin for several reasons. First, the presence of children is said to give meaning to adult life. A number of older consultants have remarked to me that if they did not have youngsters to care for, their houses and lives would be empty and without meaning. A second important consideration is that children are the primary source of social security in Kaliai. Young people are expected to provide assistance to their elderly kin as they become increasingly feeble and dependent. Elderly people, especially widows, adopt children because they need help in gardening and in collecting firewood and water, but they are not yet ready to become totally dependent and a burden on others. Menopause does not usually mean an "empty nest" for a Lusi woman. Clearly, the reason why post-menopausal Lusi women do not suffer from the "empty nest syndrome" is that they do not permit the nest to stay empty.)

Seniority

Birth order and relative age are at least as significant as gender in structuring the content of interpersonal relations. Firstborn children are the most important issue of a marriage, and older sisters, for example, have authority over younger brothers. By the same token, younger people are expected to respect and defer to their elders, who are responsible for the behavior of their juniors. The elder years are the prime of life, but they are also the years when physical ability begins to decline. This is compensated by the rule that no younger person should sit by and allow an elder to carry a heavy burden or do truly strenuous work. Of course, Lusi women differ in character, and no one expects a lazy, foolish, slovenly young woman to become responsible, wise, and careful just because she becomes an elder. However, a *tamparonga* who aggressively participates in the cycle of ceremonial exchanges and trade that gives excitement and color to Lusi life will be esteemed and obeyed, especially if she is married to a village leader.

Ceremony, Trade, and Exchange

Lusi men organize, manage, and receive the credit for the ceremonial exchanges that are the focus of Lusi social and economic life. A man who successfully controls and manipulates the system of ceremonial exchanges achieves renown and becomes a *maroni*, a leader. As noted above, there is no equivalent status for a Lusi woman. Nevertheless, women and the things they produce are critical to the functioning of the system, and women have economic autonomy.

A woman owns and controls her own sources of wealth and cash. An unmarried woman owns the coconut palms that she plants; furthermore, those trees and the money she earns from the copra she produces from them are hers, even after she marries. Married women consider themselves to own, in common with their husbands, the gardens, pigs, and coconut palms they have acquired during their marriage. Although the husband ultimately controls this property, he is expected to consult his wife before committing its use. A woman has autonomous control over the money she earns selling garden produce in the local market. She also owns the pandanas trees that she plants and the sleeping mats she makes from their leaves. Women's activities are, therefore, of considerable importance to Lusi economic life, especially because pandanas mats are the chief item of women's wealth and the primary export of the people of Kaliai.

The Lusi are deeply involved in a two-faceted system of exchange that structures and expresses both internal and external relations. Internally, ceremonial exchange celebrating rites of passage structures social relations within Lusi society. Externally, there is a system of trade that links the people of northwest New Britain with those of the Vitu Islands, the Siassi Islands, and the Rai Coast of New Guinea (Harding 1967; David Counts 1979, 1981). Two items, both produced by women, are essential in integrating this system. These items are *vula* ("shell money"), which is also produced by the Kove to the east, and pandanas sleeping mats. In Kaliai, *vula* is the standard of value against which all other items are measured: when Lusi recount the amounts given in bridewealth or distributed to honor the dead, they recall the pigs that were killed and the fathoms of shell money that were given away (Counts and Counts 1970). Women are the primary makers of *vula,* but it is usually owned by, given by, and exchanged between men: women who invest shell money in a distribution are usually acting as agents for male relatives; however, there is nothing to preclude a woman from owning it, and she may give and receive it in her own name.

In contrast, pandanas mats are entirely woman's wealth and are not distributed by men. Although their value is never recounted when men discuss the wealth that was distributed in ceremonies they sponsored, mats are critical to all exchanges. They are always part of the total given in internal distributions, and they are the unique item that the people of Kaliai contribute to the external trading system. They have practical utility, for they are used as sitting and sleeping mats, as raincoats, and as shrouds for the dead. They also express hospitality and establish social relationships. They are brought out for the comfort of honored and important guests, and when they are ceremonially given—as when they are thrown down before a child on the event of its first public dance performance—they establish a sharing relation between the woman and the child she honors. Pandanas mats are the stuff by which social ties are established and expressed. Their social importance is not limited to the Kaliai area, for Kaliai mats are prized throughout the area where they are traded.

The internal distribution system, in which women are most active, works in the following way. A couple routinely incurs numerous economic obligations during the course of its married life. The first of these, the one used here as an example, is usually the presentation of its firstborn child. The husband is responsible for sponsoring this expensive ceremony, and he is usually assisted and advised by the oldest ranking male of his kin group, probably a man he calls "father" or "older brother." The wife has obligations that parallel those of her husband. She must collect, for distribution, a supply of mats equivalent to the shell money accumulated by her husband. She is also responsible for preparing and distributing huge amounts of feast food. All guests (there may be several hundred) must be well fed during their visit, and there should be enough food for visitors to carry some home after everyone has eaten. The young wife is assisted in organizing this formidable task by the senior woman of her kin group, usually a woman she calls "mother" or "older sister." As a woman ages, she becomes more experienced in ceremonial procedure and she builds a network of women whom she has helped and who will reciprocate when she needs mats and cooked foods. As the women who were her advisers die or become dependent and withdraw from active life, her daughters marry and call on her to help them meet their responsibilities.

As a woman ages she has fewer older kin to whom she must defer and more younger kin for whom she is responsible and who owe her respect. If her husband is a *maroni*, she is increasingly obliged to provide the female wealth items and foods that he requires if he is to pursue his career successfully. Consequently, although she cannot make a name for herself as female equivalent of a *maroni*, an elder woman may direct and organize economic exchange activity, both in her own right as a senior female and as the wife of an important man.

Marital Violence

As I mentioned earlier, the relationship between husband and wife may be marked by violence, and wife beating is not uncommon. The violence is not always one-way. Wives also attack their husbands, sometimes with the intent to maim or kill. I know of three such instances, all precipitated by the husband's adulterous affairs or by his plans to marry a second wife.

The reaction of others to domestic violence varies with the cause of the conflict. Generally, it is not unreasonable for a man to beat his wife if she neglects their children or draws blood while punishing one of them. Conversely, others—especially women—express sympathy with the violent response of a wife who has found her husband with another woman. There are community controls that contain domestic violence. For example, a person who publicly attacks her or his spouse may be subject to sanctions carried out by supernatural beings. Also, because men and women from the same village often marry, the relatives of an abused spouse are likely to witness the attack. I know of no case in which the kin of an attacked husband intervened. But men who beat their wives excessively or unjustly are subject to physical attack by her coresident kin, supernatural sanctions invoked by her relatives, and ultimately the possibility that an abused and shamed woman will permanently leave her husband or kill herself. I know of examples of the invocation of all of these sanctions by abused wives or their kin (Dorothy Counts 1980b).

The relationship between spouses mellows, however, as people reach middle age. This is true even in relationships that are characterized by violence. Why does this mellowing occur? Van Arsdale notes that whereas among the Asmat young women are sometimes beaten to death, grandmothers are not struck. This is, he says,

> not so much out of deference to their age or infirmity as out of fear of the public uproar they could create. Some were so vociferous and eloquent that their husbands would not even argue with them, let alone beat them. These women reprimanded their spouses at the top of their lungs before a rapt audience of fellow villagers, young and old, who took delight in hearing an imaginative catalogue of the unfortunate husband's sexual inadequacies. (1981:115)

Van Arsdale's reasoning does not explain Lusi behavior. I am not sure why it is that the old Asmat women are permitted to publicly berate their husbands without fear of reprisal, while young women are not. Young Lusi women certainly have mouths, and although it is uncommon for a young wife to take a quarrel into the public arena, it does happen. Furthermore, if her cause is just, if for instance she finds her husband copulating with another woman in her own house, she may well have community sympathy and support.

An alternative explanation is suggested by Quinn, who argues that wife beating reflects the intimacy and tensions that exist within the marital relationship (1977:190). By the time they become elders, a Lusi couple whose marriage has survived the first turbulent twenty years are likely to have resolved most of the sources of tension, or at least have learned to contain those tensions at a relatively nonviolent level. In addition they have acquired common interests that consume their energies. They are concerned with the proper presentation and marriage of their children; with the prosperity of their common property; with the maintenance of peaceful reciprocal relations with both sets of affines; with the establishment of a "name" for the husband, whose prestige devolves onto the wife; and with the duty of elders to organize and direct the activity of their children and followers. While it is not approved behavior, it is not unexpected for an angry young husband to beat his wife or for a mistreated young woman to run away with a lover, to threaten to kill her husband if he tries to take a second wife, or even to commit suicide. Such behavior, however, is not appropriate for responsible elders, and perhaps for this reason it is uncommon behavior.

Summary

Lusi women are, in a sense, silent partners. Their participation in and contribution to Kaliai life are critical to the maintenance of society; yet this participation seldom receives public acknowledgment. For example,

1. Children are said to have physical and essential ties to their fathers but not their mothers. They are considered to belong to their father's patrikin group. A mother must forge her ties to her children through nurturance.

2. The contribution women make to economic life is not publicly proclaimed, yet ceremonial exchange and trade would not exist in their present form without the female production of mats and shell money.

3. The contribution that women make to the successful enterprise of their male kin is publicly acknowledged only in folk tales, where the mother who socializes her fatherless son in the esoteric knowledge reserved to males is a common theme.[3] The character and ambition of successful women is attributed to the influence of fathers, not mothers, and their activities directly enhance the prestige of husbands and sons, not themselves.

This generalization does not change significantly as women reach elder status. The independence that a *tamparonga* enjoys is not the result of a fundamental change in the way of life she knew as a young woman. A postmenopausal woman continues to do the same sorts of things she did when she was younger, except that as she becomes a senior female, she assumes increasing responsibility for the behavior of her juniors, and she assists her younger female kin to meet their obligations.

The key here is responsibility. The factors suggested by other scholars, and discussed at the beginning of this chapter, do not seem to affect significantly the life of a Lusi *tamparonga*.

1. Menopause brings no radical changes. A woman no longer produces menstrual blood, but a postreproductive woman is not perceived as being less feminine than a fertile one. As long as she is sexually active, she continues to produce odors and substances that are contaminating and dangerous to vulnerable people. There is, however, some neutralization of gender in the very young and the very old. Consequently, an old woman may be invited by her male kin to remain in the village when the spirits are abroad, and she may, in an emergency, enter the men's house and handle the sacred paraphernalia stored there. Conversely, an old man may baby-sit young children and even sweep the plaza in front of his men's house, a task usually done by women. These are, however, exceptional circumstances that do not significantly affect everyday life, nor do they affect the rights and obligations of the elderly.

2. The end of a woman's fertility does not signal an end to responsible

parenthood. Older couples and individuals, including widows, adopt and care for young children until they themselves become dependent.

3. A postmenopausal woman holds no new offices or positions and inherits no rights in land or property that she did not enjoy as a young woman.

4. A woman becomes a *tamparonga* when she has adult children who marry and bear children. Because the rules of residence are normatively virilocal, a woman is more likely to have coresident adult sons than married daughters. She derives no significant degree of power from her role as mother-in-law, however. Young wives are not helpless, and a woman's authority over her son's wife is limited by the same sorts of considerations that limit the power of a bigman over his followers. Both have authority and receive respect in proportion to the responsibility they are prepared to undertake. An adept, responsible woman who is the wife of a bigman will be known as the "bone (or support) of the village." But a Lusi must delicately balance the exercise of power and authority. One must "use it or lose it," but it is also possible to "abuse it and lose it."

In closing, I should note that the permission that an old woman may receive to be present during the climax of male ceremonies is not evidence of any increase in authority or esteem. Women do not seem to resent their exclusion from male secrets, nor do they necessarily consider the invitation to witness these secrets an honor. In 1981 one of my friends, who is now in her sixties and blind, was invited to remain in the village while the spirits were released. She proudly refused and left with the other women as she had always done, to join them in feasting and making lewd fun of the men's "secrets."

NOTES

This chapter is based on a paper that I presented at a symposium on middle-aged women at the 1982 American Anthropological Association meetings. I wish to thank Judith K. Brown, the symposium organizer, for her helpful comments on earlier drafts of this chapter.

My research was conducted in West New Britain Province, Papua New Guinea, in 1966–67, supported by the U.S. National Science Foundation; in 1971 supported by the Wenner-Gren Foundation and the University of Waterloo; in 1975–76 supported by the Canada Council and University of Waterloo sabbatical leave; and in 1981 suppported by the Social Sciences and Humanities Research Council of Canada and sabbatical leave from the University of Waterloo.

1. Few older women are beaten regularly by their husbands. I do, however, know of one middle-aged woman whose husband has threatened to kill her on several occasions and who has attacked her with an axe and a bushknife as well as

with his fists. More detailed information on wife beating in Kaliai can be found in Dorothy Counts (1987, 1990).

2. The data that support my statement were supplied by the Kaliai clinic. They were collected by the missionaries when the clinic was run by the Kaliai Roman Catholic Mission and include chronological ages of local people as estimated by European mission personnel. According to these data, the average age at which the women of Kandoka (a Lusi-Kaliai village and the site of most of my field research) bear their last child is 44.58 years (but see Lancaster and King, p. 7).

3. In a number of Kaliai tales, widows teach their sons how to train hunting dogs, how to manufacture and use spears and shields, and other esoterica. These stories probably reflect cultural truth, for it is clear from my discussions with women that many of them know male secrets (one elderly woman corrected her husband when he made a mistake in telling a secret story describing the origin of masked ancestor figures) and that men know that they know.

REFERENCES

Brown, Judith K.
  1982   Cross-cultural Perspectives on Middle-Aged Women. Current Anthropology 23(2):143–56.
Counts, David R.
  1979   Adam Smith in the Garden: Supply, Demand and Art Production in New Britain. *In* Exploring the Visual Art of Oceania. S. M. Mead, ed. pp. 334–41. Honolulu: University of Hawaii Press.
  1981   Taming the Tiger: Change and Exchange in West New Britain. *In* Persistence and Exchange. R. W. Force and B. Bishop, eds. pp. 51–58. Honolulu: Pacific Science Association.
Counts, David R., and Dorothy Ayers Counts
  1970   The Vula of Kaliai: A Primitive Currency with Commercial Use. Oceania 41:90–105.
Counts, Dorothy Ayers
  1980a   Akro and Gagandewa: A Melanesian Myth. Journal of the Polynesian Society 89:33–65.
  1980b   Fighting Back Is Not the Way: Suicide and the Women of Kaliai. American Ethnologist 7:332–51.
  1982   The Tales of Laupu. Port Moresby: Institute of Papua New Guinea Studies.
  1987   Female Suicide and Wife Abuse in Cross-cultural Perspective. Suicide and Life Threatening Behavior 17(3):194–204.
  1990   Beaten Wife, Suicidal Woman: Domestic Violence in Kaliai, West New Britain. Pacific Studies 13(3):151–69.
Counts, Dorothy Ayers, and David R. Counts
  1982   "I'm Not Dead . . . Yet!" Aging, Death and the Dead: Process and Experience in Kaliai. Paper delivered at the Annual Meetings of the Association for Social Anthropology in Oceania. Hilton Head Island, S.C.

Friedl, Ernestine
    1975   Women and Men: An Anthropologist's View. New York: Holt, Rinehart, and Winston.
Gutmann, David
    1969   The Country of Old Men: Cross-cultural Studies in the Psychology of Later Life. Occasional Papers in Gerontology 5. Ann Arbor: University of Michigan 'and Wayne State, Institute of Gerontology.
    1975   Parenthood: A Key to the Comparative Study of the Life Cycle. *In* Life-Span Development Psychology. N. Datan and L. Ginsberg, eds. pp. 167–84. New York: Academic Press.
Harding, Thomas
    1967   Voyagers of the Vitiaz Strait: A Study of a New Guinea Trading System. American Ethnological Society Monograph 44. Seattle: University of Washington Press.
Keith, Jennie
    1980   "The Best Is Yet to Be": Toward an Anthropology of Age. *In* Annual Review of Anthropology 9. B. Siegel, A. Beals, S. Tyler, eds. pp. 339–64. Palo Alto, Calif.: Annual Reviews.
Kessler, Evelyn S.
    1976   Women: An Anthropological View. New York: Holt, Rinehart, and Winston.
Ortner, Sherry
    1974   Is Female to Male as Nature Is to Culture? *In* Woman, Culture and Society. M. Rosaldo and L. Lamphere, eds. pp. 67–87. Stanford, Calif.: Stanford University Press.
Quinn, Naomi
    1977   Anthropological Studies on Women's Status. *In* Annual Review of Anthropology 6. B. Siegel, A. Beals, and S. Tyler, eds. pp. 181–225. Palo Alto, Calif.: Annual Reviews.
Reiter, R. R., ed.
    1975   Toward an Anthology of Women. New York: Monthly Review Press.
Van Arsdale, Peter
    1981   The Elderly Asmat of New Guinea. *In* Other Ways of Growing Old. P. Amoss and S. Harrell, eds. pp. 111–24. Stanford, Calif.: Stanford University Press.

PART 2

Intermediate Societies

Intermediate (or "middle-range") societies have larger populations and more complex social structures than those discussed in the previous chapters. They exist on the margins of complex or industrialized societies, in which they are politically and economically incorporated to some degree, while remaining socially and culturally distinct. Nominally Islamic or Christian, their religious practices have a clear local character. Although subsistence depends in part on cultivation, wage work (often in urban or other distant locales) is also important.

Older women in intermediate societies often have opportunities to attain public positions of influence and power, and they may do so independently of their husbands and male kin. Among the Maori and the Malagasi speakers of Mayotte (described by Karen P. Sinclair and Michael Lambek respectively), some middle-aged women participate in national politics. Sinclair reports that older Maori women are important social actors and that they have great public visibility when they take charge of religious festivals.

Among the Garífuna, women enjoy greater freedom and exert more influence over others during middle age. As Virginia Kerns notes, they are exempt from the many social restrictions that pertain to the reproductive cycle and childbearing. Older women (not men) are also the major enforcers of a moral code that in effect limits the sexuality of young women. Among the Maori and in Mayotte, middle-aged women clearly have influence over their juniors, and it is rooted in moral obligation. These women have created networks of supporting kin and are now in a position to draw on what is owed them.

7 Motherhood and Other Careers in Mayotte (Comoro Islands)

Michael Lambek

The anthropological literature frequently presents a static picture of sex roles. Although it is now commonly argued that women have a good deal of informal power, even where they lack formal authority, women are viewed as using the power to respond to particular situations, usually those constructed by men. In this chapter I suggest that the women of Mayotte, Comoro Islands, Western Indian Ocean, develop long-term strategies of action. My point is not to show conscious, instrumental manipulation on the part of women, but to demonstrate that the overall course of their lives is as much a product of their own actions (albeit in the face of serious constraints) as is the course of men's lives. Following the theme of this book, I will pay particular attention to middle-aged women, but I will argue that "middle age" is not a culturally recognized category in Mayotte and has no exclusive privileges or obligations associated with it. Hence, the question becomes one of assessing the degree to which the period of later adulthood represents the "fruition" of earlier plans, decisions, and interests. My aim is to present a broad picture of women's lives in rural Mayotte—one that emphasizes continuity, as well as change, and incorporates the range of diversity in the experience of women within the society.

Aging in Mayotte

Mayotte is a tropical island of some sixty thousand inhabitants, located approximately halfway between the Swahili coast of East Africa and Madagascar. Approximately one-quarter of the inhabitants are speakers of Kibushy, a dialect of Malagasy, while the remainder speak Shimaore, a

Bantu language. I worked in a pair of villages of Kibushy speakers, which were formed in the midnineteenth century by a mixture of immigrants from the Sakalava states of northwest Madagascar and indentured laborers from East Africa. Two further strong influences on the communities were the indigenous stratified Muslim society and the enterprises of the French, who took control of Mayotte in 1841 and established plantations there. The plantations declined in importance around the turn of the century. Since then the economy of the villagers has been dominated by subsistence horticulture, supplemented by fishing, raising cattle and other domestic animals, and performing occasional wage labor. In the 1970s the sale of cash crops by small independent producers was also significant. It must be clear then that Mayotte is, and has been, a society in flux, and I cannot speak of a baseline of "tradition" against which to measure change. Any shifts in the positions of Mayotte women in the course of their lifetimes have doubtless come as much from changing historical circumstance as from a playing out of a traditional pattern of the life cycle. Nevertheless, I will attempt to consider the life cycle as it appeared in 1975–76.[1]

In Mayotte there is no clearly demarcated period of "middle age." The sharpest break in a woman's life occurs with her first marriage (Lambek 1983). Thereafter, aging is a gradual process. The term *ulu be* (literally "big person") is polysemous and context dependent. At menarche it may be said that the "child" (*zaza*) is "now grown up" (*fa ulu be*). But she will still be referred to as a child until her defloration (whether properly, during the course of her first wedding, or improperly, prior to it). Defloration is a clear transformation that ends childhood. But again a woman is only an *ulu be* in reference to this event and in contrast to "children." In other contexts she will say of herself, and it will be said of her, that she is *tsendriky ulu be* ("not yet adult"). *Ulu be* also refers to both "responsible elder" (*ulu be an tanana,* "village elder" and *ulu be an mraba,* "family elder") and "important person" ("big man," "big woman"). These statuses only become unequivocal relatively late in life, if at all. However, the final stage of life is that of *bakoko,* which implies physical or mental infirmity. Whereas *ulu be* is a status that indicates social relevance, the *bakoko* is someone from whom the community has already begun to withdraw.[2]

In the local scheme, then, there is no clearly demarcated category corresponding to "middle age." Rather, there is gradually increasing social adulthood, constituted of a combination of age, social competence, and responsibility and followed by a decline into senescence. Menopause or cessation of fertility for other reasons (see Boddy, this volume) is not a socially significant transition point.

The experience of aging and adulthood is organized largely in terms of generation, relative age, and the fellowship of age cohorts. Of these, generation is perhaps the most significant. Motherhood marks a notable achievement in a woman's life, and henceforward she is addressed by a tek-nonym (*nindry ny fulany,* "mother of so-and-so"). A woman who does not give birth does not thereby lose in prestige (although she may be extremely disappointed) and will be given the name "aunt (or elder sibling) of so-and-so." Grandmotherhood marks another transition, but in most women this occurs during their thirties and well before they cease giving birth themselves. A grandmother is sometimes addressed as *dady (ny fulany),* "grandmother (of so-and-so)." When she reaches old age she is referred to either by her childhood name preceded by *dady,* thus Dady Salima, Grandmother Salima or by a nickname, e.g., Sokolon (Cyclone, noted for her volatile temper). These names are used by the entire community.

While the relationship of children to parents is marked by respect and attention that should last throughout the parents' lives, grandparents are often treated with levity by people of the grandchildren's generation (although less by those whom they have raised). Grandparents tease grandchildren when the latter are young and often have to suffer a turning of the tables when they themselves become *bakoko,* a condition for which there is not always great sympathy.

Relative age structures relationships within a single generation, so that the *zandry* ("younger sibling") should demonstrate respect for his or her *zuky* ("older sibling"), irrespective of gender. In any encounter (except where generation contradicts relative age) the younger person should initiate deferential greetings to the elder.

In community-wide ceremonial affairs, people are grouped according to age and sex. Shortly before marriage boys and girls join their respective groups of age mates, with which they will be associated until the groups disband at old age. There are approximately five or six age groups for each sex in a village (although the groups may succeed each other more rapidly in larger villages). As she or he marries for the first time, each member of a given age/sex group must sponsor a feast for the other members. In later years the groups continue to form work and commensal units on the occasion of village ceremonies and of ceremonies, such as weddings, sponsored by individuals but to which the entire community is invited and lends its assistance.[3] In general, responsibilities are divided so that elders advise, the middle-aged manage, and the young adults execute collective tasks, although there is also much overlap. For example, the age groups of older women do their share of food preparation. Respect for the wisdom and skills of the elderly is balanced by an appreciation for the energy of youth. At the same time, there is a certain tension between the old and the young, especially among the men.[4] In the arena of village politics, young adults are recognized as a significant interest group whose force must be acknowledged. The division into a number of age groups, each of which is in some competition with its immediate neighbors offsets some of the opposition between old and young.

To summarize the discussion so far, the aging process in Mayotte is gradual, emphasizing continuity rather than discontinuity. The generations succeed each other without sharp breaks, and individuals remain at the end of adulthood in much the same positions vis-à-vis significant others, parents, children, siblings, and members of the age groups, as they began. Age is essentially a matter of growth; a person gains juniors and loses seniors. The only reversal occurs in the relations between alternate generations. Grandchildren, often named for their grandparents, are viewed, in some sense, as replacing them. This offsets the authority gained with age and ensures that the greater relative influence associated with later adulthood is a matter of degree rather than kind.

Women's Careers

I have been speaking in the abstract, about structure rather than organization, and about men as well as women. In turning to a consideration of adult women, I will continue to emphasize continuity. I follow Myerhoff and Simić in their conceptualization of aging as a "career." They view aging as "a process by which the individual builds, or fails to build, a lasting structure of relationships, accomplishments, affect, and respect that will give meaning and validation to one's total life" (1978:240). In other words, the position of women at middle age is in large part a product of their own creative endeavors (in the face of certain constraints) and of their entire lives to that point. Thus I emphasize continuity within the life cycle but point to the discontinuity among the experiences of different Mayotte women. In the remainder of the chapter, I will consider certain aspects of women's life activity, emphasizing the choices open to them as well as the constraints. In general, I am concerned with how a woman acquires and consolidates sufficient material resources, social ties, and specialized knowledge to develop by later adulthood a position of relative security and authority in domestic and public life.

Marriage

At marriage a woman leaves her parents and establishes a separate household (Lambek 1983). Henceforward, she maintains her own hearth and home until she is physically incapable of doing so. She receives a house from her parents, built by her father or brothers on land to which either her mother or father has claim and thus in the same village as at least one of them. Usually it is near her mother's house. She also receives household furnishings from her kin and a wardrobe and jewelry from her husband. No return is expected upon termination of the marriage.[5] This means that in the event of a marital breakup a woman, no matter what her age, does not return to her parents but continues her existence as a relatively autonomous householder.

A wife is responsible for most of the child care, cooking, washing, and cleaning; a man is responsible for supplying the basic necessities that must be purchased: kerosene, salt, soap, etc. Wife and husband both engage in subsistence horticulture. In any given year they may cultivate several plots located on land to which either party has access. It will be clear for each plot whether the yield belongs to the wife, the husband, or both jointly, but in general it is the wife who controls and distributes subsistence products. By contrast, if cash crops are planted, they are usually the husband's responsibility and he is entitled to dispose of the earnings. For example, if a man marries a woman whose father has planted ylang ylang trees, he can choose to work with his father-in-law, who will then split the proceeds. The wife receives indirectly, as the result of her husband's purchases on her behalf. Nevertheless, it is she, along with her siblings, who inherits (inheritance is bilateral), and should the marriage break up, the land and the crops planted on it remain in her control. Thus she has a certain amount of leverage to ensure she receives sufficient support, and in the event of termination of the marriage can manage the ylang ylang herself if she so chooses. Her husband has the right to manage the cash income, but only so long as he fulfills his responsibilities. Likewise, in the case where a man is earning income from his own land, his wife expects adequate support; if it is not forthcoming, she may end the relationship.

Marriages in Mayotte are brittle, and a good marriage is defined as one in which the partners show mutual respect (*ishima*) (cf. Lambek 1991). This means that they should refrain from adultery and cooperate in the management of the household. A good marriage is thus one in which trust grows and in which the parties recognize that mutual respect and interest predominate. After a few years either the wife gains assurance that the husband dispenses the income fairly or the husband begins to share money management with his wife. In most cases a woman also has a minor source of income of her own, perhaps from a small cash crop or craft. Whereas a husband has the duty to draw from his income to maintain the household, a woman is under no such obligation.

Both women and men are economic actors in their own rights and both can own property, spend money on themselves, aid their kin, and contribute to various public activities. For some of the larger ceremonial exchanges entailing the provision of feasts to which all village members are invited, wife and husband may function as an economic unit, thereby fulfilling their individual ceremonial obligations by jointly producing the feast. The completion of these ceremonies is a major step in an individual's social career (Lambek, in press a). A husband and wife who trust each other may engage in other joint projects, such as the construction of a new house or the purchase of land. If they do not trust each other, they will put relatively more resources into projects of their respective sibling groups.

The growth of trust also means greater mobility for the wife. In the early years her husband may be reluctant to see her travel much (although even then she is hardly house or village bound), but older women pay frequent visits to kin and friends in other villages and travel to ceremonies and political meetings.

One career path for a woman, then, is the construction of a solidary relationship with a husband based on mutual trust and respect. The conjugal unit becomes a basis for joint social action, for building a family, social links, a material estate, and prestige. The main threat to a woman who invests in her marital relationship and looks to it for security is that the trust may break down, her husband may choose to initiate a second, polygynous union, or to abandon her entirely. In fact, although most men are tempted by polygyny, especially when they reach middle age and feel they can afford it, the chances of this sort of outcome appear to decline the longer the marriage lasts. Aside from feeling hurt, a woman will be outraged that her husband is choosing to direct his money elsewhere, especially if he had little enough to begin with. A woman has three choices when faced with this situation: to convince her husband to abandon his plans, to throw him out, or to put up with the situation. Many attempts at polygyny fizzle as the husband realizes that the new marriage poses too great a threat to his own investments in the previous relationship. Indeed, a slighted wife often successfully holds out for a large compensation before agreeing to resume the marriage as before. There is also a great deal of moral pressure among women not to accept the overtures of a man who is already married in the same village, especially if it is to a kinswoman. Thus a polygynous man must be mobile and capable of pursuing his social and economic interests simultaneously from two locations. It is often much easier to simply stay with the first wife should she make an ultimatum.[6]

A middle-aged woman who is left without a husband may or may not be in a difficult position, depending in large part on the ties she has made or maintained beyond the conjugal relationship. As a member of a sibling group, she has access to subsistence resources, and as an adult woman, she owns her own house and utensils. She may have a problem with a cash and labor supply, forcing her into dependence on brothers and adult sons until she can find a new husband or lover. On the other hand, she may have amassed sufficient skills or resources to support herself. Some townswomen become wealthy in real estate, renting out their houses and investing in new ones (see also Ottino 1964).[7]

Divorce in Mayotte is very easy and means simply that the parties no longer live together or support one another. A woman has a little more difficulty asking a man to leave than a man has in leaving; nevertheless, it is always possible to force him out, if necessary by conducting an affair under his nose. A number of marriages break up early, as a result of one or both parties growing tired of the union. Women often divorce because their husbands fail to provide adequate economic support. Most divorced women remain in close contact with their kin and continue their subsistence pursuits in the village. However, a young divorced woman is considerably more mobile than her married counterpart, and in fact there is no one with direct authority over her. She may close up her house and disappear for lengthy visits to kin and friends in other villages or in town. Some women engage in a series of short-lived marriages, possibly as many as twenty or more in a lifetime, thereby diversifying rather than consolidating their relations. Some travel off the island in the course of their marital adventures. Although they usually continue to return home for various periods of residence and often do marry covillagers, by middle age their position in the village is marginal unless they have children there.

Some women place (or claim to place) a high value on the diversity of their marital experiences and scorn their sisters who remain loyal to a single spouse. In middle age they are often willing parties to polygynous unions, seeing their husbands intermittently and thus retaining a good deal of autonomy.

In sum, it is difficult to compare the positions of older and younger women in the domestic economy. Wives are not objects of exchange and have the right to break free of a union, marry elsewhere, or live independently. The major constraint on all adult women is that although access to subsistence resources is relatively open, men have an easier time acquiring cash. As the cash sphere becomes ever more significant, so the position of the majority of women inevitably declines. On the other hand, it must be remembered that acquiring a steady source of cash is by no means easy for village men either and is viewed by most of them as a constant source of worry. Moreover, in the recent past most of the cash was immediately transformed into goods that were either consumed on ceremonial occasions or given to women and which they accumulated (also see Ottino 1964). This too is changing with the increasing penetration of the cash economy. On the one hand, men are forced to invest in further productive resources, and on the other, they are purchasing an increasing array of consumer goods for their own use. Many households have a running argument as to who owns the transistor radio.

Finally, although women are not particularly encouraged to participate in and have far less opportunity for wage labor than men, a few of them choose to operate as part-time entrepreneurs. For example, a number of women maintain small shops in the village. The owner of the longest-running, largest, and most successful of the village shops is an energetic woman in her midthirties who has also begun to produce her own ylang ylang cash crop. She travels to town a good deal more frequently than most of the men in the village and pursues her interests among numerous business contacts there.

Child Rearing

Kinship in Mayotte is bilateral and children belong equally to wife and husband. Moreover, because child transfers are easily arranged, no one need remain with or without children should she or he desire otherwise. Child rearing is an activity that women can pursue throughout their lives; alternatively, they can avoid it. In the circulation of children, middle-aged women play a major role, although men, young women, and the children themselves may also have an interest in the matter.

A young mother is not usually left to care for her children alone. A woman helps her inexperienced daughter in the tasks of motherhood and occasionally removes an infant or toddler from the latter's care entirely. Or a young mother without sufficient adult assistance takes in a younger sibling, niece, or nephew to help her in child care and other domestic tasks. Women often begin to have grandchildren before they have stopped giving birth themselves; at this time their compounds may be full of children. Once weaning has begun, child care may be shared informally by a group of closely related women.

Child transfers are common, ranging from informal or impermanent arrangements such as those mentioned above to those that are less frequent and more permanent. Women can ask one another for children and the requests are often difficult to turn down, especially when they come from senior kin, such as a mother or mother-in-law. Some young women find themselves constrained to give up their first few offspring to the various people who ask for them. Mothers who have a history of losing infants to disease may be said to be unable to raise children and will send out subsequent births fairly automatically. Usually this is considered to be a matter of fate rather than fault. Because stepparents are considered not to have the best interests of stepchildren at heart, the offspring of divorced or widowed parents are often taken in by a blood relative. In these ways infertile women or those whose children are already grown can acquire children to raise.

A few women do not wish to raise children and give them to relatives as soon as they can. An example is Fatima, a young woman living with her third husband. She has no full siblings and both her mother and her mother's mother are dead. Her two children from her first marriage are being raised, respectively, by her mother's father's sister (who also raised Fatima) and by her mother's mother's brother, who is also the child's father's father's brother. Fatima's child from her second marriage lives with his father's kin in his village. Her newborn baby will go to its father's relatives as soon as it is a few weeks old. In explanation, Fatima says she just "can't handle children." She becomes angry with them very quickly; moreover they hinder her when she wants to travel. Another woman doesn't like to raise children because she "doesn't know how to raise her voice."

Older women also make decisions about child rearing, and many of them choose to take in children. For example, when Amina died leaving a toddler and a baby no more than a few weeks old, her mother-in-law Velu immediately accepted them, bringing to seven the number of grandchildren she was then raising. Velu had left her latest husband because he refused to help support so many children; instead, she was being financially assisted by her own adult children. Amina's mother, Hamba, was married but raising no children at the time of Amina's death. However, she declined to take the children on the grounds that the spirit who possessed her could not stand the smell of urine and would make her sick were she to be in close contact with infants. Other people suggested this was actually Hamba rather than her spirit speaking. Four years later Hamba took in the two children (both well past the age of toilet training) of her other daughter, who had left her husband for a man in another village.

Neither of these women is typical. Velu was much admired for her love and patience with children—at one point she had even raised the child of a co-wife—while Hamba was considered somewhat selfish and unsociable. Nevertheless, the point is that women are not tied to child care and middle age does not make a difference in this regard.[8]

More burdensome than child rearing is the care middle-aged women must provide for aged and ailing parents (*bakoko*). This is considered to be the responsibility of a daughter first, although a son will contribute financially and will look in on his mother frequently. The relationship between a middle-aged woman and her aged mother is full of ambivalence. People have little patience with the very old, but a daughter is supposed to respect her mother and would be ashamed to reject her and be criticized for doing so. If she has no sisters, a middle-aged daughter cannot rely on much assistance from others and may be quite tied to the household. For example, Rehema felt guilty whenever she spent several days away from home working in distant fields. Her adult daughters, who helped willingly with the care of small children, looked after Rehema's mother very grudgingly and often neglected her. Care of the elderly, then, is a constraint placed upon middle-aged women but not upon younger ones.

By contrast, far from being a constraint that keeps a woman anchored to the home, motherhood in Mayotte is an activity that provides women with an extra source of domestic labor and widens a woman's ties. One of the primary reasons for taking in children is to have a helping hand. Moreover, a mother exchanges services with close kin who are also raising children. The ties established with her husband and his kin will be continued even if the couple separate. Thus people say that "a marriage with children never dies." If the mater is not the genetrix, she reinforces links with the latter and with the father and can expect assistance from them. Fosterage helps to cement marriage alliances and maintains links despite divorce. Women can also restructure kin ties through the establishment of "fictive" kin relationships and reinforce these links by means of child transfers. The more children she raises, the more a woman can participate in arranging marriages and subsequent child transfers. As time passes she becomes the center of an ever-expanding *mraba* ("family") with ever-greater links to other members of the community (Lambek 1988a). By maintaining an active interest in children and grandchildren, she can in turn expect their respect and support. Thus women's manipulation of social relations can partially offset their unequal access to cash. Moreover, the greater a woman's authority within the family, the more significant her role in mediating between the family and the community, acting in support of either family interests or public morality (for example, by monitoring the propriety of proposed marital unions of junior members of the family).

Let us briefly consider two women in their fifties who may be said to have made a career of motherhood. Dady Mwana (Figure 1) is a widow who has had three husbands. She has raised a daughter by the first husband, three daughters by the second husband, two male and two female junior kin of her third husband, four grandchildren, and one son of one of her foster children. One of her daughters has only a single child and lives next door to Dady Mwana, participating in her daily activities. Dady Mwana also arranged the marriages of her third husband's kin to her own relations (Figure 2), thus consolidating her family. Dady Mwana runs a small shop and makes use of one of her foster sons to replenish the stock. As a widow, she is now the focal member of a large kin group.

Halima Kolo is the middle one of three sisters. Only the eldest of the three was fertile, but while the youngest sister, whom the villagers consider slow-witted, has never raised children, Halima has raised many (Figure 3). Halima is divorced from her third husband. She cultivates ylang ylang planted by her deceased second husband on land belonging to her sibling group, is head (*ulu be*) of her kin group (*mraba*), chief of the village women, and a renowned curer.

Public Life

Finally, we may compare the roles of older and younger women in public life. It should be clear from the preceding discussion that both women and men are viewed as autonomous actors, as "social adults" who can engage in multiple activities beyond the domestic sphere and who can determine in large part where the boundaries of the domestic sphere are to lie. Older women (like older men) play a more important role than younger women in public life, but this seems to be a function of the value attributed to relative age rather than to conditions specific to being female.

All women belong to the village age groups mentioned at the beginning of the chapter. A woman becomes a full member of the village organization only in the third year after her wedding. When women participate in public work, their young daughters stay at home to carry out domestic chores. Each age group has a leader and the leader of the senior group is referred to as the "chief" of the women of the village. She and her assistants act as the spokespersons for the entire body of adult women and can often exert strong pressure on the men. The main function of the age groups is the regulation and implementation of ceremonial activity, and the chief of women negotiates with the men concerning decisions of scheduling and the like. The women determine and collect each household's contribution to an affair and redistribute the raw materials so that they may be processed by each age group working as a unit. Women are considered far better at extracting household contributions than are men. The names of each age group assert the women's views of themselves. The "Lightning" are so called because they work quickly. Other names include "Airplanes" and "Chatterboxes."

In general, the women's groups maintain a tighter control over their members than do the men's groups. This was particularly evident in the organization of the two political parties found in Mayotte in the 1970s, especially the Soldat, which advocated modernization through closer ties with France and separation from the other Comoro Islands. In the decade before Comoran independence, Soldat women led a vigorous campaign. On one memorable occasion women from throughout Mayotte gathered to surround road-building machinery and prevented its removal to one of the other islands. They spent several days·and nights there and sent

Key: Numbered individuals are those who were raised by Dady
Mwana. Black figures indicate deceased individuals.

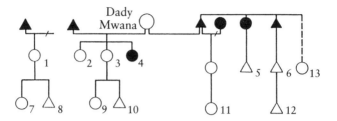

Figure 1. Children raised by Dady Mwana

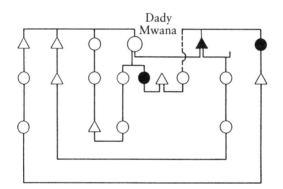

Figure 2. Marriage links among Dady Mwana's kin

Key: Numbered individuals are those who were raised by Halima.
Black figures indicate deceased individuals.

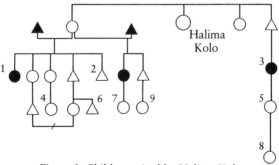

Figure 3. Children raised by Halima Kolo

messengers asking their menfolk for more provisions. Men agree that women provided the force behind the movement and that men only began to take an active role when victory appeared imminent. During 1975–76 I attended several large political congresses at which the number of women present appeared roughly to equal the number of men. The middle-aged female party leaders of each village played key roles in maintaining support for the cause and in building the intervillage party organization. During the referendum, they sat next to the ballot boxes in each village and woe betide anyone, male or female, observed by them to vote for the opposing party. The women utilized the intervillage ceremonial system to ensure broad participation. Women's political meetings were held in conjunction with performances of the *Maulida Shengy,* a lengthy religious text sung by women in honor of the Prophet (cf. Lambek, in press b). Each village had to send a specific number of performers; absent villages were threatened with having to host the next *Maulida* themselves, a considerable expense. In this way too, the skills of leadership were tied to traditional religious knowledge, a domain in which the middle-aged were likely to be preeminent.

Middle-aged women were also much more active than men and younger women in celebrating political victory. They rented all the bush taxis on the island one day and drove around singing, clapping, and ululating. In many villages the adult women planted a French flag and performed victory dances. However, with the achievement of their first aims, separation from the remaining Comoro Islands and a reassertion of the French presence in Mayotte, the women took second place to men in the party and in the government. In 1980, after the reorganization of the village administrative system, two out of the seven councillors who represented the villages in which I worked were women. One of the women was the successful shopkeeper mentioned earlier, the other an ambitious woman who operated entirely through the manipulation of kinship ties and through her position in the age-group system. There is also inequality in that the two women represent "women" whereas the men represent the entire community. Most of the representatives, male and female, were not much older than forty, reflecting the division of political roles between elders as advisers and younger adults as executors. Village authority is vested ultimately in the *ulu be,* the "elders." These include senior women as well as senior men, but the public role of the former is slight.

The key female leader remains the head of the women's age-group organization. She is in later middle age. Women identify with her and respect her. Occasionally they labor collectively in her fields on their own initiative, not out of any obligation, they say, but to repay her for all her efforts in managing village ceremonial affairs.

Middle-aged women also predominate over younger women as curers, midwives, and so on, although women can begin to learn these skills at virtually any age. Women's role in spirit possession (Lambek 1980, 1981) is particularly significant here. Possession by a spirit, especially a male one, gives a woman a new basis for communicating with her husband and other males (Lambek 1980) and may provide a means for rearticulating kinship ties (Lambek 1988a). Some women are possessed by spirits who act with a great deal of authority and direction in the affairs of the family (*mraba*) or as diviners and curers with reputations that stretch beyond the confines of the village. Such authority is built up gradually and only flourishes when a woman reaches middle age. Older women may also use spirit possession as a means to retain some of the privileges of youth (Lambek 1988b).

Finally, we may speak of women's participation in Islam. This is one area in which their status is explicitly subordinate to men, in terms of both ideology (which the women by and large do not accept) and practice (Lambek 1990). For example, in the commonly performed rituals such as the *shidjabo,* a kind of blessing, women cannot take an active role in uttering the prayers but must sit with their children as objects of the prayers. Women frequent the mosque much less than men, but many mosques do have separate women's sections. Older women go to the mosque more often than younger ones, although interest also varies by family. Women with small children say it is too much effort to keep the clothes clean enough for the mosque, but the real reason is probably that they receive no encouragement to attend. Women do play an active role in certain aspects of Islam, such as primary education, maintaining the fast, and performing liturgical music (Lambek, in press b).

Conclusion

In Mayotte there is no clear distinction between the positions of older and younger women in the domestic sphere, except to the degree that a senior woman can count on the support of her juniors. Her authority over other women is not automatic since every adult woman maintains her own household and thus a strong basis for autonomy. A woman's authority must be built up through the creation of moral obligation. A woman may attempt to build a marriage that grants her certain rights and security. The ties a woman builds with her husband(s), with her children, her foster children and their parents, her affines, and her children's affines mutually reinforce each other, granting her greater authority in a more tightly bounded cluster of kin. But a woman may also be successful if she lacks either a good marriage or children. In the public sphere the superior position of middle-aged women over younger women is more clear-cut, although only certain women can emerge as leaders in any age group.

The relationships between women of various ages are characterized by mutual support. It is my impression that younger women avoid appearing to put themselves ahead of their elders. Thus they hold back from an active participation in the mosque, in curing, or in politics, citing embarrassment and saying they are too young. This is less true of men, who are more openly in competition with one another (and who also restrict the degree of women's participation in prestigious activities). Women may adhere to a hierarchy based on age more closely than do men, but it is one that is tinged by the solidarity of the relationship between mothers and daughters.

Brown (1982) argues against the idea of a decline in women's status at middle age. The Mayotte data support this. However, they show no sudden changes but rather a pattern of continuity, growth, and florescence. Changes appear to be due more to the Mayotte conceptualization of age than of gender, but they are also grounded in the cumulative endeavors of women constructing their individual careers.

NOTES

The research on which this chapter is based has been supported by the Canada Council and the National Science Foundation (1975–76), the University of Toronto (1980), and both the Social Sciences and Humanities Research Council of Canada and the National Geographic Society (1985). I would like to thank Judith Brown for her encouragement, Jacqueline Solway for confirming the general lines of my analysis during our joint fieldwork in 1985, and the villagers of Mayotte.

1. Since this time wage labor has become much more significant. Unfortunately, its impact on women's lives cannot be considered here.

2. On the positive aspects of aging in the public domain see Lambek (in press a).

3. This is an oversimplification of the exchange system (Lambek, in press a). In general, public work is distinguished according to gender. One man participated in both men's and women's age groups. His wife belonged to the age group of another village and since he wanted to sponsor a ceremony in his own village that would require women's work, he felt he had to contribute "women's labor" on other occasions. He worked and ate with both women and men at ceremonial events, thereby acquiring double portions of meat. People considered his behavior in this one regard rather eccentric (though by no means shameful), but it represents a logical playing out of the rules regarding labor in the production of ceremonies.

4. A cross-cultural comparison of male and female intergenerational competition and hostility would be extremely interesting.

5. The expenses of the groom are not bridewealth but function rather as dowry and in the prestige system.

6. For an example of a successful strategy on the part of a wife faced with polygyny see Lambek (1980).

7. One extremely successful divorced middle-aged townswoman who saw no reason to remarry was dubbed "the financial wizard of Mamutzu [the town]" by an admiring anthropologist tenant.

8. On the other hand, menopause is often welcomed by fertile women for bringing relief from the frequent burden of pregnancy.

REFERENCES

Brown, Judith K.
  1982   Cross-cultural Perspectives on Middle-Aged Women. Current Anthropology 23(2):143–56.
Lambek, Michael
  1980   Spirits and Spouses: Possession as a System of Communication among the Malagasy Speakers of Mayotte. American Ethnologist 7(2):318–31.
  1981   Human Spirits: A Cultural Account of Trance in Mayotte. New York: Cambridge University Press.
  1983   Virgin Marriage and the Autonomy of Women in Mayotte. Signs 9(2):264–81.
  1988a Spirit Possession/Spirit Succession: Aspects of Social Continuity in Mayotte. American Ethnologist 15(4):710–31.
  1988b Graceful Exits: Spirit Possession as Personal Performance in Mayotte. Culture 8(1):59–69.
  1990   Certain Knowledge, Contestable Authority: Power and Practice on the Islamic Periphery. American Ethnologist 17(1):23–40.
  1991   Like Teeth Biting Tongue: The Proscription and Practice of Spouse Abuse in Mayotte. *In* Sanctions and Sanctuary. D. Counts, J. K. Brown, and J. Campbell, eds. Boulder, Colo.: Westview Press.
  In press a Exchange, Time, and Person in Mayotte: The Structure and Destructuring of a Cultural System. American Anthropologist.
  In press b The Playful Side of Islam and Its Possible Fate in Mayotte. Omaly sy Anio (Hier et Aujourd'hui): Journal of the Department of History, University of Madagascar.
Myerhoff, Barbara G., and Andrei Simić, eds.
  1978   Life's Career—Aging: Cultural Variations on Growing Old. Beverly Hills: Sage.
Ottino, Paul
  1964   La Crise du système familial et matrimonial des Sakalava de Nosy Be. Civilisation Malgache 1:225–48.

8 Female Control of Sexuality: Garífuna Women at Middle Age

Virginia Kerns

The social control of female sexuality, and the regulation of female fertility, can be considered cultural universals: features of social life that vary in form and specific "content" cross-culturally, but that are present in all human societies. Indeed, the regulation of women's sexuality and fertility may well constitute a central and organizing principle in human social life, one that manifests itself in many different guises. Significant cultural variation occurs along a number of dimensions, such as in the symbolic meaning of restrictions and taboos that limit female sexuality and regulate fertility; in the means by which they are enforced and the severity of the sanctions; and in the imposition of specific restrictions on certain categories of women, according to their social rank, age, marital status, or reproductive ability. In addition, perceptions and definitions of female sexuality vary cross-culturally and across the life course, often shifting at middle age.

Cultural devices that restrict or otherwise control female sexuality—enforcing abstinence ("virginity," "chastity") or fidelity to a male sexual partner—come in a remarkable variety of forms. Cross-cultural evidence that I have discussed elsewhere suggests that most restrictions apply to women of *childbearing* age. Commonly, these are enforced by middle-aged and old women, by men, or both: in other words, by *nonchildbearing* adults.[1] The distinction between childbearing and nonchildbearing adults provides a more useful framework here than the usual one, between male and female. It helps to explain why older women have supposedly "male" prerogatives in so many cultures, sometimes including greater freedom of sexual expression.[2]

A central transition in the female life course is from the childbearing to a nonchildbearing stage of life. This can be defined as the onset of middle age. Demographic and medical evidence suggests that fertility is usually lost in the forties, up to ten years before menopause.[3] Although a woman in her forties has generally ceased bearing children, she may still be involved in rearing them. Depending on her own reproductive history, she may have dependent children, grown children, both, or no children at all. In contrast to this variation in maternal status and role, the loss of fertility is a more nearly uniform experience, and so provides a more meaningful and useful criterion in defining the *entry* to middle age.[4]

The personal freedom of women seems generally to increase at middle age. More specifically, the control exercised over women by kin, by community, and by the state often decreases at midlife. Formal seclusion (or purdah), chaperonage, and other types of prescribed and purposeful "guarding" by kin are well-known means of directly limiting social and sexual contact between men and *young* women.[5] Certain forms of control by the state—especially the enforcement of laws relating to contraception, abortion, and other reproductive issues—also directly pertain to young women.[6]

At the local level, other means of control may operate. One of these, which I will call community surveillance, differs in several ways from those employed by kin and by the state. It is informal and indirect, involves many people who are not necessarily kin (or representatives of the state), and works most effectively in small, nucleated communities, where women can be watched closely. This watching is unsanctioned and occurs without conscious intent to control women's sexuality. (Community members, unlike kin and the state, do not routinely claim this as their "right.") The behavior of women is visibly the focus of intense interest and a subject of daily (if covert) comment; yet, if asked, people usually deny that they take part in such "idle talk," nor do they see it as a legitimate device to control others. Ethnographers or informants may dismiss such "gossip" or, alternatively, they may recognize it as a potent social force.

Surveillance has both an internal and external dimension and is ordinarily rather subtle. The observer sees little evidence other than a marked interest in women's affairs, both intimate and otherwise. In such a system, a woman is simply watched. She is not overtly and directly guarded; rather, she learns to guard herself. She avoids situations, places, and behavior that would compromise her reputation or bring her shame, and she does so with little conscious thought. Self-protection through self-restriction is a matter of habit.

To judge from the ethnographic record, women are generally punished more harshly than men for illicit sexual behavior, presumably due to differences in the reproductive and social consequences.[7] Female infidelity undermines confidence of paternity; maternal identity, in contrast, is inherently certain. (Or, as folk wisdom has it, "Mama's baby, Papa's maybe.") Cross-culturally, sanctions range from ridicule, criticism, and temporary loss of reputation, at the least, to permanent stigma, ostracism, confinement, beatings, gang rape, mutilation, and death.[8] Judging once again from cases in the ethnographic record, it is *young* women—those of reproductive age—who most often suffer these consequences for acts of sexual misconduct, whether real or merely suspected.

Viewed against this cross-cultural background, the Garífuna (Black Carib) have a rather benign and subtle system, one largely controlled by women and based primarily on surveillance. The acts of physical violence just listed are, with one exception, unsanctioned and unknown.[9] Middle-aged women, not men, play the major role in enforcing a moral code that indirectly limits female sexuality, especially during the reproductive years. (This is in direct contrast to an implicit and pervasive assumption of traditional social science: that men are everywhere the primary actors and agents of social control in the sexual domain.)

The usual reason that women cite for sexual restrictions has nothing to do with male authority, male proprietary rights in women, or an ideal of female chastity. These are alien concepts and at odds with various features of their social system and culture. For example, a woman's primary social identity does not center on her relationship with a man; women themselves define female sexuality, and not in ways that necessarily serve the goals of male sexuality; and sexual abstinence by men or women is regarded as unhealthy. Without making reference to men's welfare and social interests (or to their own, for that matter), women usually say that observing these restrictions is good for one's children. In their view, a young woman who is sexually unfaithful is an irresponsible mother. If she conceives, either with her spouse or her lover, the child is thought liable to suffer, both physically and socially. A good mother does not jeopardize her children in this way.

Garífuna women in Belize define themselves primarily as mothers. Maternal status eclipses marital status, which is to say that their social identity centers on having children. Having a husband is desirable but secondary. By their early forties, women have borne their last child, and most of them also have a grown child, or several. Their major responsibility as mothers, at any age, is to care for their children and protect them. Middle-aged women say that they protect their grown sons and daughters from supernatural harm by representing them in ancestral rituals. Young women fulfill this duty in part by observing a number of restrictions, or "rules" as they call them, which middle-aged women largely enforce. Because so many of the rules pertain to childbearing, older women are exempt from most of them. While the stated reason for such rules is to protect children, an unperceived effect is to limit the type of contact that young women have with men who are potential (but illicit) sexual partners. These restrictions, and changes in female sexuality at middle age, can best be understood in ethnographic context.

Ethnographic Background

Culturally and biologically, the Garífuna are of mixed, African-Indian origins and speak Central American Carib. The British deported them from their homeland, the West Indian island of St. Vincent, at the end of the eighteenth century. Today more than eighty thousand people live in about fifty settlements scattered along the Caribbean coast of Central America, from Belize (formerly British Honduras) to Nicaragua.

Several facts of social life pertain directly to perceived biological facts of life (outlined in the next section). The first of these is that maternal and paternal relatives, traced through one's biological mother and father, comprise a full set of kin. In this bilateral system, people routinely distinguish between maternal kin (*tiduhenu nuguchun,* mother's relatives) and paternal kin (*liduhenu nuguchin,* father's relatives). The specific terms of reference and address, however, are the same for both sides.

Most women and men reproduce. Virtually all say that they want children, and no one admits to the use of contraceptive devices. People speak of children in terms of their emotional, social, and material value. Children love and are loved in return. They signify one's social identity as an adult. When grown, they are supposed to "help" their parents, especially their mothers, by giving them money and food as needed. Middle-aged women, in return, may provide food and shelter for their grown children, and many foster a few grandchildren as well. For most of them, and especially those without a supporting spouse, these exchanges represent their daily work and daily bread.

While some adults never have children, virtually any woman or man is socially eligible to reproduce. That is, marriage and coresidence are not prerequisites for sexual relations and childbearing. The decision to begin a sexual relationship is a personal one, made without need for the consent of kin, public ceremony, or shared living quarters. (This is consistent with the emphasis placed on personal autonomy, which is an important social principle.[10]) Very often, a relationship begins without open acknowledgment. A common but by no means fixed sequence of events is as follows: a man and woman are attracted to each other and begin to meet privately; eventually, if the woman is fertile, she becomes pregnant; either before or after she gives birth, the couple may decide to live together; after some time, perhaps they will marry. This pattern is subject to great variation, however, depending on such factors as the couple's age, compatibility, financial means, and marital histories. One or the other may decide at any point to end the relationship on grounds of incompatibility, nonsupport, neglect, or infidelity. Such separations are more common among young men and women than among middle-aged and older couples.

Whatever the exact sequence of events, a sexual relationship always precedes marriage, or coresidence without marriage; and at first the lovers usually meet secretly. Inevitably and rather quickly in villages, where surveillance is most effective, others suspect them of meeting; and sooner or later both of them, or just the man, openly acknowledge the relationship. It sometimes happens that the man is married or known to be involved with another woman, and in such cases community opinion is divided. Other men admire him for having two women, while most women shake their heads and predict trouble between the rivals. A woman suspected of having more than one sexual partner is, in contrast, universally criticized.

In this system of kinship, the marital status of parents is of rather little consequence, and illegitimacy is an alien concept. It is quite common and acceptable for an unmarried woman to bear a child and later to enter a relationship with another man and to have children with him.[11] The crucial matter always, whatever a woman's marital status, is that she has just one sexual partner at a given time. Only a woman's fidelity to one man assures her child a full set of kin (paternal as well as maternal relatives) and an unambiguous social identity. Male infidelity may be troublesome to women, but it does not necessarily compromise the kinship status of a child, as female infidelity inevitably does.

All women claim to be faithful, and many also imply that they are unusual in this respect. Most of them have been suspected at some time of being unfaithful and have been the subject of rumors, which they categorically deny. The fact that so many men find work in other communities, returning home on a weekly or monthly basis, is said to give the women who stay at home the opportunity to "play." While daily talk is filled with allegations and innuendo, it is obviously difficult to verify these. By consensus, however, cases of uncertain paternity are extremely rare.[12]

Female Sexuality and Fertility

At the time of my initial fieldwork in Belize, I was in my midtwenties and childless. Many women asked pointed questions about my health and suggested local remedies made from various medicinal plants that might "cure" my presumed infertility. (It did not occur to them that a woman might choose to delay childbearing until her late twenties or thirties or that her marital status or any other circumstances might influence a decision to remain childless.) In the course of answering their questions and countering with my own, I found that the women I knew shared a set of beliefs about the facts of life. Certain women, however, "knew a lot more," and this tended to be age related. Middle-aged women took it as their "duty" to offer advice and information to their daughters and other young women.

Most of them spoke quite openly about sexuality and reproduction, which they regard as "natural" and "good." None of them ever avoided or hesitated to answer questions I asked, although they sometimes showed surprise and laughed at my apparent naiveté. Older women made the following observations about female sexuality and fertility, often with supporting evidence drawn from their own experience or that of female kin and acquaintances. Their observations and evidence are summarized below. I have included corroborative data from medical sources where possible. Although these sources and my informants agree on a number of the "facts," their explanations do vary in some cases.

1. Menarche generally occurs between the ages of twelve and fifteen and signals that a girl is or will soon be capable of bearing a child; several years usually elapse between the first menstrual cycle and the first pregnancy.

Women's evidence: They cited their own experience and that of kin and acquaintances. Some attributed the delay between menarche and pregnancy to the fact that a young girl's body is "not ready to make the baby," even if she is sexually active. Others explained that mothers try to supervise their adolescent daughters rather closely to prevent a premature pregnancy.[13]

Medical evidence: The age at menarche varies within and between human populations but is very rarely under ten or over eighteen years. "The first several menstrual cycles are usually irregular and anovulatory. Regular ovulatory cycles are usually established within two years after menarche, and full fertility is attained a few years after the first menstruation. . . . The period of adolescent infertility enables the girl to attain greater maturity before reproduction" (Hafez 1978:72, 78).

2. Pregnancy may occur as early as the age of fourteen, but this is uncommon and also undesirable because it puts the mother's health at risk.

Women's evidence: They cited the example of a young girl who had recently given birth at the age of fifteen, having conceived when she was fourteen. This was the only such case in recent memory. A number of women shook their heads with disapproval and expressed surprise that both the pregnancy and delivery were normal.

Medical evidence: "Adolescent pregnancies are associated with increased incidence of toxemia, uterine inertia, contracted pelvis, prolonged labor, prenatal mortality, fetal anomalies or premature labor" (Hafez 1978:77).

3. Sexual relations are not only enjoyable but necessary to good health. Prolonged abstinence (for more than a few months) can cause headaches and low backaches, as well as weight loss.

Women's evidence: They mentioned examples of women who had no sexual relations for a prolonged period of time and who suffered these symptoms. (The reason given in each case was either that the woman in question "had no man" for some time after a relationship ended or that she was in a relationship with a man who worked in a distant place.)

Medical evidence: Headaches, backaches, and changes in weight are among the symptoms of premenstrual syndrome, which is generally assumed to be a biologically based disorder (Abplanalp 1983:109, 113; cf. Martin 1988). One well-known theory is that premenstrual syndrome is due to a deficiency of progesterone during the premenstrual phase (Dalton 1964), but treatment studies do not offer conclusive support (Abplanalp 1983:115). The suggestion has also been made that some symptoms of premenstrual syndrome are related to unrelieved sexual tension (Masters and Johnson 1966:119–20).

4. Women engage in sexual relations because they "naturally" possess a strong sexual drive, but they also are "naturally" able to control this drive and confine themselves to one sexual partner.

Women's evidence: They have "felt for [wanted] sex" quite often, and virtually all of the women they know have engaged in sexual relations and regard intercourse as pleasurable. Many consider men to be naturally promiscuous ("like dogs," as some put it), but they say that women are "strong" enough to be faithful to one sexual partner for an extended period of time. No woman admitted to me that she had ever been unfaithful, yet many confided that they suspected other women of having affairs. When I asked why those women had been unfaithful, I was told that the self-control of some women wavers sometimes, and that of most men most of the time (also see Staiano 1986:109).

5. The sexual drive does not diminish greatly as fertility declines, and it persists after menopause.

Women's evidence: They named older women who had ceased bearing children but who, by self-report, remained sexually active. (As one postmenopausal woman put it succinctly and directly, "I'm still hot!")

Medical evidence: According to Masters and Johnson (1966:246), "there is no reason why the milestone of the menopause should be expected to blunt the human female's sexual capacity, performance, or drive." They find no physiological basis for any decline in the frequency of sexual activity at menopause or after (also see Gosden 1985:139–40).[14]

6. All young women are "naturally" capable of bearing healthy children. Infertility and other reproductive problems (including miscarriage, stillbirth, and birth defects) are due ultimately to "unnatural" (supernatural) causes.

Women's evidence: They pointed out that most women reproduce. They named several childless women and explained that they were the victims of sorcery or malicious spirits or they had caused their own reproductive problems by (allegedly) once aborting themselves or by ignoring supernatural taboos.

7. If a woman spends an extended period of time alone with a man, other than a close relative, it can be assumed that he made sexual advances, which she accepted. If she meets him secretly at night, she obviously intends to have sexual relations with him. (To be alone with him means simply to be out of public view, especially in a place where others are unlikely to see them. Being together for more than a few moments raises suspicions that a man and woman are planning a tryst. Close relatives, who are prohibited as sexual partners, include all lineals and first cousins, who are classificatory siblings.)

Women's evidence: Such a man and woman, they say, have no other reason to spend time alone together.

8. If a woman has multiple sexual partners, and if pregnancy results, determining paternity—and hence, the paternal relatives of the child—is problematic. No method of determination is absolutely conclusive.

Women's evidence: They cited the few cases of "washpan babies," children suspected to be the issue of extramarital relationships. (Some also use the term for babies born to single mothers who are thought to have had two sexual partners during the period of time when conception occurred.) When paternity is in doubt, middle-aged and older women informally examine the child. Most of them are said to be able to identify newborn infants as "for" their sons or not. (This is a skill that men and young women claim not to have.) The infant's facial features are considered the most important evidence, but other physical features also provide clues.

Older women pointed out that a young woman who is unfaithful and who becomes pregnant puts the paternity of her unborn child in doubt. There is no means of entirely dispelling it. Years later "people will still have a lot to say" about the circumstances of conception and birth.

Medical evidence: Until very recently, there was no scientific means of conclusively establishing paternity. Only since the mid-1980s has a new technique, DNA fingerprinting, made it possible to determine paternity.[15]

9. The age at menopause varies from the midthirties to the midfifties, but fifty is about average.

Women's evidence: They cited the case of one woman who had stopped menstruating in her early thirties. I questioned the woman, who was then in her late thirties, and she confirmed this. Hers was the earliest age reported. Women generally mentioned "about fifty" as the age when menstruation was very rare or had ceased altogether.

Medical evidence: "The average age of onset of menopause is 50 years (range: 37 to 56 years). . . . Menopause is completed after one year of amenorrhea, normally by 55 years of age" (Hafez 1978:215). "Most studies have found median ages of menopause between 49 and 51 in Western nations" (Gosden 1985:10).

10. Fertility declines before menopause. Women may reproduce in their early forties, but not after forty-five or so.

Women's evidence: They named a number of women who had borne their last children in their early forties, but they knew of no case in which the mother gave birth at the age of forty-five or after. Reproductive data that I collected in one community support this claim (see also McCommon 1982:109). Every woman between the ages of forty-five and sixty who had children had given birth to her last surviving child by the age of forty-four. About two-thirds of them did so by the age of thirty-eight.

Medical evidence: "Surveys of contemporary societies have shown that the average age at which fertility is lost (age at last delivery) is about 40" (Gosden 1985:94). "Declining fertility in aged women is partly due to less frequent ovulation. . . . It is estimated that 1 out of 20,000 to 60,000 births occurs past the age of 50" (Hafez 1978:223).

To summarize: in this noncontracepting population, most women are capable of childbearing from the age of puberty until their midforties. People also consciously recognize that a young woman who is unfaithful may bear a child of uncertain paternity. Further, they think that women have an active interest in sexual relations from adolescence through middle age, and potentially until they grow frail in old age. Despite this shared knowledge, no one ever suggested directly that *young* women should therefore be watched or otherwise controlled and that *older* women could do as they like. Men and women of all ages value personal autonomy, object to "interference" by others, and deny that they "interfere" themselves; and no woman admits to infidelity.

Following the Rules

Initially, Garífuna women of all ages struck me as remarkably independent, both in mind and manner. I was to find that they are not bound by certain restrictive customs that so clearly limit the personal liberty of women in many cultures. Over time, however, I did learn of various restrictive "rules," as they are called, that apply to women. Most of these are situational, and thus temporary, rather than absolute, permanent restrictions. They pertain to various phases of the female reproductive cycle (menstruation, pregnancy, and the postpartum period), hence to women of childbearing age. Middle-aged and old women, who have ceased bearing children and are approaching or have reached menopause, are exempt from most of these. They are also the most active exponents and enforcers of such "rules."

Nearly all of the rules are perceived as protective devices. A woman who follows them protects herself and others from physical harm, which takes various forms: sickness, loss of specific physical powers and senses, or even death. In some instances a malevolent spirit is the agent of harm, but the woman's failure to follow the rule is the root cause. Such a woman brings physical suffering upon herself, her child, or other people, and her reputation suffers as well. She also has to contend with reproach and repeated warnings from her mother and other middle-aged and old women. Some young women scoff openly at a number of these rules, dismissing them as superstition. Yet most do as they are told, or pretend to do so, if only to keep the peace.

The following few rules illustrate the many that apply to women during menstruation, pregnancy, and after childbirth. A menstruating women should stay close to home and avoid social gatherings.[16] The scent of menstrual blood is said to attract malevolent spirits, who then attack someone nearby (but not the woman directly). A pregnant woman is also advised by older women to stay at home to avoid seeing strange sights that may "mark" her unborn child. She should also avoid conflict, they say, since her anger can "spoil" the fetus in some way. After giving birth, the woman customarily stays inside the house or near home for nine days. This is said to protect her own health.

Such restrictions are situational, temporary, and pertain to women of childbearing age. The rule of sexual fidelity might appear absolute, yet the harmful effects of female infidelity vary, depending on when they occur in the reproductive cycle. A woman who has more than one sexual partner and conceives, or a woman who is unfaithful during pregnancy or soon after giving birth, risks the worst consequences. Older women warn that having an affair during pregnancy can lead to infertility in the future or can cause congenital defects in an unborn child. (The father's semen, in contrast, is said to "nourish" the fetus.) If a woman is unfaithful after giving birth, and before the child is weaned, she will suffer a wasting illness and her child may sicken as well.

Aside from causing physical harm, female infidelity is viewed as socially damaging to children, and often in a lasting way. Specifically, a woman who conceives a child while she is suspected of "playing" with a second man creates confusion about which man is the child's father. She thereby denies her child a full set of kin, and future certainty about who is permitted or prohibited as a sexual partner.[17] Since a man may justifiably leave an unfaithful woman, she and her children will lose his financial support. Even her mother suffers in that case, being obliged to help her daughter and grandchildren with food and shelter.

Middle-aged women speak of female infidelity as a form of negligence toward children. They say that an unfaithful woman is an irresponsible mother because her young children will suffer. (No one ever said that a woman whose children are grown could cause them harm in this way.) With the exception of new fathers, men who have affairs are not held responsible for hurting their children.[18] Others criticize them only, and rather mildly at that, for "making trouble" between women.

A subtle and complex system of incentives and constraints, largely directed toward young women and enforced by middle-aged and old women, limits illicit sexual relations that may result in children of uncertain paternity. Many young women simply follow the rules to avoid criticism by other women and in an attempt to keep their names out of the community rumor mill. Some say that they fear a sickness, known as *idahadu* and caused by others' criticism, more than the supposed supernatural consequences of infidelity.[19]

Certain social devices also limit any chances for illicit relations by limiting the nature and frequency of contact between men and young women. Informal segregation and surveillance are the most important of these. The customary division of labor has the effect of physically separating men and women for most of the day. Men work at a distance from home, fishing or doing wage labor, while most household tasks are allocated to women. Moreover, a young woman is supposed to work in the vicinity of her house and to leave her yard only with a specific destination in mind. Stopping for a lengthy tete-à-tete, even in public view, with an unrelated man raises suspicions that she is arranging to meet him at night. (People will always feign disinterest in such private conversations, yet these are usually grist for the rumor mill.) Most women, whatever their age, claim not to "drift about" in the community. In fact, however, middle-aged women visit quite freely, and old women do so without the least fear of critical comment.

Generally speaking, the younger the woman, the more others take note of where she goes and with whom. When young women leave their houses at night—to attend a community event, for example, or to buy something at a shop—they routinely take children or female companions with them. If they leave the village during the day to work at their "farms" (swidden plots) or to collect firewood or coconuts, they also go in company. The stated reason for taking companions to the bush is that a lone person is more likely to be "bothered" (harmed) by the malevolent spirits who live there. Some of these spirits also enter the community at night, hence the need for companions after dark. By going about with others, young women protect themselves from gossip and criticism, as well as from these bad spirits.

Middle-aged women are noticeably less concerned about being seen alone or in company, although they clearly value companionship over solitude. If expedience demands, an older woman will not hesitate to leave a ritual event at night by herself or to go off alone to collect firewood. Nor will she express fear about doing so. Immunity from supernatural harm is said to increase with age.

In short, a variety of customary beliefs and practices restrict the personal liberty of young women, but have little effect on older women. They promote female fidelity and confidence in paternity, in part by limiting the type and frequency of contact between men and young women. If a woman of childbearing age is unfaithful, she may cause lasting harm to others, and especially to her children. While "people always have a lot to say" about such cases, they show noticeably less concern about a middle-aged woman whose eye wanders. Men and women occasionally told me about specific older women whom they suspected of having affairs, but they showed rather little interest in the details. ("Well, that's nobody's business," was the way a woman summed up one such case.) The female sexual drive is not thought to diminish sharply at middle age, but childbearing is known to end by the early to midforties.

Summary

The control of female sexuality (and fertility) during the reproductive years is everywhere a central fact of social life, and an important feature of the female life course. Cross-culturally, the means of control differ. There is also variation in the degree of cultural "consciousness" about the purpose and effects of restrictions, the extent to which middle-aged women are subject to or enforce these restrictions, and the types and severity of sanctions used. The ethnographic literature provides the most detailed descriptions and analyses for the highly formalized systems of control found in stratified societies with extreme gender inequality (for example, purdah in the Middle East). These formalized systems are quite visible to ethnographers and to their informants, who speak explicitly of the need to "protect" (control) young women, to prevent illicit sexual acts, and to uphold family honor (see Boddy and Vatuk, this volume).

The Garífuna provide a contrasting case, and one noteworthy in several respects. Their object of concern is not to ensure virginity before marriage or life-long fidelity to one man—both of them ambitious goals, common in stratified complex societies and requiring elaborate systems of control and severe sanctions. The Garífuna do not hold these as ideals. Their aim is primarily, and more simply, to prevent a young woman from having more than one sexual partner at a given time (thus promoting confidence of paternity). Middle-aged women are visibly more involved than men in enforcing restrictions that socially limit women of childbearing age. The threat or use of physical coercion is not a sanctioned means of control, and expressions of disapproval are directed solely against the young woman in question. Only her reputation suffers. (Family honor is an alien concept, and conflicts with prevailing ideas about personal autonomy and personal responsibility.) A set of rules that apply to women at various points in the reproductive cycle, and a system of surveillance, provide the main means of control. Middle-aged women, who are no longer capable of bearing children, enforce these rules but are themselves largely exempt from them.

The personal freedom of women increases at middle age, and the perception of female power shifts from the negative to the positive as reproductive capacity declines. All women, whatever their age, are thought able to do good (by creating, protecting, or sustaining life) or to do evil (by harming others or destroying life). Young women, however, are more able and likely to cause serious, lasting harm by neglecting or willfully breaking the restrictive rules that apply only to them as childbearers. Older women, who act together to enforce these rules and others that support the moral and social order, have the perceived power to protect and preserve, and so to serve the common good.

NOTES

This chapter is based on ethnographic fieldwork and interviews conducted between 1973 and 1981. I am grateful to the Wenner-Gren Foundation, the Fulbright-Hays Commission, and the University of Illinois for funding my research. Thanks also to Rita P. Wright and Marie Tyler-McGraw for comments on an earlier draft of this chapter and to Barbara J. King for bibliographic suggestions.

1. See Kerns 1979, 1983:190–94; cf. Brown 1982 and this volume.

2. In some cultures, older women are said to be "like men" and to enjoy "male" prerogatives (e.g., Counts, p. 63; Vatuk, pp. 156, 157). These women share one primary characteristic with men: they cannot bear children. Perhaps their privileges are better understood as those of nonchildbearing adults, rather than as "male" privileges extended to "females" later in life (Kerns 1983:193).

3. According to Gosden (1985:94), "Surveys of contemporary societies have shown that the average age at which fertility is lost (age at last live delivery) is about 40. . . . Therefore, the average age of sterility precedes that of menopause by up to 10 years." He notes, however, that while the "natural fertility of women wanes from the third decade of life, . . . a residual capacity for pregnancy remains in some individuals until menopause" (Gosden 1985:117); and that "demographic

data do not distinguish women who are sterile from those in whom residual fertile capacity exists" (Gosden 1985:94).

Demographers use various age intervals to define the childbearing period: fifteen to forty-nine, fifteen to forty-four, twenty to forty-four. In general, however, "so little childbearing takes place after age 44, even in high fertility populations, that almost no distortion results from attributing all such births to the age group 40–44 years of age" (Bogue 1971:5–6).

4. This definition of middle age differs somewhat from Brown's (1982 and this volume), which centers on having grown children. It reflects my specific interest in defining the entry to middle age, as well as some findings of my ethnographic research. In the communities I studied, about 10 percent of the women over the age of forty-five were childless. Some women in their midforties had only dependent children. While they varied with respect to maternal status and role, all of these women were considered to be beyond the age of childbearing. In keeping with the cultural emphasis on relative age (seniority), young adults usually referred to their mothers and other middle-aged women as "old" (*waia*) and to their grandmothers as "old old" (Kerns 1983:94ff.). Women in their forties and fifties spoke of themselves as "old" in relation to their children, and "young" in relation to their parents.

5. For example, see Flinn 1988; Hrdy 1981; Dickemann 1981; Fox 1977.

6. See Ross and Rapp's (1981) discussion of families, kinship systems, communities, and "world systems" as social contexts that shape sexuality; also see Caplan 1987.

7. See Broude 1980; cf. Frayser 1985:214; Schlegel 1972.

8. See, for example, Broude 1980; Sanday 1981:15; Frayser 1985; Levinson 1988:443; Kerns 1991; Boddy, p. 45.

9. Wife beating is unsanctioned and uncommon. In each of the cases I witnessed or learned about, the man suspected his spouse of having an affair (see Kerns 1991).

10. Individuals have the right to make their own decisions about most matters, ranging from important events in their personal lives to routine daily activities, and they do not take kindly to "interference" by others. This is as true for women as for men (see Kerns 1983:75–88).

11. In two Garífuna villages in Belize, there were sixty women who, at forty-five years or older, were past the age of childbearing and who had borne two or more children. Slightly over half had children by two (45 percent) or more (7 percent) men.

12. In two communities, there were three women past the age of childbearing who were thought to have produced a child by an extramarital liason (a so-called "washpan baby"). These children comprised less than 1 percent of all surviving children born to women of that cohort.

13. See Flinn's (1988) discussion of "daughter guarding" in rural Trinidad, where men take an active role and where the purpose differs. Fathers try to prevent their unmarried daughters from entering relationships that will keep them from making stable, "good" marriages. In Jamaica, "mothers seek to guard daughters from sexual liaisons with the wrong type of man" (MacCormack and Draper 1987:152).

14. Kinsey and his colleagues also found little evidence that the physical processes of aging cause a woman's sexual capacity to decline "until late in her life," by which they seem to mean the sixties or after (see Kinsey et al. 1953:353, 715; also see Vatuk, p. 156).

15. For a brief explanation of the DNA fingerprint technique and its potential uses, see Lewin (1986:522).

16. Many women claim to have followed this rule only in adolescence and at their mothers' insistence (see Kerns 1983:97).

17. As an example, many people cited the case of a young man who for a time unwittingly courted his half-sister. He carried the surname of his mother's husband, but relatives of the husband doubted that the young man was kin. His mother was said to have been having an affair at the time of his conception while living with the man she later married.

18. For a brief time after a child is born, the father should avoid sexual relations with women other than the child's mother. Failure to follow this "rule" (one of several that pertain to new fathers, and that have been categorized as couvade) is said to cause the infant to sicken and even to die (see Kerns 1983:99–100).

19. Although no one could cite a recent case of *idahadu,* all of my informants spoke of others' negative emotions (criticism, envy, hostility) as a potential cause of physical illness (see Kerns 1983:82, 87; Staiano 1986:119).

REFERENCES

Abplanalp, Judith M.
    1983   Premenstrual Syndrome: A Selective Review. *In* Lifting the Curse of Menstruation: A Feminist Appraisal of the Influence of Menstruation on Women's Lives. S. Golub, ed. pp. 107–23. New York: Haworth Press.
Bogue, Donald
    1971   Demographic Techniques of Fertility Analysis. Chicago: Community and Family Study Center.
Broude, Gwen
    1980   Extramarital Sex Norms in Cross-cultural Perspective. Behavior Science Research 15(3):181–218.
Brown, Judith K.
    1982   Cross-cultural Perspectives on Middle-Aged Women. Current Anthropology 23(2):143–56.
Caplan, Pat
    1987   Introduction. *In* The Cultural Construction of Sexuality. P. Caplan, ed. pp. 1–30. London: Tavistock.
Dalton, Katarina
    1964   The Premenstrual Syndrome. Springfield, Ill.: Charles C. Thomas.
Dickemann, Mildred
    1981   Paternal Confidence and Dowry Competition: A Biocultural Analysis

of Purdah. *In* Natural Selection and Social Behavior: Recent Research and New Theory. R. D. Alexander and D. W. Tinkle, eds. pp. 417–38. New York: Chiron Press.

Flinn, Mark V.
1988   Parent-Offspring Interactions in a Caribbean Village: Daughter Guarding. *In* Human Reproductive Behaviour: A Darwinian Perspective. L. Betzig, M. Borgerhoff Mulder, and P. Turke, eds. pp. 189–200. Cambridge: Cambridge University Press.

Fox, Greer Litton
1977   "Nice Girl": Social Control of Women through a Value Construct. Signs 2(4):805–17.

Frayser, Suzanne G.
1985   Varieties of Sexual Experience: An Anthropological Perspective on Human Sexuality. New Haven, Conn.: HRAF Press.

Gosden, R. G.
1985   Biology of Menopause: The Causes and Consequences of Ovarian Ageing. New York: Academic Press.

Hafez, E. S. E.
1978   Human Reproductive Physiology. Ann Arbor, Mich.: Ann Arbor Science Publishers.

Hrdy, Sarah Blaffer
1981   The Woman That Never Evolved. Cambridge, Mass.: Harvard University Press.

Kerns, Virginia
1979   Social Transition at Menopause. Paper presented at the Annual Meeting of the American Anthropological Association. Cincinnati.
1983   Women and the Ancestors: Black Carib Kinship and Ritual. Urbana: University of Illinois Press.
1991   Preventing Violence against Women: A Central American Case. *In* Sanctions and Sanctuary. D. Counts, J. K. Brown, and J. Campbell, eds. Boulder, Colo.: Westview Press.

Kinsey, Alfred C., et al.
1953   Sexual Behavior in the Human Female. Philadelphia: W. B. Saunders.

Levinson, David
1988   Family Violence in Cross-cultural Perspective. *In* Handbook of Family Violence. V. B. Van Hasselt et al., eds. pp. 435–55. New York: Plenum Press.

Lewin, Roger
1986   A Matter of Maternity. Science 233(4762):522.

McCommon, Carolyn S.
1982   Mating as a Reproductive Strategy: A Black Carib Example. Ph.D. diss., Pennsylvania State University.

MacCormack, Carol P., and Alizon Draper
1987   Social and Cognitive Aspects of Female Sexuality in Jamaica. *In* The Cultural Construction of Sexuality. P. Caplan, ed., pp. 143–65. London: Tavistock.

Martin, Emily
   1988   Premenstrual Syndrome: Discipline, Work, and Anger in Late Industrial
      Societies. *In* Blood Magic: The Anthropology of Menstruation. T. Buckley
      and A. Gottlieb, eds. pp. 161–81. Berkeley: University of California Press.
Masters, William H., and Virginia Johnson
   1966   Human Sexual Response. Boston: Little, Brown.
Ross, Ellen, and Rayna Rapp
   1981   Sex and Society: A Research Note from Social History and Anthropology.
      Comparative Studies in Society and History 23:51–72.
Sanday, Peggy
   1981   The Socio-cultural Context of Rape. Journal of Social Issues 37(4):5–27.
Schlegel, Alice
   1972   Male Dominance and Female Autonomy. New Haven: Human Rela-
      tions Area Files Press.
Staiano, Kathryn Vance
   1986   Interpreting Signs of Illness: A Case Study in Medical Semiotics. New
      York: Mouton de Gruyter.

9 A Study in Pride and Prejudice: Maori Women at Midlife

Karen P. Sinclair

Maori women approach middle age with far more responsibilities than at any other point in the life cycle. But they now possess commensurately more power and authority with which to execute them. No longer completely constrained by pollution beliefs or burdened by the demands of young children, they are free to assume a more prominent, public position (Flint 1975; Kerns 1980). Ceremonial and ritual roles, hitherto limited to men, are now, to some extent, available to women. But it would be a mistake to characterize this point in the life cycle as discontinuous with women's previous experiences. Clearly, the diminishing of gender distinctions reported so extensively elsewhere (Brown 1982a, 1982b; Griffen 1982) contributes to the authority of Maori women. But women who now find themselves operating in these heady new dimensions have in fact been preparing for the prestige and independence that will characterize their later years. Continuity and consistency mark women's lives. In a colonial situation, such as exists in contemporary New Zealand, the importance of coherence in female experience cannot be minimized.

Although there are exceptions, women's lives seem to improve dramatically at middle age. As Brown points out, "Overwhelmingly the cross-cultural evidence indicates positive changes. Middle age brings fewer restrictions, the right to exert authority over kinsmen, and the opportunity for achievement and recognition beyond the household" (1982b:143). In a similar vein, both Griffen (1982) and Kehoe (1973) have commented on the restrictions inherent in maternity; child care not only limits social opportunities but women of childbearing age are often imputed attributes deemed contrary to the exercise of supernatural power. In middle age these constraints are relaxed. In short, women become more effective social actors, capable both of managing resources and manipulating their ideological and social worlds to lend meaning to their performance (Dominy 1983:2).

By virtue of their position as an indigenous minority, Maori women are called upon to operate in two contexts: one defined by Maori rules and traditions, the other by the conventions that govern the European social system. Gender and social identities are therefore enacted in different arenas.

As Maori men and women age, they participate more fully in ritual and ceremonial affairs. At this time of life, social, ritual, and political responsibilities supplant earlier concerns with domesticity and wage labor. Maori elders are expected to preside over crucial aspects of Maori social life; their responsibilities and obligations make them focal points at feasts, funerals, and on all occasions that distinguish the contemporary Maori situation. For it is at these times that Maoris may celebrate, mourn their dead, and demonstrate their commitment to their place as Maoris in New Zealand society. To participate merely by attendance requires very little; to take an active role requires years of training, expertise, and dedication.

Middle age finds the Maori man at the apex of his social power. If he has learned and practiced his task well, he is a skilled speaker, capable of persuasive public oratory and decisive behind-the-scenes manipulation. In addition, he has the advantage of an ideology that unequivocally asserts the superiority of men. Few women would question the formal structure that stresses the ascendancy and public dominion of men. At the same time they clearly recognize their own contribution to the informal, not always acknowledged, aspect of ceremonial and ritual life. Indeed, the organizational and ritual importance of middle-aged and elderly women is a critical counterpoint to an ideology of male preeminence. As women age, they depend increasingly on other women to buttress their public position. Thus the cooperation and assistance that women grant one another throughout the life cycle provide a necessary impetus to wider female participation. Women have forged close, intimate bonds, not only by working with and alongside one another—for men do this as well—but by making the subtleties of social relations their province. Thus as they reach middle age, they have more than allies and support; they have become the arbiters of community standards.

Without the security and pride of high status so often associated with men, women have been more prepared to deal with Europeans. Whatever humiliations were attendant upon such transactions, women now have an understanding of the larger culture that men lack. Furthermore, because they have maintained closer ties with their own children, they can use their knowledge of the Pakeha (the New Zealand term for individuals of European descent) to guide the younger generation through the difficulties of culture change. It is these skills that have made women, rather than men, mediators in the intricate social fabric that confronts the contemporary Maori.

The women who are the subjects[1] of this chapter are members of a religious movement, *Maramatanga*. Involvement in the movement accelerates and reinforces their growing importance and influence; for to participate in a movement like this is to participate actively in the definition and formation of Maori identity. Middle-aged women use their spiritual expertise to embark on new careers (as healers for example), to travel abroad as members of church groups, or simply to consolidate and justify their increasing prestige and influence. Religious activity does not change but rather reinforces the authority that maturity grants to women.

This chapter then is an investigation of why women's status increases at middle age. That it does in the Maori case is at first glance somewhat surprising. For colonialism often diminishes the stature of women (Boserup 1970; Bell 1981) and Maoris already have in place an ideology that affirms female inferiority. But the confluence of tradition and innovation has worked in this instance to enhance the position of women. The fusion of traditional rules, which accord women greater authority as they age, with the ambiguities of colonialism, which permit them greater scope to exercise this influence, has allowed women to fashion a significant social contribution.

Maoris in Contemporary New Zealand

In slightly over two centuries, New Zealand has been transformed from the stratified Polynesian chieftainship of the aboriginal Maoris into a complex Western democracy. This process has placed the burden of accommodation on the Maoris, who have had to respond to social and political forces that laid siege to their former way of life. The adjustment has been neither uniform nor painless; calls to battle and religious innovation have taken their place next to judicial land reform, passive conversion to Christianity, and, more recently, organized political protest. Two hundred years after the arrival of Captain Cook, Maoris acknowledge only reluctantly European hegemony over their ancestral lands.

Their discomfort is not without justification.[2] On most measures that indicate standard of living or quality of life, Maoris emerge considerably below Europeans. Moreover, the situation tends to be self-perpetuating, as Forster and Ramsay point out:

> Entering the labor market with few skills and less than the Pakeha standard
> of education, they must take those jobs which pay least; their standard of

living restricts the potential opportunities and encouragement that can be given to their children. Without supported opportunities or unusual circumstances, the children are likely to find themselves in a position not unlike that of their parents. Thus the situation can all too easily become self-perpetuating. (1971:202)

Today only 10 percent of the New Zealand population identifies itself as Maori. But this represents a larger proportion since the last census, and growth appears to have come from an increase in the number of children born. Thus the Maori population is much more youthful than the Pakeha populace and is growing at a much more rapid rate. These demographic changes will inevitably affect relations within Maori society and between Maoris and Europeans.

Another significant change in Maori life is the increase in urbanization. Continuing a movement away from rural areas that began shortly after World War II, young Maoris have looked to the cities for employment and stimulation that are absent in rural areas. Too often, however, they are ill equipped to make the necessary adjustments, and urban life frequently fails to meet their expectations. Rather, a host of social problems emerges. According to Walsh,

> Over two thirds of the Maori urban population is under the age of 25. Between 1961–66 three-quarters of the Maori youth aged 16–19 years went to live in urban areas. In 1967 over half the Maori children born were born in urban areas. This poses serious questions of adjustments to city living additional to those expected for any migration to a strange environment. First generation migrants all over the world tend initially, to live in the decaying central core of the city and overcrowded conditions and high crime rates are not unusual. (1973:12)

Under these circumstances, many relationships have to be redefined. The links between town and country Maoris must be reassessed. The traditional leadership of rural elders seldom reaches effectively into the urban milieu.[3] Yet the connections between youth in the cities and their families in rural areas are far from tenuous. Moreover, these ties are made and reinforced by women, who have demonstrated their ability to adapt and make themselves significant in the contemporary Maori world. Indeed the Maori family continues to be important. The resilience of this particular pattern has been discussed by James Ritchie:

> After suffering almost every major impact that culture change can bring we still find that the Maori family preserves its own model and that Maori individuals seek to recreate the kind of community that family model best fits. Currently, neither education, entrapment in the affluent society, discrimination, nor inducement has been potent enough to destroy Maori

patterns. . . . For such times ahead as we need to consider, it is likely that the satisfactions of Maori family and community life will make these alternatives attractive and habitual for a very large number of those who call themselves Maoris. (1972:75)

Relationships between Maoris and Europeans have, apparently, become more problematic. It is difficult to know whether the problem has actually intensified or if it is only now that difficulties in this area are being acknowledged. Anti-Maori prejudice can no longer be denied. St. George affirms its existence: "Prejudice in New Zealand there is, and the studies show that Pakeha New Zealanders do direct prejudice against Maori New Zealanders, and that they also hold prejudicial attitudes towards various other national groups that are distinctly negative where color of skin is concerned" (1972:15). Widespread stereotypes further distort ethnic relations (Metge 1976; Arbuckle 1976). Pakehas view Maoris as musical, happy-go-lucky children while they are perceived by Maoris as selfish and individualistic, without the commitment to kin and community that makes Maori life valuable. Perhaps the most poignant aspect is to be found in the fact that Maoris have come to accept these negative stereotypes of themselves, frequently maintaining that they are unattractive failures (Archer and Archer 1970).

New Zealand society, then, confronts the Maoris with many uncomfortable situations. Unwilling and unable to emulate Europeans, they have discovered that their own culture is not valued by the larger society. They have learned that pride in Maoriness must come from within their own group; only through concerted efforts will traditions be sustained. Underemployed in rural areas, with little expertise in understanding the perplexities of urban life, Maoris face serious problems of adjustment. Indeed the strains evidence themselves in many ways. There has been an increase in domestic violence, crime, and admission to mental hospitals. Walsh attributes the rise in diagnosed schizophrenia to "difficulties in maintaining dual cultural identity or in choosing between different sets of cultural values" (1973:30). Solutions have tended not to be enduring; each generation has had to come to terms anew with the difficulties of being Maori in contemporary New Zealand.

Gender Ideology

Gender ideology traditionally affirmed the superiority and preeminence of Maori men. While some aspects of gender asymmetry have been muted over time, the priority of men remains axiomatic. Thus women, who in their own right command considerable respect, will automatically defer to men. The source of men's position in general derives neither from their accomplishments nor from their abilities, but from a cultural ideology that views men as ritually undefiled and women as dangerously polluting. While these beliefs have many consequences, one is the greater freedom accorded men and the commensurately stronger restrictions placed on women.

Female sexuality and reproduction traditionally carried implications of chaos and destruction. In Maori mythology, women were presented as ambiguous creatures, embodying notions of life and death, fertility and sexuality. As befitting such anomalous beings, women were circumscribed by rules that limited and restricted their social participation. Pollution beliefs kept women in their place and narrowed their spheres of social action. On one level, notions of female pollution erected boundaries between male and female domains: women were prohibited from all building sites and excluded from all major ritual activities. Heuer maintains that "the presence of women, or more precisely of the female organs, was deemed destructive to sacredness, as was the presence of cooked food. For this reason, there were no female priests; women were, however, not infrequently seers or mediums for lesser gods" (1969:477–78).

The reproductive capacity of women was subject to great cultural elaboration. Women could purify sacred areas by walking over them or restore a warrior's lost courage in the same manner. Thus female genitals, if defiling, were also clearly powerful. Their ambiguous life-giving powers were handled with suitable gravity. Menstruating or pregnant women were denied access to entire areas of the social and physical landscape. Were they to violate these rules, the results threatened to be immediate and spectacular: crops would fail, animals would flee, warriors would fall in battle (Best 1905:215; Heuer 1969:466–67).

While such beliefs and proscriptions clearly make use of Maori conventions regarding life and death and blood and fertility, there is also a message with a clear sociological dimension. Women are disruptive to the harmony and order of social life (Douglas 1978:61). They must be controlled and contained. Moreover, the checks and limitations placed upon the activities of women make a clear public statement expressing female inferiority. Pollution beliefs not only attest to the difference between men and women but express as well the cultural conviction that legitimacy is a male preserve. To require a menstruating woman to keep away from male activities can make this point quite effectively. "To blame her carelessness in this respect for his failure in fishing or hunting or farming is a way of using the cosmos to constrain other people" (Douglas 1978:62).

Many of these prohibitions are no longer relevant or effective in the contemporary context. However, notions of female contamination continue.

Young girls are taught never to bare their genitals nor to step over a man. Sitting on a table, while indelicate behavior in a man, is a deliberate defilement when done by a woman. If hot water is in short supply and baths are to be shared, it goes without saying that men, who come in with dirt from the fields, have the first bath. Women must take the second bath, for grime and grease are not as dirty or as polluting as whatever women will leave behind in the water.

Officially, gender ideology stresses complementarity. There is no presumption of equality. While there is a strong emphasis on interdependence, the public and symbolic quality so often associated with the role of men suggests a dimension that is lacking in female experience. Thus Salmond writes: "Women do have a role to play in the ceremonial area. They call, wail and chant ancient songs. But theirs is largely a supporting role and in most areas they are excluded from the central activity of speechmaking" (1975:43).[4]

Women, however, derive some benefit from this separation: it affords them opportunities to establish ties with other women and to create a network of alliances that will serve them well in their later years. These networks are formed early and become stronger over the life cycle. To a large degree they are a response to the enduring boundaries between men and women.

Gender Roles and Female Networks

From a child's earliest years, there is a separation of male and female domains. Peer groups, becoming important first in childhood, continue to be significant throughout the life cycle. Even before adolescence, boys and girls begin to exist in separate but proximate social worlds; young girls are more constrained by domestic responsibilities while young boys are freer to range further afield. More significantly, however, young girls are far more attuned to one another's feelings and develop more intense emotional attachments than do boys of the same age (James Ritchie 1972; Earle 1958).[5]

Married by their late teens, most women spend the next two decades involved with a growing number of young children. Despite the availability of birth control, women who are now middle-aged refrained from family planning. Consequently, they have frequently produced anywhere from six to thirteen children. Although Maori family patterns preclude the isolation of young mothers so typical in other Western societies, most women described this point in their lives in distinctly negative terms. They expressed feelings of loneliness and desolation that were mitigated only by their closeness to and dependence upon other women. In rural areas such women depended far more on one another than on their spouses. Indeed, in addition to assistance with cooking and child care, women often provide one another a refuge from the afflictions of marriage: neglect, unrealistic demands, and verbal and physical abuse. Women feed, dress, and care for one another's children, thereby lessening the tyranny of domestic preoccupations. Clothing and food are rapidly redistributed, allowing scarce resources the widest application. Thus mothers aid daughters, aunts support nieces, cousins and sisters attend one another. Contemporary Maori households, then, are managed by a cooperative network of women who prepare and distribute food, shop, and tend to the needs of children.[6]

These networks are not confined to mundane events. At feasts and ceremonials, they are activated to accomplish the many details involved in the extension of Maori hospitality. When young, girls perform menial tasks; as middle-aged women they initiate and control the ritual occasions so crucial to modern Maori sensibility.

The participation of young women in ceremonial occasions is confined to the tasks of dishwashing, table setting, waitressing, shopping, and food preparation. While the work often borders on drudgery, young women nevertheless witness the effectiveness of female management and the importance of women's contribution. In the face of their own experience, they are not daunted by a formal ideology that only recognizes male accomplishment. At this time they are also being prepared for the more active ritual role that they will be expected to assume as they mature.

In ceremonial affairs women have a supportive, auxiliary role, at least while they are premenopausal. Men continue to dominate public ritual events by their expertise in oratory and genealogy. By singing and chanting, women give group confirmation to individual male performances. It is significant that women always appear publicly in a group while men, in general, engage in individual productions. Women bestow group sanctions, or in rare cases, signal group approbation.

The ritual and formal status of men and women changes as they progress through the life cycle. In old age, they are *kaumatuas,* elders. Men are referred to as *koro,* women as *kuia.* Both terms denote grandparenthood, as well as respected elder. Most middle-aged individuals will accept *Koro* or *Kuia* as a term of address from grandchildren but eschew the general label. They do not want to be seen as fitting too snugly into the elder category. For Maoris, middle age connotes a period of vigor and visibility that may be contrasted to the ceremonial, but relatively inactive, importance of elders.

As women reach middle age, the focus of their activity broadens: they now participate more publicly and effectively than do younger women.[7]

By raising the call to the dead and welcoming new arrivals onto the *marae* (the ceremonial courtyard), older women mark the commencement of ritual events. But the competence of middle-aged women is best seen in the manipulations that go on in preparation for a major ceremony. Here years of mutual cooperation have achieved a finely honed machinery that goes smoothly into action, almost without thought, when the occasion warrants. Women depend on their peers and on their daughters and nieces for performances that will ensure the essential order of Maori ritual. Stores are brought in, cakes and breads are baked, meals are prepared, tables are set, dishes are washed, beds are prepared, meeting houses arranged, and children cared for. In addition women also "make flax mats, embroider pillow cases, purchase mattresses, order linen, crockery, and cooking utensils" (Salmond 1975:170). By sounding out the early cry for the dead, by weeping with those closest to the deceased, women engineer many of the details that demand attention at times of community crisis. The prominence of middle-aged women in *marae* ritual, as well as their backstage domination of the details that facilitate such events, translate into effective control over both domains. Without them visitors would be neither welcomed nor fed and much of the distinctiveness of Maori ceremonial would be lost.

Moreover, middle-aged and elderly women serve as *pani,* the formal mourners who, for the intervening days between death and burial, are removed from ordinary social life with its mundane concerns and remain with the deceased. The traditional structure asserts itself here, since women are involved with the details of death. But only those who are past childbearing age carry this burden. Significantly, the mourning ritual (*tangi*) is a major marker of Maori ethnicity; the domination of women at this time bestows on them a critical role in passing down tradition. The colonial situation has transformed a necessary, if inevitable, encounter with the defilement of death into a socially sanctioned positive assertion of ethnic identity. Its main practitioners, believed in the past to be already contaminated, have emerged as significant social actors.

In addition, many middle-aged women are involved in the political lives of their communities. By serving on the numerous tribal committees that direct the various currents of social life, women make a direct contribution to decisions regarding the structure of Maori affairs. Fund-raising, the organization of major cultural events, and the maintenance of the *marae* are often accomplished under the competent gaze of older women. Their political influence is buttressed by the kind of support they derive from their network. Women will often reach a decision among themselves. There are few areas in Maori life where consensus on the part of older women can afford to be ignored. Furthermore, organizations such as the Maori Women's Welfare League provide women a path to local and even national recognition.

In church affairs, women, and not men, serve on district and parish committees. Maintaining ties with the church reflects more than the domestication of religion, for in such tribunals, which are often overwhelmingly European, the tricky area of interethnic relations is an explicit item for discussion. The church has also come to depend on women to do most of its community public relations work.

At middle age, a woman's nurturant role is far from over. The relative poverty of most Maoris makes the autonomous, self-supporting nuclear family an elusive ideal. Grandmothers baby-sit or take over the long-term care of their grandchildren, and for most, domestic life is incomplete without at least one young child at home. Women also persist in mediating and adjudicating the difficulties of culture change faced by their adult children. Their continued closeness to their offspring and their awareness of the difficulties they face have provided middle-aged women both with allies and with a precise knowledge of the contemporary social situation. By contrast, few men concern themselves with the problems of drug possession, urban gangs, or domestic disputes that routinely confront their children.

In groups or individually, these women also instruct the community in traditional arts and crafts. They teach weaving and basketry, mat making and flax dying, Maori songs and language to schoolchildren, church groups, their own youth, and curious Europeans. For Pakehas, they often provide examples of a noble heritage distilled for contemporary New Zealand consumption. But for Maoris, these women represent a capacity to use traditions to define, but not to limit, a behavioral and symbolic repertoire that is exclusively Maori. Their continued intimacy with their grown children and their awareness of the complexities of the contemporary situation draw the younger generation to them.

Traditional gender ideology, therefore, no longer constrains middle-aged women, but it frames the nature of their experience. Women who are today middle-aged have learned to operate in an essentially female universe and have grown adept at executing the responsibilities defined as suitable for such individuals. As women age, the restrictions of gender diminish. Female solidarity, the result of a lifetime of sexual segregation, has been transformed into control over younger women and into political influence within the community.

The contingencies of the colonial situation have enhanced the authority and influence that Maori women were traditionally permitted to claim. Institutions outside the community—e.g., the church and the schools—generally gain access to Maoris through women. By their continued involvement in these institutions and by their enduring commitment to their children and grandchildren, women have come to understand a social world dominated by Europeans. They are not always pleased by what they see, but they are prepared to adapt to it, for flexibility has been necessary throughout their lives. They are therefore willing both to uphold tradition and to ease its passing. Thus the colonial situation, which has so often diminished the stature of Maori men, has enhanced the prestige of Maori women.

Maramatanga

Becoming a cultural minority in the land of their ancestors has been a difficult adjustment for Maoris. In the past two hundred years, many prophets have come forward. Some have offered deliverance from the tyranny of the Pakeha, others have presented their followers with the means to accomodate the intruding presence. All have attempted to create a meaningful social order, one in which to be a Maori is to be a valued social participant. The middle-aged women discussed in this chapter belong to one such movement. Through the ideology of the movement and by adherence to its ritual, these women are more prepared than most to assume an active voice in the determination of Maori affairs.

The movement is nominally Catholic. But its ideology depends on traditional religion and on the Maori prophetic heritage as much as it relies on the dogma of the orthodox Catholic Church. The members of *Maramatanga* (the name suggests knowledge and enlightenment) see themselves as the logical culmination of the Maori prophetic tradition. They refer to themselves as the *kaimahi* (the workers), the *hungaruarua* (the chosen few), and to their beliefs as the *tikanga* (the correct way). The three hundred people who constitute the movement, although geographically dispersed, are all related to one another and are all descendants of the original prophet. While he was an individual clearly endowed with spiritual gifts, it is his legacy that sets his followers apart. For he is seen as the "last of the prophets." In subsequent years no leader has been necessary, for members hold that they now all have access to the spiritual world. Deceased friends and relatives (known as *wairua*, the spirits of the dead) commune with their descendants, warning of coming adversity, counseling in times of trouble, and supplying the living with a continuous source of songs, which win them acclaim in major cultural competitions.

The history of the movement, going back fifty years, is dominated by women. Although men participate, it is women who today tend to receive messages, who return as *wairua*, and who maintain a close monitoring of human/spiritual relations. This is not surprising, for women's participation in *Maramatanga* gives them a voice equal to that of men. Women can and do engage in public speechmaking and have moved into many domains previously reserved only for men. Middle-aged and elderly women, who are free from domestic pressures, participate more vigorously than any other segment of *Maramatanga's* membership.

The rituals of the movement depend largely on a knowledge and understanding of traditional art forms; oratory, singing, and chanting must be performed with skill and facility. The extent to which women participate competently indicates their capacity to master and to retain traditional cultural forms. Such activities clearly preserve the past, but far more important, they sustain the value of the present. By defining the work of the ancestors as worthwhile, as worthy of preservation, they have legitimated their position as Maoris in contemporary New Zealand. Moreover, the triumphs that accompany participation (the successful pilgrimages, the admired songs, the victories in cultural competitions) all enhance women's status and prestige in the eyes of the membership.

On several occasions throughout the year, kinship ties and individual commitments are activated in a series of celebrations, known as *ras,* which commemorate important events in the spiritual history of the movement. At such times, the members who are able gather to discuss spiritual matters and to avail themselves of Maori hospitality. Commensality and solidarity are often explicit themes; traditional inequalities based on rank, genealogy, and gender are deemed insignificant.

At the *ras,* the participation of middle-aged women is especially marked. As the most mobile group, their attendance is far more regular. More significantly, their organizational skills facilitate the feeding and housing of several hundred people over several days. Middle-aged women, therefore, sustain and are sustained by their participation in *Maramatanga.*

Many women attribute the ease with which they are able to assume their increased ritual obligations to spiritual assistance. But the *wairua* have done more than assist them in the execution of their anticipated duties. Under their auspices, several women have become healers. Others have less spectacular gifts. Nevertheless, it is assumed that each has something to contribute and should therefore be accorded the respect due to an important, productive member of the community.

To a much greater degree than men, women use what they have learned from *Maramatanga* to take an active role in the affairs of the wider society. Several women participate at all levels of church organization. Far from being alienated from Catholicism, members have assumed an elite role in the administration of the Maori Mission. Such positions have led them to take trips abroad (to Samoa, to the Philippines) and to travel extensively in New Zealand. The assurance that they can depend on the guidance and counsel of their *wairua* helpers, grants many the confidence to journey freely. Men, who are usually employed and therefore unable to leave their jobs, are not as likely to participate as fully or to derive the benefits that full participation conveys.

Membership in *Maramatanga* allows women to confront and overcome their marginality. As Maoris and as women, they are at a serious social disadvantage. However, these liabilities become somewhat less significant in the face of women's demonstrated spiritual ascendancy. Religious activity thus encourages women to redefine their roles; they have ceased to be passive complements of men. Both because of the easing of restrictions as they age and through the avenues opened to them by *Maramatanga,* women at middle age can embark on a new social identity.

Conclusion

The confluence of social change and aging has frequently proved devastating for women. But Maori women living in rural areas have found that the individual life process and the larger social process have together increased their prestige.

In both its traditional and contemporary forms, Maori society has used age and gender as principles of social differentiation. For women, the liabilities inherent in one are overcome by the other as they approach middle age. At this point in their lives, they are free in a number of ways and from a number of constraints; pollution rules, child care, and male monopolies no longer inhibit them. However, their independence is relative. Women are still perceived as defiled and defiling, grandmothers continue to oversee the young, and certain areas remain proscribed regardless of a woman's age. Nevertheless, when compared to the confined and circumscribed lives of younger women, their gains are considerable.

The women discussed in this chapter have the additional advantage of religious experiences that reinforce their authority and provide channels for their accomplishments. The equality accorded to them as members of the movement, along with the preparation they receive in ceremonial forms, facilitates their assumption of a more active role in the wider community. In this manner, women have assisted the process of accommodation between two different cultural traditions.

Despite the dramatic social change that these women have witnessed, there has been considerable continuity in their lives. Women rather than men have been prepared to assume an expanded social role. This is in keeping with the fact that these women have spent an entire lifetime in accomodation and cooperation. Early in the life cycle, women learned to depend on one another and to exercise cooperative control over their domain. In middle age these youthful allegiances are transformed into political alliances, while the informal influence of earlier years becomes recognized formal authority.

Certainly women seldom command the respect that is given to men as a matter of course. Their virtues pale in the face of more manifest masculine accomplishment. Yet as they age, women gain status and influence in the Maori community for precisely the same reasons that they gain respect and attention from Europeans. Their authority in one sphere informs their performance in the other. Within these complex contexts, middle-aged women are important social actors. For men the reverse is true. High prestige in the Maori community does not assure their appreciation by Europeans. On the contrary, the colonial situation would seem to make failure inevitable for Maori men since succeeding in one sphere preordains failing in the other. Thus the effect of colonialism in New Zealand has been the reverse of what we have come to expect. The importance of Maori men is no longer assured, whereas the contribution of Maori women appears to be guaranteed.

Epilogue to the Second Edition

Fieldwork for this chapter was carried out for twenty-two months between 1971 and 1973 and for four months in 1982. During 1982 my focus was specifically on the life cycle of Maori women. In 1987 I was again in New Zealand, from January until May.[8] At that time it became clear that New Zealand society has been undergoing changes that can, with little exaggeration, be described as revolutionary. Maoris have adopted a far more activist stance as they seek to renegotiate their resources and their participation in the New Zealand political order. In the area in which I did my fieldwork, it is women who are leading the activities that herald a Maori renaissance. It is middle-aged women, who speak Maori and are adept at various traditional crafts, who are educating a new generation.

The Maori renaissance has become apparent at all levels of New Zealand society. The attention that the *Te Maori* exhibit achieved while in the United States and its triumphal return home, the development of Maori literature, and the resurgence of Maori language have instilled greater pride in being Maori. Moreover, this is now being translated into sources of national concern as the Waitangi Tribunal (discussed below) is in the process of adjudicating land and resource allocation. Two generations of Maori have now grown up in the cities. The degree of cultural fragmentation that has resulted, the resulting disarray and despair, cannot be glossed over. While the contrast with the women of *Maramatanga* is perhaps that much more stark, it is especially critical to emphasize the distinctiveness of rural areas. Nevertheless, the social stability of the area in which *Maramatanga* has flourished has been compromised by the descent in New Zealand's economic fortunes. Employment schemes have offered some solutions but they are far from panaceas.

In 1987 I also realized that in my earlier work I had underestimated the pervasiveness of traditional gender ideology. Men who are admired often stand silent; they neither assert themselves nor seek attention, but this does not mean that they are not important. I noticed that women deferred to men, even when both they and I knew that the abilities of individual men were problematic. Perhaps because the traditional gender ideology has become emblematic of Maori culture, women in this time of a Maori renaissance continue to uphold it.

Recent Changes in New Zealand Society

From the start of my earliest research, I was impressed with concerns with *Maoritanga,* a term that can loosely be translated as "Maoriness" or "pride in Maori culture." Indeed, in 1973 proponents of the movement suggested that the relationship between the religious ideology and spiritual orientation of *Maramatanga* was consistent with *Maoritanga.* Many of the rituals, especially pilgrimages, addressed issues of cultural integrity and survival. Similarly, at universities around New Zealand young men and women were agitating for respect and autonomy.[9] By 1982 land had become a critical focal point in defining a Maori identity and distinguishing Maori and Pakeha views of New Zealand's natural heritage. This did not become an explicit theme in this chapter because the rural area in which I worked had no problem with land; on the contrary they not only managed and controlled a great deal of land but their subtribe, through an incorporation, has succeeded in buying back leases from Pakeha farmers. In this, as in other ways, they are surely an exceptional group. Nevertheless, land remains a critical focus of interest even if not an issue of immediate concern. In 1975, a march from the far north of the North Island to Parliament in Wellington, in the far south, led (significantly) by a woman, Whina Cooper (see King 1983), placed Maori sensibilities about land at the forefront of New Zealand consciousness. As the eighties began, attention was turned to land that had been confiscated for wartime purposes. It was not used for this, a golf course had been built, and the land appeared to be permanently alienated. After a protracted struggle, the land was returned, but the people were asked to pay for "improvements" they had not requested. This kind of treatment and duplicity was the subject of Grace's book *Potiki,* published in 1986 (Beatson 1989:28). Similarly, Bastion Point, the site of expensive, largely Pakeha housing, was reclaimed by the local tribe. To make their point, they staged a sit-in. "After a long occupation they were removed by police with logistic assistance from the army" (Beatson 1989:29).

While the issue in all of the above was certainly land, a Maori version of events was being insinuated into the New Zealand consciousness. In short, these early signs of activism were clarion calls to what Donna Awatere was to call "Maori sovereignty." Her book, published in 1984, urged Maoris to understand that they were living in a monocultural society, that being white conferred privileges, while being brown assured second-class citizenship. The loss of land, the domination of New Zealand by the Pakeha stood for the loss of Maori culture at the hands of people who believed themselves, erroneously, to be morally superior. One of the more interesting aspects of this new activity (although it reflected feelings and thoughts that were certainly not new) was the prominence of women: Whina Cooper, Donna Awatere, Eva Rickard, Patricia Grace. These were older women who gained prestige over the life course and younger women who dedicated themselves to a new brand of political activism. These young women activists would come in time to question the sexism implicit in traditional gender ideology. While this does create a break between generations of Maori women, who under most conditions are natural allies, there can be little doubt that this new discourse was introduced and promulgated by women (see Dominy 1990 for an especially compelling analysis).[10]

While all of this was happening at home, the *Te Maori* exhibit toured the United States. A collection of art from New Zealand museums, the exhibition opened in New York at the Metropolitan Museum of Art, at the St. Louis Museum, the San Francisco Art Institute, and the Chicago Field Museum. At each venue, elders from different areas came to the United States to welcome the art and to greet the visitors. In all areas the art and the people were an unquestionable success. The exhibit was accompanied by a book of essays that while explaining the art in very anthropological terms, addressed directly the question of cultural hegemony. Hirini Moko Mead, an anthropologist who was the most instrumental individual behind the exhibit, suggested a new way of understanding the development of Maori art. In this manner, he attempted to retake control of Maori cultural categories, to wrest cultural description from the Pakeha and restore it to the Maori. The success of the exhibit vindicated Maori pride in their artistic heritage and validated their assumptions that Pakeha ignorance and prejudice had precluded an appreciation of Maori sensibilities. In 1987, when the exhibition went on a tour of New Zealand, it was regarded as a substantial cultural triumph. But the beginnings of what has been called a "Pakeha backlash" were to be seen, most notably in an article tellingly entitled "Te Pakeha" appearing in the April issue of *Metro* (see Wall 1987), a glossy urban monthly for Auckland.

Land Rights and the Waitangi Tribunal

Nowhere is Maori activism more pronounced than in the area of land rights. While the Maori renaissance of the 1980s has stressed a revival of Maori arts and language, with preschool "language nests" proliferating around the country, there has been a vigorous reexamination of traditional Maori land claims. Land has become a critical link between the past and the future (Greenland 1984:86; Kawharu 1989). The history of European settlement is now understood as Pakeha land grabbing. Indeed the economic concerns that motivated New Zealand's development have been called into question by Maori radicals, who have asserted that this process deprived the Maori of both their land and their culture. In the continuing debate Maori spiritual links to the land are contrasted to the Pakeha's purely economic interest (Greenland 1984). More to the point, the contemporary problems of the Maori are laid at the feet of a society based on materialism and nonhumanistic values.

One of the results of this latest round of Maori activism is to emphasize the dissonance between the myth and reality of New Zealand's ethnic situation (Levine 1987:423). These themes, along with questions of land and resource ownership and management, are being enacted in the Waitangi Tribunal. Under the Treaty of Waitangi Act, 1975, and its amendment in 1985, the tribunal, which has been hearing claims involving rights to fishing grounds, control over resources, and land ownership, has restructured Maori-Pakeha relations. Anthropologists and historians (Levine 1987; Sorrenson 1987) have suggested that the treaty is being reinterpreted and Maori perspectives are, for the first time, being given a fair hearing. Inevitably, both Maori and Pakeha perceptions of the past must change as the tribunal introduces a Maori view of history into New Zealand discourse. Far more important, the range of resources available to Maoris is likely to shift and with it a balance of power. The other side of this, of course, is a backlash of Pakeha resentment (see, for example, Booth 1988).

Maori Women in the New New Zealand

As I have noted, in the area in which I worked, women are leaders of activities that are central to the Maori renaissance. Middle-aged women, who speak Maori and who are skilled in traditional crafts, are passing on their knowledge to the young. The *kohanga reo* ("language nest," where Maori is taught) is an outstanding success in this community, and the woman in charge is recognized nationally for her work.

Two or three women have dominated the organization and implementation of work in the community. They have come into middle age with confidence and with ability, eager and prepared to educate others. The general mood in New Zealand has changed, and teenagers and young adults are now particularly receptive to learning about their Maori heritage. A weekly language course for adults, led by these women, was well attended. The culture group that they lead continues to sing songs from *Maramatanga,* and persists in dominating the *Hui Aranga,* the Easter feast of the Ascension organized by the Maori diocese of the Catholic Church. These women go to committee meetings all over the country, and frequently travel beyond New Zealand's boundaries.

In this community the persistence of traditional values, especially in regard to kinship, is evident. Here, where notions of hierarchy prevail, people gain respect as they age. Kinship continues to be important. Thus elders, leaders of kin groups, are still able to exert a reasonable amount of influence. But in 1987 I realized that this was true only so long as young people did not move to the city and lose contact with their families. When children go to the city, or when they move out of the community, many of the available community sanctions disappear.

While unemployment has risen throughout New Zealand, it is especially high among Maoris (see New Zealand Planning Council Monitoring Group 1986) To alleviate this, especially for young people, the government has started several work schemes. The goal of these work schemes is to provide the training necessary to become employed. In keeping with the times, many of these schemes or modules incorporate Maori elements such as music and carving. In 1987, the situation was paradoxical. Young men and women worked on schemes that were clearly enjoyable and worthwhile but offered no prospect for permanent careers. They were being trained in areas where there could be no expectation of long-term employment: guitar playing, *marae* landscaping, *hui* (feast) catering, traditional Maori carving. Several people in charge of such activities suggested that training in auto mechanics would be far more useful. However, the prohibitive cost of establishing such facilities led to far less satisfactory alternatives. (An exception to this pattern was the administration module in which young women were taught office skills.) The advantages of such modules are that essentially unemployed youth are taken off the streets and paid the minimum wage. In a rural area, they remain under the watchful eyes of their elders, feeling proud of their *Maoritanga* and embedded in the complex web of relationships that mark these communities. Young married couples can maintain some independence when both are working on these schemes.[11] However, once there are children, their finances become much more problematic. In rural communities they can depend on patterns of sharing to sustain them. Urban dwellers are not nearly so lucky. But, as indicated above, these schemes cannot offer permanent resolutions to Maori unemployment. Indeed, they often leave their participants without work and even more skeptical of the system than before. Ironically, the comfort of kin and peers often keeps young people in rural areas with high unemployment so that even those with significant skills are reluctant to try their luck in urban areas. Inevitably, unemployment and poverty are perpetuated. Yet when the young do leave, they venture beyond the scope of their elders and away from the protective embrace of the community. Not uncommonly, these young people are worse off when they undertake such a move (see James 1988).

The stability of rural communities contrasted to urban areas is especially notable when it comes to domestic violence. In rural communities, the stresses of parenthood are relieved by reliance on kinship relations. Women who simply cannot cope can rely on extended family members to step in. There is no such relief available in the city. This introduces a new set of difficulties for urban dwellers: "The lack of multiple parenting puts a heavier strain on nuclear parent caretakers who have little cultural preparation for stress of this kind" (Ritchie and Ritchie 1981:196).[12] Moreover, the Maori tendency toward early independence is often in conflict with Pakeha neighbors who believe that children should remain at home and not be out and about exploring.

These unprecedented and unrelieved strains must be set against assertions for the well-being of women as they reach middle age. They are much more likely to be at ease if their children are not facing such conflicts. Should their children be away from them in urban areas, their influence wanes; drugs, alcohol, and domestic violence mark Maori urban life and are largely beyond the purview or control of these middle-aged women. For the most part, the women of *Maramatanga* are comfortable with their children's progress through adulthood. But they are especially fortunate, and their exceptional circumstances were not adequately highlighted in my chapter.

Moreover, the stresses caused from domestic abuse and inadequate resources are clearly demonstrated in an analysis of Maori health statistics. Armstrong and Armstrong (1988:8) write: "The latest life expectancy estimates (1980-82) show life expectancies at birth to be 69.8 years for Maori females and 76.8 for non-Maori females, a 7-year difference that continues for life expectancies at age 20 and 40 years reducing to a difference of 4 years at age 60. This consistent difference throughout most of the lifespan is due primarily to higher rates of mortality at almost all age groups in the Maori population."[13]

Poverty and stress aggravate illness in the female population. Here lung cancer and ischemic heart disease are the major causes of death. These are joined by respiratory diseases (chiefly bronchitis, emphysema, asthma, and other chronic obstructive pulmonary diseases), stroke, cancers of the lung and breast, and diabetes mellitus (Armstrong and Armstrong 1988:10).

The success of the women in this study must be understood against the general difficulties faced by Maori women. Clearly, membership in *Maramatanga,* their continuing ties with their children, the stability of their community, and their role as innovators has contributed to their success. Indeed, they were implementing national trends in a local arena. In 1987, I found these women were even more successful, more productive than they had been in 1982. But even as I marveled at their expanded social universe, I understood that their success was extraordinary.

There can be no doubt that the Maori women who belong to *Maramatanga* can redefine and reconstruct a definition of appropriate behavior. In this regard, *Maramatanga* held out considerable attraction. For women who had always been involved in death work, the movement offered a unique opportunity to maintain faith with the past and to rebel against death (see Braude 1989). For women, a renegotiation of gender roles became possible. For both men and women access to divine authority was a critical counter to Pakeha assertions of secular domination. In this context, women, speaking with spiritual assistance, could circumvent the authority of men. When this is added to their demonstrable social preeminence, the influence of women is formidable. But I think it would be a mistake to overstate the degree to which women are comfortable making their abilities explicit. Rather, most women choose to represent their enlarged participation as a continuation rather than a reevaluation of their traditional roles. Yet, while they are willing to consider what would surely be called radical alternatives, they are very reluctant to undercut men publicly, and they remain firmly committed to the ideology that continues to grant men power.

Although the most important changes since this chapter was originally written have occurred in the larger society, all Maoris are now far more active, more assertive, and much more willing to question Pakeha authority. In quiet ways (the *kohanga reo,* for example) and in not so quiet ways (the land march led by Whina Cooper), middle-aged women have taken the lead. The Maori renaissance is a cultural and social reality. The most remarkable and salutary effect of this new Maori activism is that a distinctly female voice can now be heard. The women of *Maramatanga,* who have held onto their past, are now prepared to speak for the Maori future.

NOTES

1. The research presented in this chapter was gathered over a two-year period, 1971–73, during the summer of 1982, and in 1987.

2. In a preliminary report of the 1981 census, 10 percent of Pakeha men were classed as professional/administrative while a bit over 2 percent of Maori males fell into that category. Similarly, less than a third of European males were laborers while almost half of the Maori men were so labeled.

In 1969 (the only statistics available as I wrote this chapter) Maori infant mortality was 29.8 per 1,000 compared to 18 per 1,000 for Pakehas. Similarly, while a European man can expect to live 69.2 years, the life expectancy for Maori males is 59. In education, 47.3 percent of the Europeans had a school certificate or more while only 13.1 percent of the Maoris had reached this level of educational attainment (cited by Walsh 1973).

3. In the rural area in which I have worked, there is more continuity and stability. Women are therefore able to take their place in the community with greater confidence. Since middle age represents the culmination of many themes initiated earlier in the life cycle, the relative stability of the rural setting assures their position.

It is important to point out that while middle-aged rural women do make a comparatively successful adjustment, Maori women are clearly subject to great stress. Their death rate from lung cancer is the highest in the world, while hypertension is a very common affliction (Blank 1980).

4. Older women comment freely on the content and imagery employed by speakers. Salmond writes: "It is notable that whenever a man over-steps the bounds of *marae* protocol, it is nearly always the women who carry out corrective action. . . . If a speaker becomes insulting or cuts across major rules of *marae* procedure, the older women apply the ultimate sanction of the *whaka-pohane*. They stand, turn their backs on him, then bend over and raise their skirts in pointed derisory comment" (1975:127).

5. Evidence for a more widespread occurrence of this phenomenon may be found in Whiting and Edwards (1973).

6. A similar point is made by Stack (1974) for black women in the United States.

7. It is commonly reported that the status of women is likely to improve when there are important roles available (Bart 1969; Griffen 1977; Datan, Antonovsky, and Maoz 1981).

8. Research in 1987 was funded by an NEH Travel to Collections Grant, a Josephine Nevins Keal award from Eastern Michigan University, and an Eastern Michigan University Faculty Research Fellowship. From 1988 to 1990, I have received released time to write through the support of Eastern Michigan University, which has awarded me both a Faculty Research Fellowship (1988) and a sabbatical leave (1989–90) and an NEH Fellowship for College Teachers.

9. Those of us working with Maoris were certainly aware of *Maoritanga,* however defined, as a major cultural focus. Joan Metge, for example, wrote in 1976: "When asked to identify Maori ways in detail, Maoris usually focus on a few of

central importance, notably language, land, tribe, *marae,* and *tangihanga,* providing a sample rather than comprehensive coverage. For them, Maori ways are so closely interwoven that mention of these few calls up a host of associated ideas....I have come to the conclusion that without working it out consciously Maoris use these key 'ways' as symbols for Maoritanga as a whole. This is a perfectly legitimate way of proceeding, known in literary terms as synecdoche—using the part to stand for the whole. The problem is that Pakehas too often take the symbols at face value as constituting the whole and fail to appreciate their full ramifications" (48).

10. There are of course men who are prominent Maori activists. The presence of women is notable, however, given traditional gender ideology. This indicates that there are wide arenas within the New Zealand landscape that are now open to renegotiation.

11. It is not that independence is such an important value in these communities. However, the parents of these young people are themselves hard pressed and are often unable to contribute much to their sustenance. Somehow when pressed, they always manage to, but it puts an enormous strain on already scarce resources.

12. The Ritchies (1981:196) note that patterns of alleviating stress in the West are not yet available to women. Their conclusion is that while Western women under duress might abuse substances or manipulate, Maori women are more likely to act out.

13. They go on to note that while late fetal and neonatal death rates have shown an encouraging drop, death in the immediate postnatal period (twenty-eight days) and in the first year were significantly higher than for non-Maoris. "Contributing to the high rates in the Maori population are a higher proportion of younger mothers, high rates of smoking during pregnancy, low birthweights, and higher rates for congenital anomalies and for sudden infant death syndrome" (Armstrong and Armstrong 1988:9).

REFERENCES

Arbuckle, Gerald
    1976 The Church in a Multi-cultural Society. Greenmeadows Seminary, Hastings, New Zealand. Unpublished manuscript.
Archer, D., and M. Archer
    1970 Race, Identity and the Maori People. Journal of the Polynesian Society 79:201–18.
Armstrong, M. Jocelyn, and Warwick Armstrong
    1988 New Zealand Maori Women's Health: Status and Self-help Action in the 1980s. Paper presented at the Annual Meeting of the Association for Social Anthropology in Oceania. Savannah, Georgia.
Awatere, Donna
    1984 Maori Sovereignty. Auckland: Broadsheet Publications.

Bart, Pauline
    1969 Why Women's Status Changes in Middle Age: The Turn of the Social
        Ferris Wheel. Sociological Symposium 3:1–18.
Beatson, Peter
    1989 The Healing Tongue. Studies in New Zealand Art and Society. Palmerston
        North: Sociology Department, Massey University.
Bell, Diane
    1981 Women's Business Is Hard Work: Central Australian Aboriginal Women's
        Love Rituals. Signs 7:314–37.
Best, Elsdon
    1905 The Lore of the Whare Kohanga. Journal of the Polynesian Society
        14:205–15.
Binney, Judith
    1986 Nga Morehu. Auckland: Oxford University Press.
Blank, Arapera
    1980 The Role and Status of Maori Women. *In* Women in New Zealand
        Society. P. Bunkle and B. Hughes, eds. pp. 34–51. Sydney: George Allen
        and Unwin.
Booth, Pat
    1988 Learning to Live with the Waitangi Tribunal. North and South (June):
        78–87.
Boserup, Ester
    1970 Woman's Role in Economic Development. New York: St. Martin's
        Press.
Braude, Ann
    1989 Radical Spirits. Boston: Beacon Press.
Brown, Judith
    1982a A Cross-cultural Exploration of the End of the Childbearing Years.
        In Changing Perspectives on Menopause. A. Voda, M. Dinnerstein, and
        S. O'Donnell, eds. pp. 51–59. Austin: University of Texas Press.
    1982b Cross-cultural Perspectives on Middle-Aged Women. Current Anthro-
        pology 23(2):143–56.
Datan, Nancy, Aaron Antonovsky, and Benjamin Maoz
    1981 A Time to Reap: The Middle Age of Women in Five Israeli Subcultures.
        Baltimore: Johns Hopkins University Press.
Dominy, Michele
    1983 Gender Conceptions and Political Strategies in New Zealand Women's
        Networks. Ph.D. diss., Cornell University.
    1990 Maori Sovereignty: A Feminist Invention of Tradition. *In* Cultural
        Identity and Ethnicity in the Pacific. J. Linnekin and L. Poyer, eds. pp.
        237–59. Honolulu: University of Hawaii Press.
Dougherty, Molly
    1978 An Anthropological Perspective on Aging and Women in the Middle
        Years. *In* The Anthropology of Health. E. E. Bauwens, ed. pp. 167–76. St.
        Louis: C. V. Mosby.

Douglas, Mary
    1978   Implicit Meanings. London: Routledge and Kegan Paul.
Earle, Margaret
    1958   Rakau Children from Six to Thirteen Years. Victoria University of
    Wellington Publications in Psychology, no. 11. Wellington.
Flint, Marcha
    1975   The Menopause: Reward or Punishment? Psychosomatics 16:161–63.
Forster, J., and P. Ramsay
    1971   Migration, Education and Occupation. *In* Social Process in New Zealand.
    J. Forster, ed. pp. 198–232. Auckland: Longman Paul.
Grace, Patricia
    1986   Potiki. Auckland: Penquin.
Greenland, Hauraki.
    1984   Ethnicity as Ideology. *In* Tauiwi. P. Spoonley et. al, eds. pp. 86–102.
    Palmerston North: Dunmore Press.
Griffen, Joyce
    1977   A Cross-cultural Investigation of Behavioral Changes at Menopause.
    Social Science Journal 14:49–55.
    1982   Cultural Models for Coping with Menopause. *In* Changing Perspec-
    tives on Menopause. A Voda, M. Dinnerstein, and S. O'Donnell, eds. pp.
    248–62. Austin: University of Texas Press.
Heuer, Berys
    1969   Maori Women in Traditional Family and Tribal Life. Journal of the
    Polynesian Society 78:448–94.
James, Colin
    1988   New Zealand Maori Challenge. Far Eastern Economic Review 141(37):
    36–42.
Kawharu, I. H., ed.
    1989   Waitangi: Maori and Pakeha Perspectives on the Treaty of Waitangi.
    Auckland: Oxford University Press.
Kehoe, Alice
    1973   The Metonymic Pole and Social Roles. Journal of Anthropological
    Research 27:266–74.
Keith, Jennie
    1980   "The Best Is Yet to Be": Toward an Anthropology of Age. *In* Annual
    Review of Anthropology 9. B. J. Siegel, A. R. Beals, and S. Tyler, eds. pp.
    339–64. Palo Alto, Calif.: Annual Reviews.
Kerns, Virginia
    1980   Menopause and the Post-reproductive Years. National Women's Anthro-
    pology Newsletter 4(2):15–16; 4(3):26–27
King, Michael
    1983   Whina. Auckland: Hodder and Stoughton.
Levine, H. B.
    1987   The Cultural Politics of Maori Fishing: An Anthropological Perspective
    on the First Three Significant Waitangi Tribunal Hearings. Journal of the
    Polynesian Society 89:421–43.

Mead, Hirini Moko, ed.
  1984   Te Maori. New York: Abrams.
Metge, A. Joan
  1976   The Maoris of New Zealand. London: Routledge and Kegan Paul.
New Zealand Planning Council Monitoring Group
  1986   The New Zealand Population: Change, Composition and Policy Implications. Report no. 4. Wellington: New Zealand Planning Council.
Orange, Claudia
  1987   The Treaty of Waitangi. Wellington: Allen and Unwin.
Ritchie, James
  1972   New Families, New Communities. *In* Racial Issues in New Zealand. G. Vaughan, ed. pp. 89–96. Auckland: Akarana Press.
Ritchie, James, and Jane Ritchie
  1981   Child Rearing and Child Abuse: The Polynesian Context. *In* Child Abuse and Neglect. J. Korbin, ed. pp. 186–204. Berkeley: University of California Press.
Ritchie, Jane
  1957   Childhood in Rakau. Victoria University of Wellington Publications in Psychology, no. 10. Wellington.
St. George, Ross
  1972   Racial Intolerance in New Zealand: Problems and Insights. *In* Racial Issues in New Zealand. G. Vaughan, ed. pp. 9–18. Auckland: Akarana Press.
Salmond, Anne
  1975   Hui: A Study of Maori Ceremonial Gatherings. Wellington: A. H. and A. W. Reed.
Sorrenson, M. P. K.
  1987   Toward a Radical Reinterpretation of New Zealand History: The Role of the Waitangi Tribunal. New Zealand Journal of History 21:173–88.
Stack, Carol
  1974   All Our Kin: Strategies for Survival in a Black Community. New York: Harper and Row.
Wall, Carroll
  1987   Te Pakeha. Metro 70:36–48.
Walsh, A. C.
  1973   More and More Maoris. Christchurch: Whitcombe and Tombs.
Whiting, Beatrice, and Carolyn Edwards
  1973   A Cross-cultural Analysis of Sex Differences in the Behavior of Children Aged Three through 11. Journal of Social Psychology 91:171–88.

PART 3

Complex Societies

In many complex, agrarian societies, such as India and traditional China, a woman is socially defined throughout life in terms of her relationships to men: initially, her father and brothers; after marriage, her husband and sons. A new bride has an unenviable position as she takes up residence in the household of her husband's kin. The chapters by Sylvia Vatuk and Douglas Raybeck illustrate the many disabilities young women face and show that only the birth of sons and increasing maturity lead to an improvement in their lives. The position of Malay women in Kelantan differs significantly, and Raybeck attributes this to their control of important economic resources.

Among Arabic-speaking Muslims in Northern Sudan, Janice Boddy shows how fertility, and especially giving birth to sons, governs a woman's social position in early adulthood and middle age. Ultimately, her goal is to become (with her husband) the cofounder of a lineage section, yet she must pass many hurdles to attain this position. Older Chinese women, as Raybeck notes, may also achieve great (but presumably informal) influence over lineage and community affairs.

In these societies, middle-aged women have certain opportunities and advantages, but they face a variety of potential problems and disadvantages. An Indian woman, as mother-in-law, has considerable power; yet her son's marriage may also mark the end of a sexual relationship with her husband. An older woman in Northern Sudan can become a powerful and respected grandmother of a patriline, or, depending on the outcome of her marriage, she may find herself without the support of a husband, sons, or other male kin. As Raybeck suggests, an opportunity to achieve greater power and prestige carries a certain cost: the possibility of failure.

10 Bucking the Agnatic System: Status and Strategies in Rural Northern Sudan

Janice Boddy

The reaches of the Upper Nile north of Khartoum, Sudan, are bounded by a chain of settlements, mud-brick hamlets strung end to end, interspersed with larger villages at railway depots and now and then an administrative town. These settlements cling tenaciously to the river, forming a barrier between fertile, cultivable Nile silts and desert sand. Their inhabitants are Arabic-speaking Muslims whose traditional occupation, farming, has been eclipsed for some decades by labor emigration owing both to a shortage of arable land[1] and to the perennial urban promise of comfort, adventure, and better wages.

Hofriyat (a fictitious name) is one such village whose population is depleted of men between the ages of fifteen and fifty for much of the year. Roughly half of its eighty-nine households are comprised of adult women and young children supported by remittances from husbands and male kin, whose presence is felt only during vacations, religious holidays, funerals, and weddings. Some men move away permanently, find wives in distant locales, and neglect their kinship responsibilities in Hofriyat; but these are few. Despite the lures of the city, the majority remain firmly attached to the village area where they were born and feel keenly the obligation to select a wife from within its confines. Marriage among Hofriyati ideally takes place between close kin, between a man and a woman whose families are previously bound by a thick net of moral obligation. Should a man wed a nonrelative from outside the village area, he is scorned by his neighbors as one whose wife is a ewe or she-goat from the market, so uncertain is her pedigree, so greatly has he relied on the word of unrelated individuals to vouch for her character. Just as the market ewe might seem to be a good deal at the time of its purchase only to prove otherwise once its owner gets it home, so the wife formerly unknown to villagers might appear sweet, honest, and hard working at the time of her wedding, but prove difficult, demanding, and, worst of all, untrustworthy shortly thereafter. Similarly, a village woman who marries a nonrelative or outsider takes a greater chance than does one who marries close. Harmony and cooperation in social relations are highly valued qualities and most threatened by marriages between villagers and nonkin.[2]

But a hidden dimension in all of this is the issue of fertility. In Hofriyat human fertility is appropriately exercised only between close kin, for morality inheres in kinship, and social life, consisting as it does of patterned, controlled behavior, depends upon the bearing and nurturance of off-spring by people who are obligated to each other both naturally and contractually. Socialization, in a sense, begins in the womb and is bound to be successful only if the womb has been impregnated by a morally appropriate and legally designated sire.

The fertility of Hofriyati women is at once their most valuable and, as we shall see, their most elusive asset. Since reproductively active women are effectively barred from occupations outside the home and are, with the remainder of Hofriyati, party to the cultural conviction that the role of a woman is to produce descendants for her husband, fertility is the salient feature by which female self-image is defined.[3] I suggest, as do other authors in this volume, that a woman's entry into middle age is deter-mined by the state of her fertility: it is the postreproductive phase of life. Yet in Hofriyat there is a subtle difference, for here the state of a woman's fertility is judged not only in terms of her biological capacity to reproduce but also by her legal status. Furthermore, a legally postreproductive woman in Hofriyat may share with her chronologically senior counterpart a certain freedom from constraints and also opportunities for acquiring power and social recognition that middle-aged women in non-Western settings seem typically to enjoy. Not surprisingly, in the case at hand such opportunities have much to do with fertility: middle-aged women may attain the power to manipulate the fertility potential of others either by arranging their first marriages or by becoming the focal points for future marital alignments. Since descent among Northern Sudanese Arabs is agnatic and marriages ideally are contracted between people who are related through men, some consideration of where women figure in this scheme is necessary if we are to understand the type of power available to them and the strategies they might use to achieve it.

Women in the Social Structure

The residents of Hofriyat are organized into several related patrilineages, few of which presently exhibit corporate characteristics. Ideally these lineages are endogamous; preferred marriages are those between patrilateral parallel cousins, or *awlad 'amm*. In practice, however, lineages are endogamous only to the extent they are corporate.[4] First marriages usually involve close cognatic kin irrespective of descent affiliation, the salient criterion of marriageability being the demonstration of some prior relationship, whether patrilateral, matrilateral, bilateral, or purely affinal. Most first marriages, those held to be morally appropriate because they unite "close" kin, are based on a cross or a parallel sibling link in the second or third ascending generations. Significantly, Hofriyati make no real distinction between agnatic and uterine links when determining the relative closeness of kin.

Yet a distinction is made when it comes to future genealogical reckoning. Because of a secondary system of kin classification, which assigns cousins of the same generation the status of siblings, marriages that ultimately are based on relationships traced through women may be brought forward in time, thereby in most cases erasing all traces of uterine kinship. For example, a prospective couple whose fathers are the sons of female matrilateral parallel cousins are spoken of as *awlad 'amm* because their fathers are classed as brothers (Figure 1). In future generations these may be considered real brothers, the original classificatory designation, as preserved in the marriage, providing grounds for bringing village genealogy into line with present realities.

Moreover, though kinship is traced bilaterally through the living, in ascending generations the doctrine of patrilineality takes precedence, encouraging a progressive suppression of close uterine relationships in favor of more remote agnatic links (Boddy 1989:75–88; cf. Kronenberg and Kronenberg 1965). Here again marriages that originally were contracted between cognates will appear to their descendants as marriages of *awlad 'amm*.

In thus rewriting the past, Hofriyati both generate future marriages and reinforce the ideological fiction that lineages are endogamous and unambiguously agnatic. Though links traced through women are indispensable to contemporary social arrangements, rarely are they remembered as such when traced beyond the grandparental generation. Further, women's names usually disappear from genealogical memory within a generation or two of their deaths. To be incorporated into genealogies on a more permanent basis is to be immortalized—a coveted status and the province of reproductively successful men. The social recognition permitted to women is both elusive and temporally limited.

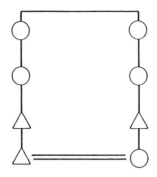

Figure 1. A marriage between classificatory *awlad 'amm* based on a kinship link traced ultimately through women, in the future to be considered a marriage of the children of brothers.

These features of Hofriyati social organization bear relevance for the ways by which a middle-aged woman might work to attain or to surpass her allotted potential following divorce or the death of her husband. The dissolution of her first marriage usually jeopardizes a woman's quest for elevated social status relative to her peers (Boddy 1989:177–85). Yet some women are able to profit by it, to seize the chance for a second beginning which, if tempered by equal amounts of skill and luck, might enable them to achieve positions of influence later on.

Women and the Life Cycle

The sexes in Hofriyat are segregated; women are pharaonically circumcised[5] and relatively secluded. They inherit both as wives and as daughters and may pass on property to their husbands and children. A woman's property, both movable and immovable, whether inherited, received as a gift from her husband, or, occasionally, earned is hers alone. In her lifetime it may be disposed of as she desires, however constrained she might feel to conform to the wishes of male kin.

She has no rights over the allocation of her fertility, however, at least in her younger years. A woman's first marriage is arranged by her parents and elder brothers with an eye to the possibilities for marital arrangements in future generations, especially should significant amounts of heritable property be at stake (cf. Peters 1978). Bridewealth (*mahr*, sometimes translated as "dowry") is nominal, and is said to be held in trust by the woman's father for her use or upkeep in the event of divorce. A woman remains an active member of her natal family after marriage. Her close male agnates retain life-long moral and economic responsibility for her, which is shared in part by her adult sons should she be widowed or divorced. She is expected to return to her parents' home at the dissolution of her marriage. Moreover, though virilocal residence is said to be the rule, a woman often lives in her natal household most of her married life. She is home for extended periods of time surrounding each pregnancy and, should her husband work outside the village, may remain there indefinitely. In sum, while rights to use a woman's fertility are conferred upon her husband at marriage, jural rights and obligations are not similarly transferred and remain with her own minimal descent group.

It is necessary to stress that marriage in Hofriyat is best viewed not as an end in itself but as a means for both parties to attain elevated social status through reproductive success. In marriage a man acquires access to his wife's fertility, and she acquires legitimate means to activate it. Reproduction for village women takes place solely in the context of a marriage. Alternatives not only are unthinkable, but constitute a grave affront to family honor, punishable by death at the hands of her agnates.[6]

When a woman marries for the first time, usually between the ages of fourteen and eighteen, her symbolic status is high. As a virgin bride, she is the idealization of femininity and the embodiment of key cultural values (Boddy 1988, 1989). Enclosed by pharaonic circumcision, her womb is the locus of morally appropriate, socialized fertility that has been rendered potent through marriage (Boddy 1982).

However, the corresponding social status of a bride is low: she is a married woman, yet childless. She can expect a gradual improvement of her position relative to affines and peers as she produces children for her husband in the course of a stable and preferably monogamous marriage, especially if most of her offspring are sons. Her ultimate goal is to become, with her husband, the cofounder of a lineage section. Her claim to prestige rests with her demonstrated fertility and subsequently with the prominent role she plays in arranging her children's marriages. When they themselves reproduce, she is assured of becoming a respected *ḥabōba*, literally, "darling," the grandmother of a patriline and a woman who might speak her mind in public, who is listened to, who is reputed to be skilled at social maneuverings.

The respect that she commands at this point is often well deserved, for to become a powerful *ḥabōba* is no small feat. It requires diligence and a long and fruitful marriage, the likes of which are difficult to secure in Hofriyat. Women alone bear responsibility for the reproductive problems that so frequently plague a marriage. If she suffers stillbirth, miscarriage, the death of an unweaned infant, or the birth of a daughter as her first child, a woman's procreative ability may be called into question and her marriage terminated. If she is young, she may quickly remarry at the insistence of male kin, provided a suitable spouse can be found and she can be pressured to comply. For the dissolution of her first marriage guarantees a woman an increased measure of personal autonomy at the same time as it brings about a diminution of her status. She now has the ostensible right to choose among her suitors or to remain unwed.

Presuming a woman passes the crucial test of demonstrating her fertility, the next hurdle in her marriage is likely to come at any time between her late twenties and her forties when menopause signals the end of her reproductive career. It is then that a Hofriyati woman might well find the marriage she has worked so hard to establish threatened by divorce or co-wifery. Perceived fertility dysfunction is not the only provocation for such action on the part of village men. For it is a mark of a man's prosperity to have a wife unencumbered by child-care concerns, who has time to spend ministering to her husband's personal wants. Thus he may take a second, younger wife as much to enhance his prestige as to increase his descendants.

But since few men have sufficient means to support two households adequately,[7] such gambits regularly fail and divorce of the first wife often results. Should she remain unrepudiated, the first wife will nonetheless see her quest for *ḥabōba* status menaced by the diversion of her husband's procreative attentions and the impending division of his estate among a greater number of heirs. Co-wifery that results in permanent separation and withdrawal of financial support is perhaps the most devastating blow to a woman's aspirations, for without divorce she is precluded from resuming her reproductive career through remarriage. Finding herself in this predicament, a woman might seek the intervention of her brothers to secure her liberty.

Divorce, separation, and co-wifery do not exhaust the range of career crises a woman might experience. She might, of course, be widowed. Should her husband die while their children are still young, a leviratic marriage is usually arranged. However, depending on the circumstances, she may refuse her husband's kinsman, preferring the relative autonomy that postmarital status brings.

Middle Age or Postreproductive Status

What seems to emerge from the foregoing discussion is that the crisis that Hofriyati women are apt to face prior to menopause is the official or legal cessation of their reproductive careers. The status of a divorced woman or a widow precipitates—whether for good or for ill—many of the changes that a woman who remains stably married throughout her reproductive years experiences when she is no longer able to reproduce. Should a divorced woman or widow remarry (as is likely to happen when she is young and no serious fertility disorders have been discerned), her newfound mobility and autonomy will be curtailed to some extent. Yet the choice of husband is largely her own. She now has the freedom to allocate her fertility where she will (though her male kin ought to be consulted) or indeed, to withhold it. Both options have important implications for a woman's long-range goals, a point to which I will return.

What I wish to emphasize here is that if we adopt the view that middle age for women universally refers to the time of life surrounding menopause, we succumb, in essence, to a Western biological model according to which physical changes provide absolute reference points in the course of a woman's life. For us the onset of menses, loss of virginity, pregnancy, and the cessation of menses have traditionally signaled momentous alterations of social context, a resituation of relationships and of female self-image. In Hofriyat, to focus on menopause as the crucial criterion of middle age is to miss the point. Much as virginity in Northern Sudan may be socially defined as potential but unactivated fertility (Boddy 1982) and is a status that can to a certain extent be renewed through reinfibulation[8]—as Hayes (1975:622) suggests—so too might middle age be defined in social terms as the deactivation of procreative ability, as a status that can, under certain conditions, be partially reversed. In Hofriyat a woman's "social age" is linked inextricably to the state of her fertility. Menopause is but one event among several that might usher her into midlife, a status variously intermediate between bridehood and senescence, heralded either by legal or by physical cessation of reproduction and bringing with it increased personal autonomy and enhanced opportunity to manipulate the social environment for her own ends. However, if midlife is not coincidental with menopause, the status might also bring a loss of prestige.

Political Strategies and Opportunities for Advancement

Whatever the individual circumstances, the termination or suspension of a woman's reproductive career frequently jeopardizes her aspirations to become a powerful and respected *habōba* later on. Middle age in Hofriyat is marked, in part, by a narrowing of former career possibilities and available strategies. It may sometimes affect women in dramatically negative ways, particularly if male kin are absent or deceased. One woman of my acquaintance who has twice been married and twice divorced, whose only child is a daughter herself divorced and childless, and whose close male kin are no longer living must rely on the charity of her neighbors to survive. For this she suffers the chides and barbs of her juniors and the pitying looks of her contemporaries.

Yet most Hofriyati women in the postmarital midlife status are better advantaged, having male kin who are committed to their financial support. Indeed, some welcome the status in spite of its ominous implications, seeing in their comparative autonomy fresh possibilities for social advancement. For such a woman might, in a sense, circumvent the agnatic system earlier described and both achieve a position of respect and, like the conventional *ḥabōbat* (plural), assure herself a passing place in village genealogies.

Previously I discussed some peculiarities of kinship calculation in Hofriyat, noting that despite the undeniable significance of uterine relationships in determining marriageability and inheritance, the doctrine of patrilineality, plus a system of generational classification, operates to suppress the memory of such links in ascending generations. Thus, even if she is cofounder of a lineage section, a woman's name and achievements are seldom remembered for more than a few generations, unlike those of her male counterparts. Moreover, should she have experienced a prevenient end to her reproductive career, it is doubtful that a woman's memory will survive a generation after her death. In her later years she can expect to exert little influence over the disposition of the fertility of others. She is unlikely to become a key figure in the negotiations of future marriages whether during her lifetime or thereafter.

However, should she be in a position to remarry, she might alter her prospects significantly. Hofriyati entering their second marriages are far less constrained to marry close kin than they are in their first. This, coupled with the fact that a previously married woman is quite free to choose among her suitors, means that she might opt for a lineage-exogamous union. Her choice, if astute, might counterbalance any drawbacks (e.g., co-wifery) in the conjugal arrangement, for she might now become the point of articulation between two and in some cases three patrilines that do not acknowledge close relationship due to a lack of known intermarriages in previous generations. Her second marriage might thus provide the link necessary for future marital considerations among unrelated descent groups. For if a woman provides just one child for each of the lineages into which she was wed, then all children of her consecutive husbands are considered siblings, hence unmarriageable. But a marriage prohibition between individuals in one generation ensures preferred marriageability among their offspring in the next. Thus might a woman who is precluded from becoming the *ḥabōba* of a patriline come to exert influence over the marriages of her husband's descendants by his other wives for generations to come. In a sense, then, her central position allows her to usurp prerogatives of the legitimate *ḥabōbat*.[9] Even should her second marriage prove infertile, it nonetheless creates possibilities for intermarriages between her husband's and her own natal groups, for marriages occasionally are contracted on the strength of demonstrated prior affinity between lineages.

Furthermore, a woman who becomes a pivotal figure in village genealogies also becomes a reference point for the potential alienation of heritable property, a notable consideration when her siblings and her husband's siblings negotiate marriages for their respective offspring. A woman who comes to occupy a node in the descent structure of Hofriyat might also gain influence as a result. In posthumous recognition of the continuing significance of her position, her name is not soon suppressed in the constructions of village genealogists. Indeed, in contrast to the vertically organized and segmented patrigenealogies commonly recounted, there exists a second type of genealogy in Hofriyat, constructed horizontally and known as a *nisba awlad khalāt,* a genealogy of matrilateral parallel cousins. This form is wholly devoted to tracing, for a single generation, the intricate web of kinship that is obtained between lineages due to the first and subsequent marriages of related women.

However, many premenopausal women who are propelled into the status of "middle age" do not remarry. For some, especially those with several children, this is a matter of preference: one widowed woman told me she had provoked the dissolution of her leviratic marriage because she resented its constraints; she viewed it as incompatible with her vocation in the *zār* spirit possession cult.

On the other hand, women who are deemed infertile are likely to remain unwed whatever their desires. Yet the relative jural minority of these women and their expanded mobility and autonomy in certain domains have permitted a few of them to pursue other interests advantageously. Two of these are worthy of note. One woman, childless and divorced, undertook government-sponsored training in midwifery and is presently the only licensed practitioner in the district. She derives a substantial income from her salary and from gifts from those she assists. Since her job takes her into nomad camps in the desert and into neighboring villages where she has no kin, she would be hard pressed to function in this capacity were she married and secluded. It is only because her reproductive career is now officially behind her that she has the autonomy she requires.

The second instance concerns an older woman who was divorced when fairly young after producing a daughter as her first child. This woman returned with her child to live in her parents' home after her husband left the village; upon her parents' deaths, she was allowed by her siblings to retain possession of that house and at the time of my fieldwork was considered its sole owner. She and her daughter were supported by her brothers from their father's small farm and she worked to supplement her income by selling cooked food to villagers. Then, with the proceeds of her business, she began to purchase and distribute raw materials for the cottage crafts that occupy women in their spare moments, dealing with itinerant traders or placing orders through male kin. Next, she made use of her relative freedom from seclusion to sell finished basketry in the local market. Over the years she has otherwise diversified her trade. Through her entrepreneurial activities, she has amassed considerable wealth; twice now she has taken herself on the pilgrimage to Mecca.

Though she is not the *ḥabōba* of her husband's descendants, this woman is widely respected, for she is on her way to becoming the actual, if not formally accredited, founder of a lineage section. She was instrumental in arranging the marriage of her daughter to her brother's son, a landless but industrious sharecropper, then gave the couple money with which to buy a plot that someone no longer living in the village wished to sell. With her help, this family has continued to acquire land little by little, both through mortgage and through outright purchase. Marriages recently arranged between her daughter's daughters and her brothers' descendants point to the gradual crystallization of a corporate descent group. What is significant here is that an endogamous patrilineage is emerging that is focused on the financial success of a woman, based upon the future inheritance of her daughter, and is directly attributable to the premature curtailment of her reproductive career (Figure 2).

Conclusion

In Hofriyat marriage inaugurates a woman's reproductive career: divorce, widowhood, or menopause may bring it to a permanent or temporary close. Middle age for Hofriyati women is neither identified with a specific chronological age nor absolutely associated with a particular physical manifestation. Instead, it is the social status accorded a woman whose fertility is no longer active, whether jurally or biologically. Much as Brown (1982) has described, the status of "middle age" is characterized for a woman by enhanced personal autonomy, that is, the capacity to make certain decisions for herself and a relaxation of some of the constraints by which she was bound in her childbearing years. It is also associated with her expanded maneuverability in the social arena. This frequently leads to the furtherance of uterine kinship ties in future marital arrangements, however fleeting their recognition in village genealogies.

Postmarital middle-age status coupled with ongoing jural minority in certain respects means that village women with close male kin are assured of economic support while being freer to explore a limited range of career

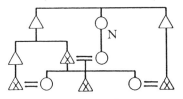

(x : cooperate in farming)

Future rewrite:

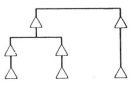

Figure 2. A Corporate descent group crystallizing around the entrepreneurial success of a woman, N, and the eventual disappearance of her position from future genealogies.

alternatives. These in turn may enable them to approximate the position of *habōba* in other than usual ways. This is the positive side of things. Middle age can, however, bode disaster for a woman cast adrift who has no male kin. These circumstances, plus the fact that middle age generally implies the narrowing of former possibilities even as it implies the broadening of others, suggest that this period of a woman's life is approached with ambivalence, if not with trepidation.

NOTES

1. The reasons for the perceived scarcity of land for cultivation are numerous: periodic changes in the course of the Nile through its floodplain may either cause good silts to be lost to inundation or remove the source of water for flood-bank irrigation. Added to this are the problems of land fractionation due to formalized land registration and adherence to Islamic inheritance rules, desertification and the stated decline in productivity of *wadi* (stream bed) plantations, increasing population pressure in certain areas, and the expense and uncertain availability of fuel for diesel irrigation pumps.

2. Covillagers are considered to be kin of some sort by definition, however tenuous their genealogical links in recent generations.

3. For more on this point, see Boddy (1988, 1989).

4. Lineages in Hofriyat appear to go through cycles of consolidation and

dissolution. Families often "incorporate" when their members acquire land or some other lucrative resource (e.g., a diesel pump), but since all heritable property is individually owned and strictly divided among heirs, they tend to dissolve when their membership proliferates and ownership becomes fractionated.

5. Pharaonic circumcision as practiced in Sudan involves surgical removal of the clitoris, labia minora and all or part of the labia majora. This is followed by infibulation, whereby skin from either side of the wound is pulled together and held in place by thorns or by suture. A small opening often no broader than the circumference of a matchstick is left for the elimination of urine and menstrual blood; once healed the genital area is covered by a layer of thick, resistant scar tissue. For further consideration of this operation, its implications, functions, and significances, see Boddy (1982), Dareer (1982), Gruenbaum (1982), and Hayes (1975).

6. Since sexual segregation is the norm in Hofriyat and tensions between spouses frequently run high over the issue of honor, companionship in a marriage is both rare and unexpected. It may develop with age, however, should the union prove stable.

7. According to the tenets of Islam, a polygynous man must treat his wives equally. In Hofriyat this is taken to mean that each must have her own house.

8. When a woman gives birth, the opening left in the scar tissue of her circumcision wound must be surgically enlarged to release the child. Once delivered, her wound is immediately closed up again (reinfibulated), she is given gifts of jewelry similar to those she received at her wedding, and she is re-presented to her husband as a "bride."

9. Thus, the power available to older women in Hofriyat is a kind of "limited good": the acquisition of power for oneself entails the loss of power for others, a system that tends to pit women against each other competitively.

REFERENCES

Boddy, Janice
    1982   Womb as Oasis: The Symbolic Context of Pharaonic Circumcision in Rural Northern Sudan. American Ethnologist 9(4):682–98.
    1988   Spirits and Selves in Northern Sudan: The Cultural Therapeutics of Possession and Trance. American Ethnologist 15(1):4–27.
    1989   Wombs and Alien Spirits: Women, Men, and the *Zār* Cult in Northern Sudan. Madison: University of Wisconsin Press.
Brown, Judith K.
    1982   Cross-cultural Perspectives on Middle-Aged Women. Current Anthropology 23(2):143–56.
Dareer, Asma El-
    1982   Woman, Why Do You Weep?: Circumcision and Its Consequences. London: Zed Press.
Gruenbaum, Ellen
    1982   The Movement against Clitoridectomy and Infibulation in Sudan: Pub-

lic Health Policy and the Women's Movement. Medical Anthropology Newsletter 13(2):4–12.

Hayes, Rose Oldfield
1975 Female Genital Mutilation, Fertility Control, Women's Roles, and the Patrilineage in Modern Sudan: A Functional Analysis. American Ethnologist 2:617–33.

Kronenberg, A., and W. Kronenberg
1965 Parallel Cousin Marriage in Mediaeval and Modern Nubia, Part 1. Kush 13:241–60.

Peters, Emrys L.
1978 The Status of Women in Four Middle Eastern Communities. *In* Women in the Muslim World. L. Beck and N. Keddie, eds., pp. 311–50. London: Cambridge University Press.

11 Sexuality and the Middle-Aged Woman in South Asia

Sylvia Vatuk

Judith Brown has observed that in many non-Western societies women's lives "appear to improve with the onset of middle age," rather than becoming less satisfying, as is commonly the case in our own society (1982:143). One reason for this, she suggests, is that restrictions on a woman's physical mobility and on her freedom to interact socially with others, which may be imposed in earlier periods of her life, are often relaxed in middle age. A key factor in the increased freedom and independence enjoyed by the older woman is her inability to conceive and bear offspring. In cultures that regard the processes and substances exuded in menstruation and childbirth ritually contaminating to males, it is easy to see that menopause might entail social advantages.

Furthermore, in cultures characterized by what Mediterraneanists have called an "honor and shame" complex (see, for example, Peristiany 1965; Schneider 1971), the perceived need to control women's sexuality by imposing limitations upon their freedom of movement should lose much of its urgency when they become infertile. As Brown explains, "once their sexuality can have no consequences, women are often regarded as asexual. Beyond childbearing, a woman can no longer bring dishonor upon her family by sexual adventuring" (1982:144). While Brown's statement to the effect that a postmenopausal woman cannot shame her family with an illegitimate pregnancy needs no further elaboration, the same is not true of the notion that the loss of reproductive functions means the end of a woman's sexuality in the broader sense. This cultural assumption is worth exploring in greater depth.

Many ethnographers, from research in various parts of the world, have reported such conceptions: the postmenopausal woman is considered "asexual," treated "like a man," thought to be sexually unattractive to men or lacking in the desire or ability to be sexually active. However, I have not been able to discover in the literature any attempts to examine or analyze the content or the internal cultural logic of such conceptions. Most ethnographers, indeed, seem to take for granted, as obvious and self-evident, the idea that female sexuality ceases at menopause. This may be, at least in part, because the ethnographers are themselves members of cultures in which the asexuality of the postmenopausal woman is also popularly and widely assumed; therefore they may regard the issue as unproblematical—a cultural restatement of a biological given. Yet we know from recent studies of the physiology of female sexuality that although aging brings about distinct changes in the mechanism of sexual responsiveness and functioning, under favorable personal and cultural conditions women can and in fact do remain sexually active for many years after the climacterium (see Masters and Johnson 1966). Such scientific findings from disciplines other than our own prompt a closer look at the assumptions underlying the notion that women cease to be sexual persons when they lose the ability to bear children.

For this purpose I propose to look at cultural constructions of female sexuality in South Asia, where, as in the societies Brown refers to in her article, there is a prominent concern for the sexual modesty of women and a concomitant plethora of social institutions designed to restrict young women to the "private," domestic arena; limit their physical mobility, social contacts, and activities; and make them generally dependent on and subordinate to the authority of the male members of their families. In South Asia, too, as many observers have noted, female seclusion and veiling, demands for deferential behavior toward men, and limitations on women's freedom are gradually relaxed as old age approaches (see, for example, Mandelbaum 1970:88–90; Jacobson 1977:105–7; Vatuk 1975:155–58, 1987). These changes are associated with increasing ability to exercise power and influence over others and carry out decision making within the family and kindred, particularly after a woman's sons mature and marry and their wives take over the more burdensome and confining household chores.

Some scholars of South Asian societies have made the specific association suggested by Brown between the older woman's improved social status and her physiological status as one whose childbearing capacity has ended. David, for example, speaking of the loosening of restrictions on the behavior of older women among Tamil-speaking Sri Lankans, suggests that this is related to the fact that the postmenopausal woman is "incapable of affecting family honor by improper behavior with males" that might lead to a pregnancy (1980:99). Hershman makes a similar point about the position of the Punjabi woman after menopause: "With the shedding of her shameful sexuality a woman becomes more like a man and she has the ability to exercise power according to the strength of her own personal character" (1977:275). To put these statements into their broader context, let us examine in greater detail South Asian cultural conceptions about the nature of men and women as sexual persons and about the effects of the aging process, and menopause in particular, upon female sexuality in its various manifestations. In order to do this, it will be necessary to draw very widely on a variety of ethnographic, literary, mythological, and psychoanalytic sources, in addition to my own field research, which has not focused directly on this issue. Unavoidably, the ensuing discussion will contain sweeping generalizations and display a seemingly careless disregard of regional and subcultural variation within South Asia as a whole. However, some insights should emerge that can provide an impetus for more solidly grounded empirical investigations by others.

Attitudes toward Sexuality

Most scholars in general agree that sexual desire in South Asia is accepted rather matter-of-factly as an impulse whose satisfaction provides an incomparable source of pleasure for women and men alike. There is no sense that sexuality is bad, dirty, or sinful in itself. It is regarded as a positive force, not only for the transitory delight it affords, but more important, for its unique ability to bind together husband and wife for the foundation of the family unit and the procreation of offspring. However, it is recognized that because of the very compelling strength of physical desire, those under its sway may be impelled to behave in ways that have potentially destructive consequences—for the individual, for the social groups to which he or she belongs, or for society at large. Thus, when directed at socially inappropriate objects, incestuous, adulterous, or intercaste matings may result; when desire for the love object leads to an exclusive preoccupation, other socially significant relationships or obligations may be neglected. Furthermore, sexual feelings may distract an individual from the pursuit of other important worldly or spiritual goals. And while beneficial and even necessary in moderation, sexual activity when indulged in to excess can be quite physically harmful and debilitating, especially for the man. It is hardly surprising, therefore, that there should be considerable cultural emphasis in South Asia upon the proper and careful regulation and control of sexual impulses—not only for women, but for men as well.

On the one hand, the control of sexuality is achieved through a variety of social practices, including varying degrees of seclusion and veiling of women and the enforcement of strict standards of modesty and decorum in mixed-sex gatherings. A major purpose of these is to ensure that sexual expression is confined, as far as possible, to the marital relationship, between partners selected by their parents from within the appropriate social units, and according to customary rules concerning prohibited degrees of kinship. Even within marriage the frequency and timing of opportunities for sexual relations are considered a legitimate area for social control, especially in the early years of marriage when most couples live within an extended family setting. Thus a newlywed pair's access to privacy is limited by elders—an extended working day is imposed upon the young bride, open display of interest or affection in the presence of other people is proscribed, and space within the house is rarely allocated to the couple for their exclusive use on a long-term basis. While it is recognized that sexual concerns are paramount for a recently married couple, and properly so, it is felt to be important for the integrity of the larger family group that such preoccupations not interfere with the even routine of household affairs or the solidarity of previously established relationships among its members. The fact that in the long run the latter is almost inevitable perhaps gives even greater force for this imperative in the early stages of married life.

The Stages of Life

Not only in social institutions, but also in cultural conceptions about the ideal life course of the person, the theme of control of sexuality is prominent, at least in the Hindu traditions of the region. The most familiar textual formulation of this, from the Manusmrti, outlines four stages of life for a man and, after his marriage, for his wife as well (see Bühler 1886). While such a schema is not, of course, rigidly adhered to in practice as a detailed guide for action, it nevertheless provides a conceptual framework for appropriate role performance at each major stage of the family developmental cycle, which has considerable immediacy for men and women at all social levels, even for those not directly familiar with the textual materials from firsthand reading.

The textual description of each of the stages of life—the four *aśramas* —includes specification of the appropriate attitudes and activities for that period. These specifications pertain to various facets of life—work, food, abode, etc. But at each stage central attention is paid to appropriate sexual behavior. An active sexual life, in this schema, is appropriate only to one life stage, that of married adulthood, the years of rearing offspring. In the first stage of life, up to the time of marriage, a man's primary duties are to learn and to serve his religious preceptor faithfully; he must strictly abstain from sexual activity of any kind. During the second stage of life, on the contrary, a man and his wife are positively enjoined to engage in sexual relations and to procreate, while concerning themselves with the associated matters of supporting and managing a household and becoming involved in wider social and community affairs. The third stage begins when a couple's sons marry and begin to have children in their turn. Now a man ought to begin turning over the management of the household to the younger generation and devote most of his attention and time to the spiritual quest. This is a transitional stage: a man should gradually begin to loosen the bonds of affection and reciprocity that tie him to others by physically leaving his home and by subjecting himself to an increasingly ascetic regimen. While a man may take his wife with him upon his departure from home, he should not permit her presence to distract him from his spiritual aims—they may live together, but should not engage in sexual activity. In the fourth and final stage of life, a man should cut all ties with family and society, including his wife, and spend his remaining days roaming homeless in the world, renouncing all pleasures and attending single-mindedly to the goal of salvation. It is significant, insofar as this life-cycle model sheds any light upon conceptions of *female* sexuality in South Asian Hinduism, that the period of a woman's active sexual life is delimited by the requirements and timing of her husband's worldly and spiritual needs, rather than by any physiological changes in her body or any secular or religious aspirations of her own.

As this model of the ideal life cycle illustrates, the expression of sexuality in South Asian cultures is subject not only to social or external control imposed upon the individual by others, but there is also a very strong emphasis on self-control in the sexual realm. In general, as I shall show, these cultures tend to place more emphasis on the former mechanism in the case of women, while stressing the latter more heavily as a means of regulating men's sexual conduct. The reasons for this difference in emphasis are related to differences in male and female sexual natures, as culturally conceived. These in turn are comprehensible within the context of broader ethnomedical theories about the makeup of the human body and its various processes, of which I have room here to give only the sketchiest account.

Traditional Medical View

According to traditional Hindu medical texts (see Filliozat 1964), which outline a humoral theory of bodily constituents and functioning, the ultimate source of bodily strength and vitality, as well as of the sexual fluids themselves, is contained in the blood, which is in turn equated with somatic "heat." Semen is regarded as a kind of distilled "essence" of blood—its loss, like the loss of blood in its ordinary form, involves the inevitable draining away of a man's strength. While it is not desirable or practical for most men to avoid losing any semen at all in sexual intercourse, this theory clearly suggests that a man can retain a high level of vitality to the extent that he is able to control the expression of sexual impulses. In fact, a major and recurrent theme in Hindu mythology centers on the potentials of the use of ritual heat, generated by sexual abstinence, by gods and ascetic holy men for powerfully creative or destructive purposes (see, for example, O'Flaherty 1973; Danielou 1964; Cantlie 1977; Caplan 1987). Such notions are not restricted to the ancient classical texts—similar ideas are present in the various local folk medical theories reported by ethnographers who have worked in different regions of India and Sri Lanka. The following quotation from McGilvray, summarizing the words of some of his Tamil-speaking Hindu informants on the east coast of Sri Lanka, is typical of these explanations of the relationship between sexuality and health reported from all over the subcontinent:

> The loss of semen through sex, masturbation, or nocturnal emission drains the body of valuable blood, while the retention of semen, particularly during adolescence and young manhood, promotes a man's physical, and ultimately his spiritual development. The body of an ascetic young bachelor should glow with good health. (1982:33)

While men, according to this theory, must take special care to preserve their supply of strength-giving blood, postpubertal women are thought to have an overabundance of blood. As McGilvray's informants put it, "the monthly flow, . . . is a safeguard . . . insuring that a woman's natural surplus of blood (and hence physical strength and vitality, including sexual desire) is regularly drained away" (1982:31). This conception of the relationship between menstruation and level of sexual desire is obviously pertinent to the issue of the image of the postmenopausal woman as one who is no longer sexual. It is also relevant to the widely reported view that women are "naturally" more passionate, and thus sexually demanding, than men. This notion is found not only in the explicit statements of informants (as cited, for example, by such scholars as Hershman 1977; Carstairs 1967; Harper 1969; Bennett 1983; Dhruvarajan 1989; Tapper 1983), but also in the indirect evidence provided through analyses of ritual symbolism (see Beck 1969; David 1980; and Babb 1970).

Because of a woman's lustful nature, she presents a dual threat: to the honor of the men of her family and to the well-being of potential sexual partners. On the most superficial level, the latter threat arises out of the notion that the act of sexual intercourse inevitably drains a man's vitality. A lustful woman, particularly a woman who is not one's legitimate sexual partner in marriage, can thus be envisioned, in the extreme case, as a threat to a man's very existence (see Vatuk and Vatuk 1975). Some psychoanalytically oriented discussions of conceptions of female sexuality in South Asia have suggested furthermore that underlying a widespread fear of the consequences of female sexuality among Indian and other South Asian men is the possibility that one may prove unable to fulfill adequately a woman's sexual demands. Both Kakar (1978:95) and Carstairs (1967:167), for example, have associated this fear with what they regard as an unusually severe and prevalent concern with impotence, particularly among young males (see also Obeyesekere 1976:213–15, 1981:425–50; Lannoy 1971:114–18).

While woman as sexual partner is thus conceptualized as passionate and therefore untrustworthy and threatening to men, a counterpoised image of woman as mother and sister sees her as pure, self-sacrificing, selfless, and ever-faithful. Kakar, describing what he regards as a severe ambivalence in this South Asian male attitude toward women, says that "underlying the conscious ideal of womanly purity, innocence, and fidelity, and interwoven with the unconscious belief in a safeguarding maternal beneficence, is a secret conviction . . . that the feminine principle is really the opposite: treacherous, lustful and rampant with an insatiable, contaminating sexuality" (1978:93). Harper notes a similar ambivalence in attitudes toward women in rural Karnataka, south India (1969:81–86), as does Hershman with reference to Punjab (1977) and Hart for traditional Tamilnad (1973; see also Allen 1982; Kondas 1986). In the work of these writers, the major focus is on the implications of such ambivalence for male psychological development and sexual functioning. Roy is almost alone in considering in-depth the impact of this divided conception of femininity for female psychosexual processes over the life cycle. Among the conclusions to be drawn from her extended discussion of personality development and social adaptation among urban, elite, upper middle-class Bengali women is that, particularly as middle age approaches, this culture provides substantial rewards to a woman who denies the sexual side of her being and accepts an essentially asexual, motherlike identity, even vis-à-vis her own husband (1975:117–21). Jacobson's (1978) interesting analysis of life history data from an elderly central Indian woman, though providing a somewhat different perspective, nevertheless also supports such an interpretation.

The Aging Woman

When one turns to the question of how, in South Asian cultures, the aging process is thought to affect the nature of female sexuality, the evidence is not entirely clear. On the one hand, according to indigenous medical theory, the aging process is thought to involve an overall "cooling" of the body. This gradual dissipation of somatic heat in later life is linked to a supposed decline, for both sexes, in the supply of blood that represents the source of youthful strength and vitality, as well as sexual desire. In the case of women, this process is made evident by the ending of the menstrual flow. Thus, for a female there is a clear ethnomedical rationale for equating the infertility of the postmenopausal period with asexuality in the broader sense.

However, somewhat inconsistent with the notion that women become gradually less sexual as they age, until menopause causes their sexual desire to dissipate altogether, is the widely reported belief in South Asia that sexual intercourse with an older woman is far more dangerous for a man than is intercourse with an adolescent or young adult woman. McGilvray, for example, notes that according to his informants intercourse with an older woman can kill a man (1982:65–66). (Presumably this is the case if indulged in on a regular basis.) Kakar maintains, based on experience in his psychoanalytic practice, as well as on folklore and myth, that there is among Indian men a widespread "fear of mature female sexuality. The fantasy world of Hindu men is replete with the figures of older women whose appetites debilitate a man's sexuality" (1978:91). He connects this dread with feelings of ambivalence toward the mother, aroused in the context of early socialization. Although there is no suggestion in the literature that these images of the sexually aggressive *older* woman refer to the *postmenopausal* woman, their prominence in this culture is nevertheless of relevance to the broader issue of what happens to female sexuality with age (see below).

One might expect that since in the South Asian view the onset of menopause brings about a fundamental alteration in woman's nature, involving as it does the loss of the two key aspects of her gender identity, this physiological transition might be ritually or symbolically marked in some way. Such is not the case with menopause, and in this respect South Asia is not an exception.

Might menopause serve as an essential criterion of eligibility for significant ritual or social roles? In fact, it seems quite clear that the social status transitions that accompany middle age—the acquisition of increased power, authority, and autonomy referred to above—are tied in with family developmental processes rather than with chronological age, reproductive capacity, or sexuality (Vatuk 1987). The obvious distinctions made by Hindus and Buddhists for ritual purposes are among the virgin (*kanya*), the married woman whose husband is living (*suhāgin*), and the widow. The last is typically excluded from ritual participation, while the former two play distinct and often central roles in a wide variety of ceremonial contexts. The classification of women for ritual purposes is thus based in South Asia upon marital status—a "sociological" characteristic—and in part also upon physiology, insofar as the *kanya* is understood to be a prepubescent girl and the *suhāgin* a physically mature and sexually active woman.

Physiological status is not relevant in the definition of the widow, but her ritual exclusion is implicitly associated with the threat posed by a potentially sexually active, fertile woman who is no longer under male control (see, e.g., Babb 1970; Allen 1982; Tapper 1983). As for the postmenopausal but still married woman, I have found in the literature reference to only one minor ritual in which she is specified as the appropriate *central* character. This is a Sinhalese domestic ritual in which seven "grandmothers" are the recipients of sweets—their consumption of these offerings is supposed to assure family prosperity (Gombrich 1971). Even in this rite the qualifications for eligibility do not involve specific reference to physiological status, although Kemper (1980:750–51) is perhaps justified in suggesting that the quality of beneficence attributed to the grandmothers in this ritual derives from the fact that they are no longer menstruating.

The loss of the ability to conceive and bear children—and the accompanying bodily changes—do not appear to be culturally construed as problematical or traumatic for South Asian women. By contrast we may note that in the Western societies in which this matter has been investigated, the menopausal transition period is generally felt, by men and women alike, to be fraught with physical and psychological stresses of various kinds (see, for example, Davis 1982, 1983; Skultans 1970; Bart 1969; but also Neugarten et al. 1963). While evidence on this point from South Asia is scanty, the available literature confirms my own observations that older women in this society do not explicitly associate any physical or psychosocial difficulties with the physiological processes of menopause. This does not mean that late middle age is regarded as a necessarily healthful or problem-free time of life, but rather that any difficulties that a woman experiences during this period are not consciously perceived as being a consequence of the climacterium per se (Vatuk 1975:161–63; Flint 1975).

The end of childbearing and of the menstrual cycle generally seems to be welcomed—despite the fact that it is childbearing that gives a woman in this culture her major source of positive gender identity. Perhaps, however, this should not be too surprising: aside from the strictly practical considerations involved, it is clear from the preceding discussion that it is the social status of motherhood, rather than biological fertility itself (with its vaguely threatening and ritually contaminating sexual associations) that is culturally valued and socially rewarded. A middle-aged woman who has successfully achieved this status by bearing one or more still-living children need not regret reaching the point when she can bear no more—particularly when by doing so she is able to overcome the disadvantage that her active sexuality presented during her years as a young mother. Only after menopause, in the context of these South Asian cultural conceptions of female sexuality, would a woman be able to attain the ideal and idealized image of a pure (because sexless), wholly beneficent, and trusted mother figure.

Restrictions and Constraints

Up to this point the picture I have painted is internally consistent—the postmenopausal woman as clearly asexual, freed from the social constraints made necessary by her lustful sexuality in earlier years. However, there are other elements in the picture that do not fit so well. It has frequently been noted that the widow in this part of the world is subjected to a variety of sumptuary restrictions and ritual disabilities—the former, at least, seem explicitly designed to neutralize her sexuality as part of a process of enforced renunciation. These restrictions are imposed regardless of the age or physiological state of the woman involved: as David puts it, the symbolism of widowhood ignores menopause as a biological event (1980:98). It has rarely been noted in the literature, however, that women in late middle age—regardless of whether their husbands are living—are also subjected to restrictions on dress and physical adornment and upon sexual activity itself that have much in common with those imposed upon women who have lost a mate. Thus even though at one level the woman at this stage of life is said to be asexual, the most prominent constraints on a woman's behavior continue to center on the issue of sexuality.

First, the middle-aged woman, particularly one whose son has married, is subject to negative social sanctions if she dresses in such a way as to heighten her physical attractiveness. While she is expected to dress cleanly and to keep her hair bound and oiled, she should not attempt to adorn her person in any way. In the part of India in which I have done research—Western Uttar Pradesh and the Delhi area—this means wearing only white or light-colored clothing (no deep or bright colors) of inexpensive cotton fabric. Preferably, she should wear hand-me-downs from a daughter-in-law, and her clothing should be worn until it has totally outlived its ability to cover the body. New clothes, even if of the required color and fabric, are only considered suitable for a woman of this age on special ceremonial or holiday occasions. For these she should still avoid silk or synthetic fabrics and should not wear jewelry (except that considered normal, everyday wear) or use makeup. If she wears a sari (rather than the traditional shirt and full skirt formerly worn in this region) her blouse should not be of the tight, stomach-revealing cut preferred by younger women but long and loose, the sleeves wrist-length. To dress otherwise in middle age is to risk ridicule and the suspicion that one is attempting to attract male sexual attentions.

This kind of dress code appears at first glance contradictory in terms of the often-reported observation that postmenopausal women are permitted a casualness of dress and a degree of license in behavior that is proscribed for the young and sexually active. It is not considered immodest if a woman of this age reveals her breasts, even in front of males, and she may be seen with her skirt or sari hiked up to her knees when working—something that a younger woman would carefully avoid. Modesty of dress is not an issue at this age—in a sense, perhaps, because the outward signs of modesty also represent signs of the existence of sexuality. For an older woman to be excessively modest could thus legitimately be interpreted as a kind of sexual gesture or even an invitation. To put this another way, a woman is encouraged to abandon modesty standards to make her reinforce the cultural definition of herself as a nonsexual person, regardless of how she may personally feel. The same applies to the lewd and bawdy talk and gestures that are such a source of amusement to others when they come from an older woman. Especially significant is the fact that they are prescribed in certain ritual and ceremonial contexts—as when the women of the bride's family greet the male wedding party of the groom before the marriage ceremony. On an informal level, this kind of talk may also be heard from middle-aged and older women and is tolerated and even encouraged in a way that it would not be were the speaker still in her reproductive years. It seems to me that to allow a woman to behave in a way that is the very antithesis of the way that genuinely sexual women would behave, and even to reward such behavior by appreciative laughter and attention, is a way of encouraging her to deny the very thought that she might still be a woman in the sexual sense. From such a perspective this license is at least a double-edged sword.

A second kind of constraint that is imposed on both men and women at this time of life takes the form of strong social pressure to cease having sexual relations, even within marriage. The decision to stop being sexually active when a son marries and brings his bride into the household is consistent with the scriptural prescriptions for an ideal life plan. It is typically presented, by men particularly, in terms of spiritual considerations. My female informants usually explained this later-life celibacy as motivated by "shame" (*sharam*): it is embarrassing and even "wrong" for two couples, related as parent and child, to be simultaneously sexually active in the same household. However, those who provided details about the timing and other circumstances of their own decision to refrain from further sexual activity uniformly reported that the husband had taken the initiative—the implication usually was that they had had little choice in the matter.

It is significant that the issue of whether to continue sexual relations after the marriage of a son is not one that is necessarily considered a very private, personal one. There is a strong social expectation that sex should end at this time, regardless of the personal preferences of the pair. Physical arrangements within the home are not conducive to an older couple's continuing to sleep together. They do not normally share a private bedroom, and as soon as grandchildren cease to nurse they begin to sleep with a grandparent as their own parents seek sexual privacy at night. Any attempt on the part of the older couple to have sex would be difficult to arrange without other members of the family becoming aware of it and without it becoming more general public knowledge and a source of disapprobation. Occasionally, of course, a couple fails to conform to this norm, and even more rarely, a woman with grandchildren becomes pregnant herself in middle age. Such an event causes great embarrassment, especially for the woman—the man may still be the object of some admiration for his continuing virility but the woman is only considered "shameless."

It should be pointed out that the control of a young couple's opportunities for being together privately and engaging in sexual relations and other forms of intimacy, which I referred to earlier, is exercised primarily by the groom's mother. The fact that at this time the mother has herself been forced to renounce her active sexual life, by reason of her son's marriage, sheds a new light on this phenomenon and on the family dynamics at this period.

If, as the logic of South Asian ethnomedical theories suggests, the woman after menopause is no longer a sexual person, why should her sexuality continue to be the focus of social and symbolic controls, even while the earlier forms of control over her sexuality have been relaxed? The answer to this question may be sought in further exploration of cultural images of women and their powers, as found in ritual symbolism and myth, as well as in beliefs pertaining to the supernatural. There seems to be a clear and consistent tendency in South Asia to fear the power of women who are not under external control. Babb (1970) has pointed this out in his discussion of the qualities imputed to unmarried, as opposed to married (male-controlled) deities. Harper makes a similar point in connection with beliefs in ghosts and witches, who are typically female, often widowed and old. He reasons that fears of women are projected into the images of these supernatural beings; in turn, he explains the fear itself as arising out of the knowledge that women in ordinary life are kept in a weak and dependent position. And one of the unconscious reasons for so keeping them is the fear that they are in fact powerful beings (1969). This analysis can perhaps help us to understand the persistence of sexually focused restrictions on the middle-aged woman. It does not seem unreasonable to hypothesize that as a woman in later life finds herself working free of male authority, for a variety of reasons related to the dynamics of the family cycle, and as she becomes increasingly powerful and independent, this process should be perceived as unleashing potentially threatening forces and should call up attempts at control. Since the destructive powers of women are so inextricably associated with their sexuality in South Asian cultural conceptions, it is then perhaps not entirely surprising that these new controls should continue to center on sexual issues even though the logic of cultural theories about female sexuality requires that the restrictions placed on the woman when she was younger now be abandoned.

REFERENCES

Allen, Michael
　1982　The Hindu View of Women. *In* Women in India and Nepal. M. Allen and S. N. Mukherjee, eds. pp. 1–20. Australian National University Monographs on South Asia, no. 8. Canberra: Australian National University.
Babb, Lawrence A.
　1970　Marriage and Malevolence: The Uses of Sexual Opposition in a Hindu Pantheon. Ethnology 9:137–48.
Bart, Pauline
　1969　Why Women's Status Changes in Middle Age: The Turns of the Social Ferris Wheel. Sociological Symposium 3:1–18.
Beck, B. E. F.
　1969　Colour and Heat in South Indian Ritual. Man 4:553–72.
Bennett, Lynn
　1983　Dangerous Wives and Sacred Sisters: Social and Symbolic Roles of High-Caste Women in Nepal. New York: Columbia University Press.
Brown, Judith K.
　1982　Cross-cultural Perspectives on Middle-Aged Women. Current Anthropology 23(2):143–56.
Bühler, J. B., trans.
　1886　The Laws of Manu. Oxford: Clarendon Press.
Cantlie, Audrey
　1977　Aspects of Hindu Asceticism. *In* Symbols and Sentiments. I. Lewis, ed. pp. 247–67. London: Academic Press.

Caplan, Pat
    1987   Celibacy as a Solution? Mahatma Gandhi and *Brahmacharya*. *In* The
            Cultural Construction of Sexuality. P. Caplan, ed. pp. 271–95. London:
            Tavistock.
Carstairs, G. Morris
    1967   The Twice-Born. Bloomington: Indiana University Press.
Danielou, Alain
    1964   Hindu Polytheism. London: Routledge and Kegan Paul.
David, Kenneth
    1980   Hidden Powers: Cultural and Socio-economic Accounts of Jaffna Women.
            In The Powers of Tamil Women. Foreign and Comparative Studies/South
            Asian Series, no. 6. S. S. Wadley, ed. pp. 93–136. Syracuse, N.Y.: Maxwell
            School of Citizenship and Public Affairs, Syracuse University.
Davis, Dona L.
    1982   Women's Status and Experience of the Menopause in a Newfoundland
            Fishing Village. Maturitas 4:207–16.
    1983   Blood and Nerves: An Ethnographic Focus on Menopause. Social and
            Economic Studies, no. 28. Institute of Social and Economic Research,
            Memorial University of Newfoundland.
Dhruvarajan, Vaneja
    1989   Hindu Women and the Power of Ideology. Granby, Mass.: Bergin and
            Garvey.
Filliozat, Jean
    1964   The Classical Doctrine of Indian Medicine. Delhi: Munshi Manoharlal.
Flint, Marcha
    1975   The Menopause: Reward or Punishment? Psychosomatics 16:161–63.
Gombrich, Richard
    1971   Food for Seven Grandmothers: Stages in the Universalization of a
            Sinhalese Ritual. Man 6:5–17.
Harper, Edward B.
    1969   Fear and the Status of Women. Southwestern Journal of Anthropology
            25:81–95.
Hart, G. L., III
    1973   Women and the Sacred in Ancient Tamilnad. Journal of Asian Studies
            32:233–50.
Hershman, Paul
    1977   Virgin and Mother. *In* Symbols and Sentiments. I. Lewis, ed. pp.
            261–91. London: Academic Press.
Jacobson, Doranne
    1977   The Women of North and Central India: Goddesses and Wives. *In*
            Women in India: Two Perspectives. D. Jacobson and S. S. Wadley, eds. pp.
            17–111. Columbia, Mo.: South Asia Books.
    1978   The Chaste Wife: Cultural Norm and Individual Experience. *In* American
            Studies in the Anthropology of India. S. Vatuk, ed. pp. 95–138. New Delhi:
            Manohar.

Kakar, Sudhir
   1978   The Inner World. Delhi: Oxford University Press.
Kemper, Steven
   1980   Time, Person, and Gender in Sinhalese Astrology. American Ethnologist 7:744–58.
Kondos, Vivienne
   1986   Images of the Fierce Goddess and Portrayals of Hindu Women. Contributions to Indian Sociology (n.s.) 20:173–97.
Lannoy, Richard
   1971   The Speaking Tree. London: Oxford University Press.
McGilvray, D. B.
   1982   Sexual Power and Fertility in Sri Lanka: Batticaloa Tamils and Moors. *In* Ethnography of Fertility and Birth. C. P. MacCormack, ed. pp. 25–73. London: Academic Press.
Mandelbaum, David
   1970   Society in India. Berkeley: University of California Press.
Masters, William H., and Virginia Johnson
   1966   Human Sexual Response. Boston: Little, Brown.
Neugarten, Bernice, et al.
   1963   Women's Attitudes towards the Menopause. Vita Humana 6:140–51.
Obeyesekere, Gananath
   1976   The Impact of Āyurvedic Ideas on the Culture and the Individual in Sri Lanka. *In* Asian Medical Systems: A Comparative Study. C. Leslie, ed. pp. 201–26. Berkeley: University of California Press.
   1981   Mother Goddess and Social Structure. *In* Cult of the Goddess Pattini. G. Obeyeskere, ed. pp. 425–50. Chicago: University of Chicago Press.
O'Flaherty, Wendy Doniger
   1973   Asceticism and Eroticism in the Mythology of Śiva. London: Oxford University Press.
Peristiany, Jean G., ed.
   1965   Honour and Shame: The Values of Mediterranean Society. Chicago: University of Chicago Press.
Roy, Manisha
   1975   Bengali Women. Chicago: University of Chicago Press.
Schneider, Jane
   1971   Of Vigilance and Virgins: Honor, Shame, and Access to Resources in Mediterranean Societies. Ethnology 10:1–24.
Skultans, Vieda
   1970   The Symbolic Significance of Menstruation and the Menopause. Man 5:639–51.
Tapper, Bruce E.
   1983   Widows and Goddesses: Female Roles in Deity Symbolism in a South Indian Village. Contributions to Indian Sociology (n.s.) 13:1–32.

Vatuk, Sylvia
    1975   The Aging Woman in India: Self-perceptions and Changing Roles. *In* Women in Contemporary India. A. deSouza, ed. pp. 142–63. New Delhi: Manohar.
    1987   Authority, Power and Autonomy in the Life Cycle of the North Indian Women. *In* Dimensions of Social Life: Essays in Honor of David G. Mandelbaum. P. Hockings, ed. pp. 23–44. Berlin: Mouton de Gruyter.
Vatuk, V., and Sylvia Vatuk
    1975   The Lustful Stepmother in the Folklore of Northwestern India. Journal of South Asian Literature 11:19–43.

Douglas Raybeck

12 A Diminished Dichotomy: Kelantan Malay and Traditional Chinese Perspectives

Douglas Raybeck

There is a marked disparity between the status of Malay women in West Malaysia and the status of women in traditional Chinese society. A number of anthropologists describe the situation of women in Malay society as one of relative equality (Raybeck 1981; Strange 1981; Winzeler 1974), where women can control important economic resources, participate in important domestic decisions, and influence public political behavior. In contrast, authorities describe the status of women in traditional Chinese society as one of severe inequality, where women "were considered to be minors throughout their lives, subject first of all to the men of the family into which they were born, then on marriage to the men of their husband's family, and finally on widowhood to their sons" (Baker 1979:21–22; cf. also M. Wolf 1972, 1974; Lang 1946; Yang 1945). In Kelantan, Malaysia, it is recognized that a woman is in several respects the social equal of a man and fully capable of conducting her own affairs, while in traditional China, Confucius asserted that "women indeed are human beings, but they are of a lower state than men and can never attain to full equality with them" (Burton 1911:18–19). Thus, Confucius also stated, it was "a law of nature that woman should be kept under the control of man and not allowed a will of her own" (Burton 1911:29). I believe I can shortly demonstrate that the dichotomy between the status of women in traditional China and among Kelantan Malays diminishes considerably as women enter middle age, and I wish to examine the causes for this diminished dichotomy.

Brown argues that across cultures women entering middle age generally encounter positive changes in their circumstances. These changes often include fewer restrictions on behavior, greater authority over kin, and better opportunities for achievement and recognition (Brown 1982:143–45). She cites a number of alterations in the circumstances of middle-aged women that help to account for these improvements. These changes include the end of fertility, continued personality development, a lessening of narrowly defined feminine parenting behavior, and a woman's increasingly influential relationship with her adult children (Brown 1982:146–48). I will refer to these factors in this chapter and will attempt to evaluate their utility for explaining the positions of middle-aged women in Kelantan Malay society and in traditional China. In both societies, middle age is most appropriately defined less by the physical condition of men or women than by the condition of their children. People of middle age are those who are still socially active and who have adult children, often married, who are themselves active participants in the social life of the community. Throughout this effort, it will be useful to distinguish between the jural status of women and their usual social situations, for the accepted social circumstances of women do not wholly reflect cultural ideals (cf. Baker 1979; Raybeck 1981).

The following description of Malay women refers principally to the state of Kelantan where I conducted eighteen months of fieldwork. Kelantan is similar to another east coast state, Trengganu, studied by Strange (1981), who has provided a useful description of the position of Malay women, which I will employ to complement some of my own observations.

While Kelantan differs considerably from the more developed states of the peninsula, where wage labor and increased urbanization have altered many of the circumstances described below, there remain some rural west coast villages, such as Jendram Hilir, described by Wilson (1967), that can provide still more supplementary material on the position of Malay women.

The description of traditional Chinese society refers to circumstances before 1911; however, considerable ethnographic information is drawn from recent studies conducted in Taiwan. There is ample precedence for viewing elements of Taiwanese society, particularly those concerned with family structure, as very similar to such elements in traditional China (Cohen 1976; Freedman 1979; M. Wolf 1972, 1974). Further, a concern with the situation of women in traditional Chinese society has considerable relevance for their current position in the People's Republic. There are clear indications that older customs still influence the position of Chinese women and hinder their full participation in the communist state (Baker 1979:200ff; Parish 1975:615; Parish and Whyte 1978:215; M. Wolf 1985).

Kelantan Malay Women

The state of Kelantan on the east coast of the Malay Peninsula is noted as a stronghold of traditional Malay customs and cultural practices that are disappearing from the more developed states on the peninsula. Ethnic Malays constitute approximately 92 percent of the state's population, and the great majority of them reside in rural nucleated villages, where they practice wet rice agriculture. Their social structure is bilateral and results in the formation of relatively stable kindreds, which provide important material and emotional support for members. Most social life occurs within the confines of the rural village and is strongly influenced by cultural values that emphasize the importance of individual dignity and interpersonal harmony (Raybeck 1975). Virtually all Malays are Sufi Moslems and view themselves as sincere participants in the religious system.

The general position of women in Kelantan society is defined by a combination of traditional custom (*adat*) and the rules of Islam. Elsewhere (Raybeck 1981), I have described the manner in which Kelantanese villagers resolve conflicts between these two codes. Briefly, the indigenous perspective on women and their rights is one of rough equality with men. A woman is entitled to full economic participation, equal inheritance rights, and participation in major domestic decisions, as well as an active and influential social life. In contrast, the laws of Islam require a wife's deference to her husband, limit her rights in such important social matters as divorce, and entitle her to an inheritance half the size of her brothers'. Nonetheless, the social circumstances of women remain close to the indigenous perspective, for the Kelantanese have adopted behavioral strategies that largely uphold the letter of Islamic law while maintaining traditional village social organization and the important role of women in that organization (Raybeck 1981:15–17).

The status of young Kelantanese men is somewhat superior to that of young women. However, women's status increases more dramatically with age than does men's and reaches its zenith in middle age, when it achieves rough equality with that of men. Thus, it is instructive to examine the positions of women at various stages in their life cycle.

The Kelantanese highly value children and refer to them as "the gift of God" (*hadiah Tuhan*). Families are equally pleased by the birth of a girl or boy, and parents sometimes express a preference that the firstborn be a girl, who can be of greater assistance in the household and who, when older, may be of greater assistance than a male in the parents' old age (Djamour 1959; Firth 1966). Young boys and girls are initially treated in a similar fashion, but by the age of six or so, girls start to assume domestic duties and are encouraged to remain close to home while boys of this age have no responsibilities and are somewhat freer in their movements.

As girls approach puberty, their freedom of movement is further restricted, and the importance of their chastity and of modest behavior is impressed upon them. During this period, they are taught that they should exhibit deference to males, including their future husbands, yet they often observe that the behavior of their mothers does not conform to this admonition. A girl's first marriage is usually arranged by her parents, but she may often influence the choice of her spouse, and she is almost always able to veto the match if she disapproves. She may disapprove if she dislikes the proposed groom or because of the proposed postmarital residence. While marriage residence is technically ambilocal, women prefer to be close to their natal family, and most couples establish residence near the bride's parents (Raybeck 1975; Strange 1981:127).

A young bride will generally receive from her parents her brideprice (*mas Kahwin*) and often an additional sum, which she will bring to her marriage along with whatever property she may have inherited. Throughout her marriage she retains her right to the property she brought with her, and should she become divorced, she is entitled to her original property and half of everything she and her husband acquired during the marriage. A young wife still has some constraints on her freedom of movement, but she usually takes an early lead in managing the family finances and in selling goods at the local market (Firth 1966; Strange 1981). Thus, while a young wife is ideally expected to be obedient to her husband and to defer to him, her active economic role encourages both her independence and assertiveness in domestic decisions. As Strange has noted, "Both women and men talk about a wife's obedience more than they expect or practice it in the family milieu" (1981:135). As a wife grows older, her participation in village affairs increases and the restrictions on her movements and activities continue to decrease.

As a married woman approaches middle age, she usually becomes a more active participant than her husband in several aspects of village life, particularly in the sphere of economics (Firth 1966; Raybeck 1975; Strange 1981; Wilson 1967). It is she who manages the household finances and monitors the family budget. She also works in the rice fields at times of planting and harvesting, and she may maintain her own garden, in which she often raises cash crops for sale in the village market. She may also sell handicrafts that she and her husband have made, as well as other items such as snacks and shellfish. Such economic activity on the part of women is not confined to Kelantan; rather it is common throughout Southeast Asia (Boserup 1970; Strange 1981; Winzeler 1974). However, in Kelantan women dominate the marketing and tend to control the distribution of many forms of produce (Firth 1966:116; Strange 1981:198).

A woman's economic activities require her frequent participation in the village market, where she encounters other women sellers, who provide her with information on such socially relevant matters as prices, local politics, and the availability of marriageable girls and boys. A woman's access to such extradomestic information provides her with a lever with which she can widen her social participation. A wife is often more aware of the intricacies of village affairs than is her husband, and she takes an active role in major domestic decisions involving such concerns as the marriage of children, the purchase of land, and even political matters (Raybeck 1981:16; also cf. Firth 1966:26ff.; Wilson 1967:105). Further, a wife may rely on members of her kindred for emotional support and for assistance in caring for her children.

A middle-aged woman is not expected to be as modest as a younger woman and is free to travel beyond the village for economic and other purposes. Social visits to relatives in other states may last for several weeks while travel for business purposes seldom takes more than a day. Many Kelantanese women engage in trading operations that require travel throughout the state and often across the neighboring border with Thailand. Middle-aged women are also among the most active small-scale smugglers engaged in moving long-grained rice from Thailand to Kelantan (Raybeck 1986). Such women are also free to pursue other business concerns from which a younger woman would be barred. The most popular coffee shop (*kedai kopi*) in the village was owned and run by a middle-aged woman, although Islamic-influenced village morality holds that it is generally improper for women to frequent coffee shops.

Both older and younger wives may sometimes gain greater freedom through divorce. Divorce is extremely common in Kelantan, and while the rules of Islam make it difficult for a woman to obtain a divorce, there are social mechanisms a wife can employ that will force her husband to divorce her (Raybeck 1981:16–17). A divorced woman is free of both parental restrictions and those of her former husband. She may arrange her own remarriage, and she often establishes a specific contract that assures her of rights she would not enjoy in a standard marriage. Although divorce often frees a woman to take a more active role in village life, younger women usually soon remarry because a divorced status also carries an undesirable connotation of sexual license and impropriety. Older women, however, may choose to remain single, especially if they have property, kindred support, and adult offspring (cf. Strange 1981: 232–33). Firth has noted that the single status of older women "illustrates their assertion of their own independence, rather than the casting of them off by the rest of the community" (1966:11).

Despite the highly visible participation of middle-aged women in economic activities, their roles in the religious and political spheres are more circumscribed. Women can arrange for Islamic feasts and other religious events, but they may not publicly participate in them. Similarly, at the village level it is not considered appropriate for a woman to hold office or to be publicly active in politics. However, many middle-aged women display an interest in public politics and a pronounced ability to affect such politics (Raybeck 1981:16).

A Kelantanese woman experiences a gradual increase in status and in social participation from the time of her initial marriage through middle age. There does not appear to be a marked discontinuity between youth and middle age. Indeed, as Strange has noted, there is "no view of 'middle-age' as a discrete segment of the life cycle" (1981:76). The relatively high status accorded Kelantanese women in general and middle-aged women in particular seems best explained by their active economic role in village society (Firth 1966:32ff.; Strange 1981:198–99). However, it also seems likely that as a woman assumes greater economic responsibilities and experiences the demands of attendant increasing participation in domestic decision making and village social life, the female personality would become stronger and more assertive, as Brown suggests (1982:147). Certainly, the most assertive women I encountered in Kelantan were middle-aged or older and differed markedly from younger women in this respect. As women age, there also appears to be a lessening of narrowly defined feminine parenting behavior, as Gutmann would predict (see this volume).

Although the circumstances accounting for the relatively high status of middle-aged women in Kelantan support much of Brown's model, their status does not seem to be particularly dependent on the relationship they have with their adult children.

Traditional Chinese Women

Traditional Chinese society was consistently patricentric. Descent was patrilineal, residence patrilocal, and authority patriarchal. Although China had a complex literate society for thousands of years, most Chinese were illiterate peasants residing in rural villages and engaged in the raising of wheat in the north and wet rice in the south. Their patrilineal rule of descent formed corporate lineages that often owned land and were among the most influential elements in Chinese social life. While the Chinese could and did participate in a variety of religious traditions, ranging from animism and Taoism to Buddhism, the dominant values of traditional China focused on the family and wider lineage. These values were clearly reflected in Confucianism, which exalted the importance of the family and described appropriate behaviors for each family member. The belief in and practice of ancestor worship continually emphasized both the importance of maintaining a family line and the importance of males for this purpose.

The general position of women in traditional Chinese society, as defined by kinship rules, Confucian ideology, and the legal code, was quite low (Baker 1979; Freedman 1979:245; Lang 1946; Levy 1963:149ff.; M. Wolf 1974; Yang 1945). A woman was jurally a minor throughout her life, and although she had a right to her dowry, she had no inheritance rights to land (Freedman 1979:258; van der Sprenkel 1977:17), nor did she have much opportunity to participate in economics (Boserup 1970:89; Lang 1946). She was expected to defer to her husband in all domestic matters, and she was not expected to play any active role in the social life of the village or of the wider society. However, Arthur Wolf (1975) and other authorities (Freedman 1979; M. Wolf 1972) have argued that the circumstances of women in China were quite varied, and Margery Wolf (1972) has noted that women's situations changed markedly as they passed through various stages of their life cycle. Thus, as for Kelantanese women, it is appropriate to examine the manner in which the circumstances of traditional Chinese women change as they age.

Unlike the Kelantanese, traditional Chinese express a strong preference for male children. Sons are necessary to perpetuate the family line, to provide for the parents' old age, to worship their spirits after death, and to carry on the economic fortunes of the family. Daughters, in contrast, are seen as mouths to be fed that will contribute little to the future of the family and will leave it upon marriage. Both male and female children are usually loved and treated tenderly (Levy 1963:68; Lang 1946:238), but a family lacking boys or with too many children may actively resent the birth of a girl and give her a derogatory name as a sign of their displeasure (Yang 1945:125). Not surprisingly, boys were generally better nourished and better cared for than girls. Indeed, Ho finds evidence for extensive female infanticide in traditional China among both poor and wealthy families (Ho 1959:58ff.). Among poor families concerned with subsistence, a newborn girl might be drowned, sold to another family, or when older, sold into prostitution (Levy 1963:69). Wealthy families appear to have practiced female infanticide to avoid the expense of future dowries (Ho 1959:60).

During childhood, young girls are often disciplined with greater severity and frequency than are their brothers (Levy 1963:71; M. Wolf 1972:53–79). They are expected to assume domestic responsibilities by the age of five or six and soon learn to defer to all males of the family, even younger ones (cf. M. Wolf 1972:66). As a young girl approaches puberty, she is kept under constant observation and her freedom of movement is severely restricted. Her marriage is arranged by her parents, who usually attempt to further their interests by making a connection with a desirable family. Unlike her Kelantanese counterpart, the young Chinese woman does not have the option of vetoing the proposed marriage.

As a young bride enters her husband's family, her status in Chinese society is at its nadir: "her marriage cut her off economically and as a legal person from her own family and transferred the rights in and over her to the family receiving her" (Freedman 1979:245). Not only is a young bride required to defer to her husband and his father, but she is also under the constant supervision of her mother-in-law, who often treats her with great harshness. During the first year of marriage a bride's position is very insecure. She can be divorced for barrenness, neglect of her parents-in-law, or simply garrulousness (Baker 1979:45). At the same time, she has no right to initiate divorce, and if she abandons her husband or repudiates him, she can be legally put to death (Baker 1979: 46; van der Sprenkel 1977:144).

The major means by which a young bride may improve her circumstances is to bear a son. Her mother-in-law will be less inclined to beat her severely since the welfare of the child is tied to his mother's health. The production of a male heir also assures the continuity of the husband's family and may gradually provide the wife with some leverage in domestic matters. Frequently, her increasing influence exacerbates family tensions, for she will be more interested in the welfare of her husband and children than she will be in concerns of the wider family (Freedman 1979:246; M. Wolf 1972). The resulting friction is widely viewed as one of the principal causes of family fissioning, an event that the senior generation will attempt to postpone as long as possible.

A wife can gradually improve her situation largely by playing upon the affection of the children, particularly her sons. Margery Wolf, in a sensitive and insightful book, has described the manner in which mothers manipulate the emotions of their children so that the father is often seen as a rather remote and sometimes punitive authority figure while she is perceived as the confidante and protector (1972:158–70). During this period, as their children are maturing, many women are able to expand their influence on their husband and his family, even though the jural status of wives remains low (Baker 1979:47; Cohen 1976:91–92; Parish and Whyte 1978; M. Wolf 1972).

As wives enter their thirties, several elements contribute to an improvement in their circumstances in addition to their influence on their children. They begin to receive some status from the ideal kinship rules, which define the hierarchy of family relationships through generation, age, and sex, in that order (Baker 1979:16). This advantage could be somewhat muted since the strong emphasis on male superiority sometimes allows sex to override the significance of age, but the principle of generation is never challenged (Baker 1979:16–17). Although Chinese wives do not take a significant part in economic activities as Kelantanese women do, they increasingly assume responsibility for household management, particularly when their mothers-in-law become infirm or if the wife's nuclear family establishes a separate residence (Cohen 1976:60–61, 91–92). Also, while the male head of the family is supposed to be in charge of ancestor worship, the daily domestic ancestor worship is usually managed by a woman, who may manipulate the family's perception of ancestral behavior for her own ends (Freedman 1979:283, 308).

When a middle-aged woman in traditional China becomes a mother-in-law, her status undergoes a marked improvement. She not only continues to influence the behavior and attitudes of her sons but also controls her daughters-in-law. Further, her influence over her sons becomes more important as they take on more responsibility for the economic and social welfare of the family. As the family head grows older, he continues to receive respect from his sons, but his authority tends to wane as theirs waxes (Baker 1979:38). Margery Wolf has noted that "although young women may have little or no influence over their husbands . . . , older women who have raised their sons properly retain considerable influence over their sons' actions, even in activities exclusive to men. Further, older women who have displayed years of good judgment are regularly consulted by their husbands about major as well as minor economic and social projects" (1972:40). Indeed, as a mother and father age, it is not uncommon for the woman to become the de facto head of the household (Baker 1979:47; Freedman 1966:66–67; Parish and Whyte 1978; M. Wolf 1974:159; Yang 1945:56–57).

A middle-aged woman is capable of playing an active and important role in the social life of traditional China even though her jural status has not appreciably improved. In addition to the greater amount of participation they have in domestic decision making, older women increase the amount of time they spend in extradomestic activities (M. Wolf 1972:38). They may serve as go-betweens, arranging local marriages, and they often become more involved in local religious activities (M. Wolf 1972:224–25). There are even reports that women have exerted significant influence on lineage affairs (Yang 1945:188) and on the social life of their village. Margery Wolf makes it clear that middle-aged women may influence others through their sons and through their own force of character. Assertive middle-aged women can develop a reputation for being quite outspoken and can "terrorize the men of their households and their neighbors with their fierce tongues and indomitable wills" (1974:157). The concern about such sharp-tongued women was sufficiently common that a book of precepts for local administrators included the admonition not to summon women to court without good reason. This precept was sustained partly by the desire to protect the good name of refined women and partly so that "women who might otherwise become fierce and violent are kept within the bounds of decency and prevented from becoming troublesome, and showing fits of temper" (van der Sprenkel 1977:146).

The authority of a middle-aged woman tends to reach its zenith with the death of her husband. Although widows are supposed to defer to their adult sons, such women often act as the household heads, expecting and receiving the obedience of their offspring (Freedman 1966:66–67, 1979:259; M. Wolf 1972). Many women find themselves widowed in early middle age, often because their husbands were considerably older or because men are exposed to more hazards than are women. Significantly, many widows in Taiwan are reluctant to remarry since this would mean giving up their children and their claim to a share in their deceased husband's estate (M. Wolf 1972). Instead, they can enjoy greater independence and social leverage by remaining single and having virtually unchallenged influence over their children. Arthur Wolf found that during a fifty-year period in a Taiwanese community the great majority of widows over thirty did not remarry despite opportunities created by a shortage of women (1975:107–8).

Although a woman in traditional China experienced a gradual increase in status and in social participation following the birth of her first son and continuing through middle age, her experiences of the role of mother-in-law, and later widow, usually marked significant and relatively abrupt improvement in her social position. The circumstances accounting for her improved status conform closely to Brown's model, for a woman's social success depends heavily on her ability to influence her adult children, particularly her sons. Further, as Brown would anticipate, a middle-aged woman who has successfully dealt with the structural and interpersonal problems presented by traditional Chinese society may often develop a stronger and more resourceful personality. Margery Wolf has noted that "the contrast between the terrified young bride and the loud, confident, and often lewd old woman who has outlived her mother-in-law and her husband reflects the tests met and passed by not strictly following the rules and by making purposeful use of those who must" (1972:41). As in the Kelantanese situation, there also appears to be a lessening of narrowly defined feminine parenting behavior, as Brown and Gutmann would expect.

A Diminished Dichotomy

If we compare the social positions of women in Kelantan and in traditional Chinese society, significant differences are manifest right from birth. While the Kelantanese are equally pleased by the birth of a child of either sex and accord them equal treatment, the Chinese express a strong preference for male children, and they raise boys with greater care than girls. The difference in the positions of women in Kelantan and women in traditional China is most apparent in early marriage. A young Kelantanese wife begins her marriage with a good social position based on a variety of rights to economic participation and on the support of her family and kindred, while a young bride in China was both jurally and situationally helpless. Traditionally, she seldom controlled significant resources and was under the complete domination of her husband and his family. As I have indicated above, this dichotomy diminishes as women enter middle age in both societies, owing mainly to a dramatic improvement in the status of middle-aged women in traditional China. However, different factors seem to account best for the improved situations of women in Kelantan and in China, and this calls for another look at Brown's arguments.

Brown suggests that compared to a younger female, a middle-aged woman encounters fewer restrictions and more opportunities for social influence because of the end of fertility, personality changes, a lessening of the demand for stereotyped female parenting behavior, and, particularly, her relationship to her adult children. These reasons fit the Chinese situation very nicely, and the single most significant factor in the improvement of a middle-aged woman's status is clearly her ability to influence her adult sons (Baker 1979; M. Wolf 1972, 1974). Elements of Brown's model are also relevant to the improved circumstances of middle-aged women in Kelantan, but here the factor that best accounts for their better status is the women's increased economic participation (Firth 1966; Raybeck 1981; Strange 1981).

It is apparent that middle-aged women may encounter the improved circumstances suggested by Brown for different reasons. Yet these differing specific reasons do not lessen the utility of Brown's model since she acknowledges that the combinations of factors affecting middle-aged women may differ across societies. Furthermore, although the primary reasons for the improved status of middle-aged women in Kelantan and in China differ, they also display an important underlying similarity. Friedl (1975), Sacks (1974), and Sanday (1974) have each argued that women's status in general is heavily dependent on their abilities to control valued resources, particularly in the public sphere. It seems likely that in societies such as traditional China, where women are barred from public economic pursuits and where adult children constitute a particularly valuable resource for the family and wider kinship group, a mother's ability to control her adult children may contribute substantially to her status. Conversely, in societies like Kelantan, where women can control more classically economic resources, the significance attributed to the mother-adult child tie may well be less. In such a society, a woman can act directly to promote her own interests rather than be constrained to operate indirectly through her children.

Although most of this chapter has dealt with the advantages that can accrue to women in middle age, I wish to end on a cautionary note. If middle age tends to lessen the restrictions on women and to provide them with greater opportunities for achievement and recognition, it can also have less pleasant consequences. Middle age can also provide women with a capacity to threaten the ideal system and with the possibility of encountering a greater degree of failure.

Across cultures a middle-aged woman's threats to the ideal cultural system can result in accusations of witchcraft, the evil eye, etc. Ahern notes that the Chinese conceptual system holds women to be ritually unclean and dangerously powerful. A middle-aged woman was seen as losing her reproductive power to do great good while retaining her power to threaten male ideals through pollution because of her enduring association with birth and with other marginal and transitional phenomena (1975). Even among Malays, where women's status is comparatively high, a postmenopausal woman may be referred to as "useless" (Strange 1981:76).

Middle-aged women who experience difficulty in realizing the satisfaction and achievements that are possible for them may become quite despondent. In Kelantan, middle-aged women who were widowed, lacking in financial security, and separated from their children frequently fell ill with a psycho-somatic complaint that required the performance of an indigenous curing ceremony (Kessler 1977; Raybeck 1974:240) Indeed, there is recent evidence that the reduced ability of middle-aged women to retain calcium makes them increasingly susceptible to external stressors that may trigger behaviors associated with spirit possession and aberrancy (Raybeck 1989).

In China a middle-aged woman's difficulties could have even more serious consequences. Margery Wolf notes that in China women's suicide rate equals that of men (1975) and that women's suicide tends to occur at two crisis periods: first, when a woman is newly married and helpless; and second, in middle age when the appearance of a new bride provides a challenge for the son's affection, making it more problematic for the mother to control him (1972:163).

Epilogue: Voices Will Rise

A recent return to Kelantan, Malaysia, in spring and summer of 1989 provided information concerning the current status of middle-aged women as they increasingly encounter pressures that are transforming Kelantanese society. Although such pressures emanate from many sources, I wish to discuss briefly only three elements of modernization that have had a perceptible influence on the situation of middle-aged women: increasing exposure to media, especially Western-influenced television; a resurgent Islamic fundamentalism that emphasizes restrictions on women's activities; and an increase in wage labor opportunities. Interestingly, the last and most important of these elements seems to have an either/or effect on middle-aged women's status, leading to a reduction in some circumstances, enhancing it in other situations, but seldom leaving it unchanged.

Many village homes now possess color television sets that provide a window into a nontraditional and rather Western world. Although the government controls two of the three Malaysian stations, there are numerous Western movies and television shows that glamorize younger people and tend to shift attention from older to younger role models. Nonetheless, some of the most popular shows feature middle-aged women, such as "Murder, She Wrote." These are watched by both young and old, men and women, and tend to reaffirm existing positive attitudes toward middle-aged women and their importance.

The influence of expanding Islamic fundamentalism on the status and comparative freedom of middle-aged women seems predominantly inhibitory. There is an increased emphasis on the polite public behavior of wives toward their husbands and there are also pressures to increase wifely subservience in the home. Further, the principal advocates and adherents of the Islamic fundamentalist movement, *dakwah,* are the young, and this has succeeded in promoting friction between the generations and has undermined some of the support to which middle-aged women are generally entitled.

In recent years, there have been significant material improvements in the lives of Kelantanese peasants and these are well valued. Wage labor has become both more possible and more desirable. For some middle-aged women this has resulted in significant problems, as increasing geographic mobility tends to undermine kindred solidarity and support. An emphasis on wage labor also means that young people are increasingly willing to leave home to seek employment in urban areas, depriving their mothers of their company and of the opportunity to interact with grandchildren. For those young families who remain near their parents, the status of middle-aged women is not greatly diminished, as they supply a valued service, child care, but the basis of their status seems less certain than when it rests upon economic productivity.

I confess that I had anticipated that the effects of modernization on the status of middle-aged women would be primarily, if not uniformly, negative.

What I found is that a significant number of such women have availed themselves of opportunities for employment and remain at least as active as men, if not more so.

In addition to finding wage labor positions, many middle-aged women have established their own small businesses, and banks seem quite willing to help underwrite such enterprises. One male Kelantanese bank officer observed that older women are better at economic matters than their husbands and that they are generally more industrious. One excellent example is a woman in her forties who, with a government loan, began a small batik-producing shop ten years ago that is now Kelantan's leading batik-producing center and renowned throughout Malaysia. She is critical of Islamic fundamentalism and believes that it endangers women's status and freedom, which she asserts benefits women, men, and society in general.

The tenacity of middle-aged women's social status is recognized by both women and men throughout Kelantan. One well-educated man who has studied for six years in the United States and is the brother of a highly successful middle-aged woman observed, "Women here are more independent and self-reliant, especially the older ones. They are used to making their own living." He then went on to connect their economic activities to their greater social freedom and assertive natures.

Perhaps a better example of the contemporary attitude of middle-aged women toward their own circumstances can be drawn not from the striking economic successes but from those who undertake structured wage labor. Two middle-aged women who work as chambermaids in a hotel in Kelantan's state capital expressed their sensitivity to Islamic pressures on their behavior and the possibility it might limit their freedom. They acknowledged that they should be respectful to their husbands and do things for them around the house but they also noted that this ethic only works when the efforts are mutual. In support of this, both noted that their husbands work too but that they also share in child care and in household duties. One woman commenting on older married couples noted, "A husband who continually tries to boss around his wife will be resented, argued with, and resisted. A wife should be respectful to her husband and speak to him in a polite (*halus*) fashion, but she also expects that her words will be heard and heeded. If this does not happen, voices will rise."

REFERENCES

Ahern, Emily
  1975   The Power and Pollution of Chinese Women. *In* Women in Chinese Society. M. Wolf and R. Witke, eds. pp. 193–214. Stanford, Calif.: Stanford University Press.
Baker, Hugh D. R.
  1979   Chinese Family and Kinship. New York: Columbia University Press.
Boserup, Ester
  1970   Woman's Role in Economic Development. New York: St. Martin's Press.
Brown, Judith K.
  1982   Cross-cultural Perspectives on Middle-Aged Women. Current Anthropology 23(2):143–56.
Burton, Margaret E.
  1911   The Education of Women in China. New York: Revell.
Cohen, Myron L.
  1976   House United, House Divided: The Chinese Family in Taiwan. New York: Columbia University Press.
Djamour, Judith
  1959   Malay Kinship and Marriage in Singapore. New York: Humanities Press.
Firth, Rosemary
  1966   Housekeeping among Malay Peasants. 2d ed. New York: Humanities Press.
Freedman, Maurice
  1966   Chinese Lineage and Society: Fukien and Kwantung. New York: Humanities Press.
  1979   The Study of Chinese Society. Stanford, Calif.: Stanford University Press.
Friedl, Ernestine
  1975   Women and Men: An Anthropologist's View. New York: Holt, Rinehart, and Winston.
Ho Ping-ti
  1959   Studies on the Population of China, 1368–1953. Cambridge, Mass.: Harvard University Press.
Kessler, Clive
  1977   Conflict and Sovereignty in Kelantanese Malay Spirit Seances. *In* Case Studies in Spirit Possession. V. Crapanzano and V. Garrison, eds. pp. 295–331. New York: John Wiley and Sons.
Lang, Olga
  1946   Chinese Family and Society. New Haven, Conn.: Yale University Press.
Levy, Marion J., Jr.
  1963   The Family Revolution in Modern China. New York: Octagon Books.
Parish, William L.
  1975   Socialism and the Chinese Peasant Family. Journal of Asian Studies 34:613–30.

Parish, William, and Martin King Whyte
 1978   Village and Family in Contemporary China. Chicago: University of
        Chicago Press.
Pruitt, Ida
 1945   A Daughter of Han. Stanford, Calif.: Stanford University Press.
Raybeck, Douglas
 1974   Social Stress and Social Structure in Kelantan Village Life. *In* Kelantan:
        Religion, Politics and Society in a Malay State. W. Roff, ed., pp. 225–42.
        Kuala Lumpur: Oxford University Press.
 1975   The Semantic Differential and Kelantanese Malay Values: A Method-
        ological Innovation in the Study of Social and Cultural Values. Ph.D. diss.,
        Cornell University.
 1981   The Ideal and the Real: The Status of Women in Kelantan Malay
        Society. Women and Politics 1:7–21.
 1986   The Elastic Rule: Conformity and Deviance in Kelantan Village Life. *In*
        Cultural Identity in Northern Peninsular Malaysia. Sharon Carstens, ed.
        pp. 55–74. Athens: Ohio University Press.
 1989   Women, Stress, and Participation in Possession Cults: A Reexamina-
        tion of the Calcium Deficiency Hypothesis. Medical Anthropology Quar-
        terly 3:139–61.
Sacks, Karen
 1974   Engels Revisited: Women, the Organization of Production, and Private
        Property. *In* Woman, Culture and Society. M. Z. Rosaldo and L. Lamphere,
        eds. pp. 207–22. Stanford, Calif.: Stanford University Press.
Sanday, Peggy
 1974   Female Status in the Public Domain. *In* Woman, Culture and Society.
        M. Z. Rosaldo and L. Lamphere, eds. pp. 189–206. Stanford, Calif.: Stanford
        University Press.
Strange, Heather
 1981   Rural Malay Women in Tradition and Transition. New York: Praeger.
van der Sprenkel, S.
 1977   Legal Institutions in Manchu China. New York: Humanities Press.
Wilson, Peter J.
 1967   A Malay Village and Malaysia. New Haven, Conn.: HRAF Press.
Winzeler, Robert
 1974   Sex Role Equality, Wet Rice Cultivation, and the State in Southeast
        Asia. American Anthropologist 76:563–67.
Wolf, Arthur
 1975   The Women of Hai-shan: A Demographic Portrait. *In* Women in
        Chinese Society. M. Wolf and R. Witke, eds. pp. 89–110. Stanford, Calif.:
        Stanford University Press.
Wolf, Margery
 1972   Women and the Family in Rural Taiwan. Stanford, Calif.: Stanford
        University Press.
 1974   Chinese Women: Old Skills in a New Context. *In* Woman, Culture and

Society. M. Z. Rosaldo and L. Lamphere, eds. pp. 157–72. Stanford, Calif.: Stanford University Press.

1975　Women and Suicide in China. *In* Women in Chinese Society. M. Wolf and R. Witke, eds. pp. 111–41. Stanford, Calif.: Stanford University Press.

1985　Revolution Postponed: Women in Contemporary China. Stanford, Calif.: Stanford University Press.

Yang, Martin C.

1945　A Chinese Village. New York: Columbia University Press.

PART 4

Industrialized Societies

Middle-aged women in industrialized societies form a remarkably heterogeneous category. Differences in class, ethnicity, level of education, employment status and occupation, family structure, and personal circumstance help to create the "diverse realities" of their lives. Various "experts" in industrialized societies—such specialists as medical doctors, anthropologists, psychologists, and other social scientists—define, study, and interpret middle age. They do so with varying degrees of sensitivity to the differences among women in this stage of life.

In their comparative study, Patricia A. Kaufert and Margaret Lock draw on survey data they collected from several thousand women between the ages of forty-five and fifty-five in Japan and Canada. Despite obvious diversity, to many Japanese and Canadian physicians these women comprise a homogeneous category, "the menopausal woman." Kaufert and Lock suggest that the medical model of menopause represents an attempt to answer a question: What is to be done with women as they age?

Nancy Datan, Aaron Antonovsky, and Benjamin Maoz present empirical evidence of variation among middle-aged Israeli women. For example, their survey data reveal significant ethnic differences in the perceived consequences (emotional, social, and physical) of menopause. In addition, they identify one major area of agreement: all of the women in the survey welcomed the loss of fertility. Datan and her colleagues suggest that this attitude is a matter of developmental change in adulthood, the subject of David Gutmann's concluding chapter.

Ruth Ellenson

13 Tradition, Modernity, and Transitions in Five Israeli Subcultures

Nancy Datan
Aaron Antonovsky
Benjamin Maoz

This study of middle-aged women in five Israeli subcultures reflects the expectation that culture may shape the response to biological change. The study began in Kiryat Shmona, where Benjamin Maoz, on his psychiatric residency, observed that hospitalization for involutional psychosis was seen only among European women and not among women from Near Eastern cultures. Maoz, together with Aaron Antonovsky, a medical sociologist, found in the national health statistics that the observation in Kiryat Shmona was true for the entire Israeli population: that is, that hospitalization for involutional psychosis, while rare, occurred almost exclusively among European women.

Three hypotheses were proposed to explain this observation:

1. Differences in cultural patterns create varying degrees of stress in middle age, and this stress is greatest for the modern, youth-oriented European culture and manifested not only in the extreme response seen in involutional depression, but observable also as nonpathological stress among normal women.

2. Stress may be more or less equal across cultures but manifested as psychiatric complaints among European women and expressed as somatic complaints among Near Eastern women, since there are cultural differences in the permissible forms of expressed stress.

3. Stress may be more or less equal across cultures, but the diagnosis of involutional psychosis is only made among the European women, due to some combination of the doctor's readiness to observe psychiatric symptoms and the woman's ability to communicate psychic distress.

Antonovsky and Maoz proposed a broad-scale study to explore the consequences of cultural differences for stress in middle age. Their view was that greater stress could be anticipated among European women, who had planned and restricted childbearing. They could therefore be said to have "denied" their femininity and to view menopause as the loss of a potential that had not found sufficient fulfillment. Traditional women, on the other hand, could expect to enjoy raised status as they took on a matriarchal role. Support for this view was found in the psychiatric literature.

Nancy Datan brought to the study a perspective from developmental psychology that led to a contradictory view: the European women, who had coped actively throughout their lives, would find menopause and middle age a time of new freedom, while traditional women from Near Eastern cultures, whose only role had been that of childbearer and mother, would find the loss of fertility both salient and stressful. Support for this view was found in the developmental literature.

The Study: Purpose and Methods

The study was designed to address two major issues: (1) what is the relationship between the degree of traditionalism or modernity in a culture and the level of psychological well-being in women during changes of middle age and (2) what is the relationship between the degree of modernity (and the woman's fertility history) and the perception of the loss of fertility. These questions emerge from a comparison of the woman's life cycle in traditional and modern cultures. In traditional cultures, early marriage (at or shortly after menarche) and frequent childbearing throughout the years of fertility are the norms. In modern cultures the converse is seen: marriage—a mark of social maturity—occurs several years after biological maturity, and childbearing is limited to a few children, typically born fairly soon after marriage. It may be said, then, that the family life cycle in traditional cultures corresponds fairly closely to the biological life cycle of the woman; with increased modernity, there is increased independence of the family life cycle and the biological life cycle. The purpose of this chapter is to inquire whether the relative strength of the relationship between the biological life cycle and the family cycle in traditional and modern subcultures is expressed in women's responses to menopause.

The study was carried out in four phases. The first phase was a pilot study during which semistructured psychiatric interviews were conducted by Maoz with 55 women of European and Near Eastern Jewish origin and women of Israeli Muslim Arab origin. On the basis of findings from the pilot study, a closed interview schedule was constructed for the second phase of the study, a broad-scale survey among 1,148 women from five Israeli subcultures ranging along a continuum from modernity: immigrant Jews from Central Europe, Turkey, Persia, and North Africa; and Israeli-born Muslim Arabs. The survey questionnaire dealt with aspects of middle age, including demographic information, psychosexual history, attitudes toward climacterium, menopausal symptomatology, social roles and role satisfaction, and self-reported psychological well-being.

An overview of selected social characteristics of the five ethnic groups (see Table 1) reveals a consistent pattern of differences, from the most traditional group, the Arab women, through the North Africans, Persians, and Turks, to the most modern group, the Central European women. This pattern supports our general notion that the life cycle of the traditional woman more closely approximates the biological life cycle, while the life cycle of the modern woman is relatively more independent of the biological life cycle. Traditional women marry sooner, bear more children, and continue bearing children far longer than do modern women. In addition, traditional women are likely to be religiously orthodox—and both Jewish and Muslim traditions have elaborate taboo systems related to menstruation, pregnancy, and childbirth. Finally, traditional women tend to be illiterate, while literacy is universal among the Central Europeans. In short, it is probably reasonable to say that with successively greater degrees of modernity, the life cycle becomes progressively more independent of biological changes. This general tendency, in turn, leads us to anticipate culturally determined differences in psychological well-being and the response to the loss of fertility.

All women from the second phase of the study were invited to participate in the third phase, a medical examination; of the 1,148 women who agreed to take part in the survey, 697 consented to the medical examination. There was somewhat more readiness to cooperate in the medical examination among women in the more traditional groups, but this difference was not statistically significant. The medical examination included a pregnancy history, a general physical examination, the woman's self-reported assessment of her physical health, and the physician's overall rating of her physical and mental health.

The fourth and final phase of the study consisted of follow-up psychiatric interviews with 160 subjects, subsamples from each of the five ethnic groups in the survey, who represented the high and low extremes with respect to self-reported psychological well-being. Among other findings, considerable agreement was seen between the woman's self-report and the psychiatrist's diagnosis, although the psychiatrists had no prior knowledge of the woman's report: that is, a woman whose self-report indicated a high measure of psychological well-being was likely to be evaluated by the psychiatrist as well adjusted; and, conversely, women with low self-reports were often independently viewed by the psychiatrist as somewhat depressed. These findings were interpreted as a measure of support for the validity of the survey responses.

Table 1. Selected Social Characteristics by Ethnic Group (percentages)

	Ethnic Group				
	Central Europeans	Turks	Persians	North Africans	Arabs
	(n = 287)	(n = 176)	(n = 160)	(n = 239)	(n = 286)
Illiterate	0	29	61	60	96
Husband illiterate	0	25	49	53	66
Married before age 16	0	5	35	37	30
7 or more live births[a]	0	5	53	59	72
5 or more living children	0	14	68	68	76
5 or more children currently living at home	0	3	29	36	53
At least one child under 14 years old	16	30	47	57	56
Total childbearing span less than 7 years	70	35	13	20	10
Works outside the home (full or part-time, including family business or agriculture)	42	21	29	25	35
Currently religiously orthodox	21	30	57	85	98

[a]Percentage based on medical subsamples.

Source: Taken from N. Datan, A. Antonovsky, and B. Maoz, *A Time to Reap: The Middle Age of Women in Five Israeli Subcultures.* Baltimore: The Johns Hopkins University Press, 1981, p. 18. Used with permission.

Middle Age and Modernity

We commenced this study with contradictory views on the relationship between adjustment at middle age and the degree of modernity: the first predicted an inverse linear relationship between adjustment and the degree of modernity on the basis of the psychiatric literature; the second predicted a direct linear relationship between adjustment and the degree of modernity on the basis of the developmental literature. The survey findings showed a curvilinear relationship between degree of modernity and self-reported psychological well-being, with the highest reported well-being at the two extremes, among the modern European and traditional Arab subcultures. This finding has been attributed to the greater cultural stability in these two subcultures: the immigrant European women came to a country where the dominant cultural values were European, while the Muslim Arab villagers, living in a stable traditional setting, saw change gradually penetrate their lives.

The transitional groups, by contrast—the Turks, Persians, and North Africans—had been socialized into traditional settings and transplanted into a modern context, where traditional cues no longer served them, while they were unable to make use of the benefits of modernity, choices among a plurality of roles. The self-reported psychological well-being was lowest in the group that, by external indicators such as the degree of traditionalism in the life history and the modernity of the present life context, would appear to have experienced the greatest discontinuity: the Persians.

Each subculture viewed climacterium as a combination of gains and losses, but this combination differed by ethnic group: the Europeans saw a possible decline in emotional health; the Near Eastern Jews were concerned over a decline in physical health; and the Muslim Arabs felt there was some decline in the marital relationship. On the other hand, all groups unanimously welcomed the cessation of fertility, despite large variation in conception control and fertility history, ranging from the Europeans at one extreme, who typically bore one or two children and prevented or aborted unplanned pregnancies, to the Arabs at the other extreme, some of whom were continuously pregnant or lactating between menarche and menopause. That this response is paced by the life cycle and not shaped by prior events in the psychosexual history is suggested by the European women's attitudes toward their actual and ideal family size: two-thirds of the European women reported that they would have wanted to have borne more children but that economic or political circumstances—this group bore children at the time of the establishment of the state of Israel and the attendant war and period of economic austerity—prevented larger families. Notwithstanding the desire to have borne more children, the European women—like all other groups—did not now wish to be capable of pregnancy. We have interpreted this finding as suggestive of a developmental change in adulthood, linked (like many earlier developmental changes) to a maturational change.

Involutional Psychosis Reconsidered

Finally, the multidisciplinary approach to the question of the significance of the changes at middle age permitted us to answer the question that originally stimulated the broader study: that is, is the hospitalization of European women for involutional psychosis a consequence of differential rates of stress in different cultures, different modes of expression of stress, or differential diagnosis? From the survey, the medical examinations, and the follow-up psychiatric interviews, we were able to provide tentative answers. There was no support for the first hypothesis, that cultural patterns produced greater stress in the modern culture, manifested at the extreme as involutional depression; on the contrary, as has been shown, self-reported well-being was greatest at the two poles of the traditional-modernity continuum. There was some support for the second hypothesis: that is, there was a greater incidence of psychosomatic complaints on survey responses among the Persian and North Africans, while the follow-up psychiatric interview showed "psychological" symptomatology among the Europeans and "somatic" symptoms among all other groups. Finally, there was support for the third hypothesis: clinical depression was found to be rare but appeared in approximately equal rates across cultures in the medical examination and follow-up psychiatric interviews, and diagnosis was considered to have been improved by the use of psychiatrists from the same (or closely related) subculture as the respondents.

To sum up, our broad-scale study of normal women showed involutional psychosis to be an extremely infrequent response; we found in general that the response to middle age and to climacterium is shaped by ethnic origin, that the balance of gains and losses is specific to each subculture, that there is no linear relationship between psychological well-being and the degree of modernity, and finally, that the cessation of fertility is welcomed by women in all cultures.

NOTE

This study was an invited contribution to the symposium "Middle-Aged Women: Evolutionary, Ethnographic, and Cross-cultural Perspectives," organized by J. K. Brown for the eighty-first annual meeting of the American Anthropological Association, Washington, D.C., December 1982.

The research reported in this chapter was conducted through the Israel Institute of Applied Social Research and supported by the U.S. National Institute of Mental Health (P. L. 480 Agreement 06-276-2). A detailed treatment of the issues raised in this chapter and a full exposition of the cross-cultural comparisons reported here can be found in *A Time to Reap: The Middle Age of Women in Five Israeli Subcultures* by N. Datan, A. Antonovsky, and B. Maoz (Baltimore: Johns Hopkins University Press, 1981).

14 "What Are Women For?": Cultural Constructions of Menopausal Women in Japan and Canada

Patricia A. Kaufert
Margaret Lock

If they live long enough, all women eventually stop menstruating. By this criterion, menopause is universal. Yet the timing of even basic physiological changes depends on such factors as women's access to food (starving women do not menstruate) or their access to gynecological surgery (protection against a surgical menopause is one of the paradoxical benefits of inadequate medical care for women). These are extreme examples, but they serve to demonstrate that becoming menopausal is also the product of social rather than simply biological processes.

The subject of this chapter is not menopause per se, but the menopausal woman: more precisely, the menopausal woman in Japan and in Canada. The material comes from studies we have conducted separately but are linked by our interest in menopause, an agreement to match methods and design, and the decision to collaborate on the analysis of common data. Having created one of the very few opportunities for comparative research on menopause, we will be obliged to deal with such issues as differences in menopausal symptoms, in attitudes toward menopause, in rates of hysterectomy, and in the prescription of hormone therapy. Here, however, we want to compare the ways in which Canadian and Japanese women, and their physicians, select, organize, and interpret the bundle of physiological changes that occur in women as they age. For we see in menopause a unique opportunity for exploring how differences in class and culture, in economic and political power, find their expression through the bodies of women.

Our objective in this chapter is to explore the relationship between social reality (the diverse realities lived by women who are menopausal) and cultural construct ("the menopausal woman," a unitary construct created in part by the medical profession). Differences in the medical construction of the menopausal woman in Japan and Canada can be related to different histories and traditions in medicine. Yet, as we will also show, these quasi-medical, quasi-public representations of the menopausal woman have less to do with medical science's past than with the present and future political and economic structure of the two societies. Both in Japan and Canada, the menopausal woman is viewed as a medical and social problem; and the implicit question is What is to be done with women as they age?

Research Strategies

The comparative material that we will discuss comes from studies carried out in Japan and Canada in the 1980s, using a variety of research methods. The most structured data come from two surveys, one conducted in and around Kyoto, Japan, in 1983–84 and the other in Manitoba, Canada, in 1980–81. The Canadian survey was larger, involving 2,500 respondents, while the Japanese survey data come from about half that number of women (n = 1,326). The age band of the Canadian respondents was also wider (forty to fifty-nine years) than that of the Japanese (forty-five to fifty-five years). In other respects, however, the two surveys are very similar. Both surveys selected their study populations from general population sources and both included urban and rural women. Self-completed questionnaires were used in both surveys. The questionnaire completed by Japanese women included many questions directly translated from the earlier Canadian survey. Other questions, while dealing with the same topic area, were adapted to the Japanese context: for example, a section on medical care was extended to include questions on the use of Japanese traditional medical practitioners and medicines. In addition to the survey, the Japanese study included a series of in-depth interviews with fifteen gynecologists and fifteen family practitioners. Both studies included a set of in-depth interviews with women at, or close to, the age of menopause.

Other material comes from reviews of the North American and Japanese clinical and epidemiological research literature on menopause. The works reviewed also include those directed to a general audience: articles on menopause and the menopausal woman published in newspapers, magazines, and paperback books. Often written by physicians, these articles are not constrained by the rules of scientific presentation that prevail in the professional literature. Their mix of medical information with social and moral commentary provides a rich source of material on the ways in which Canadian and Japanese physicians construe the menopausal woman and visualize the processes of her body.

Finally, extended fieldwork in Canada and Japan has given us the opportunity to meet the variety of experts who act as interpreters of the menopausal woman. They include practicing physicians, clinical researchers, epidemiologists, psychologists, feminist filmmakers, journalists interested in women's health, and the occasional sociologist or anthropologist. Through their work and through their writing, these experts are all variously engaged in a discourse on the menopausal woman. They would become her architects, imposing their definition of who she is and how she is to recognize herself.

It is with their products, their constructions of the menopausal woman, that the first part of this chapter is concerned. The second part, which draws on demographic data from our surveys, shows the diversity among women who are menopausal: diversity in their life circumstances and in their self-definitions. The final section addresses some questions about the menopausal woman, the economic order, and the political self.

The Menopausal Woman as a Medical Construct

Most women know the script laid out in their particular society for the woman in midlife, including what symptoms she should expect from her body. Greek women, for example, expect hot flushes, while Mayan women do not (Beyene 1989). Women will know not only the repertoire of menopausal symptoms, but also the repertoire of behavior considered appropriate for a woman who is menopausal. Women in California are told that a loss in libido is a medical problem to be treated by hormone therapy, whereas a Bengali woman in India knows very well that sexual activity is inappropriate for the postmenopausal woman (see Vatuk, this volume).

Both the denial and the affirmation of sexuality are social phenomena, but for the California woman the responses of her body have been transformed into a medical problem to be medically managed. It is her physician who will tell her that the continuation of sexual activity is "normal," but that to lose the desire for sex is an expression of a disease state, the menopause, which is to be managed by hormone therapy. Just as obstetricians and pediatricians would define how women should feel and behave when becoming mothers, gynecologists and psychiatrists tell women what it is to be menopausal. What they say, however, varies from one society to another and from one period of time to another.

The Menopausal Woman in Japan

The medical literature on menopause read by Japanese physicians is not dissimilar to that read by their Canadian counterparts. Occasional traces of the influence in Japan of late nineteenth-century German medical thinking still linger in the long lists of menopausal symptoms. The main sources of clinical and epidemiological information, however, are often the same American and European studies that are quoted and read by Canadian gynecologists. When referring to physiology, the answers to such questions as Why do some women get symptoms and others not? are often essentially the same whether the physician is Canadian or Japanese. Many Japanese physicians will then go on to emphasize that the instability in the autonomic nervous system is implicated, in addition to falling estrogen levels, as causal of menopausal symptomology. The emphasis given to the autonomic nervous system in Japanese medical discourse is largely due to the cultural proclivity for using models in which theories of balance and harmony are central (Lock, Kaufert, and Gilbert 1988). If the question is repeated, however, answers may become quite different.

At the level of patient as person, physicians draw on a potent mix of psychological theorizing about the nature of woman with political statements on their proper role (or rather lack of role) that are particular to each society. To explain why Japanese physicians, for example, adopt a somewhat censorious stance toward their menopausal patients requires an understanding of relationships of class, gender, and power in Japanese society.

Discussing the faults of the middle-class, middle-aged homemaker has become one of the preoccupations of the popular media in Japan. The topic of numerous quasi-medical, quasi-psychological articles, she is castigated for selfishness, individualism, and lack of discipline (Ikemi and Ikemi 1982; Kyūtoku 1979). She is described as deficient in the strength and willpower once characteristic of the traditional Japanese woman. She is blamed for becoming the victim of an assortment of new diseases, including "the kitchen syndrome," "apartment living neurosis," and the "menopausal syndrome" (Lock 1986a).

The "menopausal syndrome" has now achieved status as a formal medical category in Japan and is discussed in the medical scientific journals. In the popular media and in less formal discussions, however, physicians attribute vulnerability less to hormonal than to moral factors.

> Menopausal syndrome is described as a luxury disease (*zeitakubyō*), a problem which occurs in women with too much time on their hands, who are selfish and concerned only with their own pleasures. Women like this are said to lack a real identity (which is bound up inextricably with one's social role [Lebra 1976]); they have no sense of self (*jibun ga nai*), and are deficient in the willpower, positive attitude, and endurance that were characteristic of their mothers. (Lock 1986a)

A few of the physicians interviewed in the study were sympathetic toward their menopausal patients rather than condemnatory. They discussed the plight (as they saw it) of women with nothing to do, closeted in small apartments, lacking meaningful occupation. Those physicians who were sympathetic were more likely to say that they offered counseling to their menopausal patients, although even this is normally little more than advice on the value of cultivating hobbies (Lock 1988). They prescribe herbal teas, but are much less likely than Canadian physicians to offer psychotropics and hormones.

The moralistic stance toward women complaining of menopausal symptoms can be traced back to the ideal codes of behavior for women in Japanese society. The behavior and discipline expected of women is based originally on rules laid down in the feudal period for the wives of samurai. The *sengyō shufu,* a term that can be glossed as a "professional homemaker" is the modern form of the "good wife/wise mother" (*ryōsai kenbo*), the "correct woman" of the Meiji period. Somewhat adapted to suit postwar Japan, the good wife/wise mother remains the epitome of the Japanese woman.

The samurai valued discipline, submission, and unquestioning obedience not only of themselves but of their wives and children. According to their Confucian-influenced code, a woman should be patient, submissive, diligent, even-tempered, compliant, and gentle. Her life should be devoted to the care of her husband, her children, and her parents-in-law. Her concern should not be for herself but always for these others. Domestic skills and an orderly household were to be valued as an expression not just of competence as a woman but of virtue. The body also became an expression of virtue. Inner discipline, for example, was reflected in a body language based on good posture, a neat appearance, elegance in the handling of objects, graceful manners. A virtuous body was considered healthy and, hence, sickness in a woman revealed a lack of discipline and of balance. According to this code, a woman was blamed both for allowing her body to become ill and for failing through illness in her responsibility to others. The moral roots of negative attitudes toward the woman complaining of menopausal symptoms can be traced in part to this idea of the good woman holding mastery over her own body.

There is another explanation, however, that has less to do with traditional codes for womanly behavior and more with the role assigned to women in modern Japanese society. This explanation depends on the answers to a question that is partly political and partly philosophical: What are women for? In the Meiji period, the answers to this question could be framed in terms of the responsibilities of the wives of samurai living within a large traditional household. After the war, many samurai values became part of the code by which the newly emerging middle class was to live. Unlike the samurai wife, however, the modern homemaker is expected to reside in a small apartment with a husband and no more than two children. The hard work, perseverance, and discipline, which were central to the traditional code for womanly behavior, are now to be funneled into the work of raising and educating children in the context of the nuclear family. The modern version of the good wife/wise mother is responsible for the success (and survival) of children within the highly structured, highly competitive system of contemporary Japanese education. (A reversed image, the woman-as-bad-mother, is blamed for children who fail or who are destroyed by the system; see Lock 1986b.)

In modern Japan, a woman is above all else "for" the education and training of children. She is responsible for inculcating the virtues seen as essential to the Japanese workplace: loyalty, discipline, and perseverance. In this interpretation of her role, the Japanese woman is essential to the maintenance and reproduction of modern society. The dilemma is that raising children is a time-limited function. Japanese families are small, and childbearing is completed relatively early. The highly active, intensive involvement of a mother in her children's education is practically over by the time most women reach menopause.

The professional homemaker is not expected to go out to work, and she cannot take up a role in public life. Neither of these options is compatible with the essentially domestic locus of the image of the good wife/wise mother. At the same time, she cannot continue to play a role designed for the period of life when her children were young. Neither the Japanese husband nor the Japanese adolescent is expected to spend much time at home. A woman should not remain overcommitted to being the good housewife, overzealous of the order of her household, or overly protective of her children. Such women are described by physicians as neurotic, blamed for their lack of balance and control (Lock 1988).

Left without an occupation and living in a society that values perseverance, hard work, and discipline, the menopausal woman is anomalous. Anomalous social categories are always troublesome, but particularly when they are a product of social changes toward which many are ambivalent. By attaching the menopausal syndrome to the leisure and lack of social responsibility, the Japanese physician engages in victim blaming. Lacking any legitimate outlet for the traditional virtues of self-sacrifice, hard work, and devotion to the family, the menopausal patient is described as selfish, idle, individualistic. Most important, she is told that she has brought her own troubles, her menopausal syndrome, upon her own head. The implications of modernization are displaced onto the body of the woman.

This portrait of the menopausal woman is not simply a product of the medical or the male imagination. The interviews with Japanese women in midlife revealed that many of them agreed to its essential lineaments. Yet, when we analyzed the data from the Japanese survey, reports of stress were more common among women living in multigenerational households than those in single-family homes. Women living only with their husbands and children were more likely to say that they were satisfied with their lives, less likely to report the symptoms associated with menopause than women living with other kin. Whatever the leisure now available, and whatever the moral stance of the wider society toward this leisure, the women themselves appeared to enjoy and be content with their lives.

The Menopausal Woman in Canada

Much of the European and North American literature on menopause shares an assumption that women are defined (and define themselves) by their relationships with others. For the adult woman, the most significant of these others are her husband and children. This echoes the Japanese idea of a woman's sense of self being contingent on her social identity as a wife and as a mother (Lebra 1984). North American physicians are told that the loss or diminution of these relationships threatens psychological well-being and that this explains the depression of their menopausal patients. The appropriate medical response, they are also told, is some mixture of counseling, psychotropics, and hormone replacement therapy.

The casual stereotype of the menopausal woman is a depressed homemaker: her children are leaving home while her husband is at best preoccupied with work and at worst divorcing a wife he no longer finds sexually attractive. In her lack of meaningful occupation, she is reminiscent of the Japanese professional homemaker except that she is to be pitied rather than condemned. Depressed and depressing, suffering a multiplicity of losses, the menopausal woman makes a sad and forlorn image.

This view of the menopausal woman owes something still to the influence of Freud. In Freudian logic, the meaning of a woman's life is based on her ability to bear children; hence, once she loses this capacity, it follows that her life has lost its purpose. Helene Deutsch, who was largely responsible for framing a Freudian interpretation of menopause, described the menopausal patient as a being without hope. The best that could be offered was a form of palliative care; for with the end of her fertility, a woman "had reached her natural end—her partial death" (Deutsch 1945:459).

Articles on the management of the menopausal patient still tend to remind physicians that the biological end of fertility at menopause coincides with the social ending of the mothering role. The menopausal patient is described as "neurotic, depressed, unable to cope with emotional crisis such as children leaving home, and constantly subject to vague complaints and gynecological disorders" (Roberts 1984). This caricature of the physician's view of the menopausal patient is British, but might as well be Canadian. It might also be Japanese for there are echoes in this of the description of the menopausal patient offered by a Tokyo physician: "These women have no *ikigai* (purpose in life). They have free time but can't think of anything to do, so they get a psychosomatic reaction. They can't complain openly so they use 'organ language' [said in English]" (cited in Lock 1988). Whether Japanese or Canadian, this image of the menopausal woman is a powerful one, suggesting that it may reflect attitudes toward women, women's roles, and the impact of aging on women, attitudes that are widely held in both societies.

Freud is now being replaced, and a new version of the menopausal woman has emerged gradually in North America over the past ten to fifteen years. Medicine has defined menopause as a deficiency condition (akin to diabetes or anemia) and a risk factor for the chronic diseases of old age. Osteoporosis and cardiovascular diseases are highlighted as the major killers, but incontinence and atrophic vaginitis are thrown in for good measure. Menopause becomes not only a threat to the lives of women but strikes at the root of their identity as continent, sexually active, mature adults.

Regardless of whether one thinks in terms of the burden of suffering and pain to the woman or the burden of cost to society, osteoporosis and heart disease are not trivial conditions. The message being put out in the medical literature, both the professional and popular varieties, is that the middle years, the menopausal years, represent the period in a woman's life when she can make the changes necessary to their prevention or delay. By changing her diet, exercising, giving up alcohol and cigarettes, and above all else by taking her hormones, a woman may ensure her own survival into a healthy old age. Her choice is between an old, diseased, and broken body or a fit and vigorous one.

Corresponding to the activist approach to the physiological tasks of midlife, the psychological literature lays out a series of actions to ward off the consequences of menopause for mental well-being. A dismal listing of the events to be expected by women is still customary in the literature on midlife. A book published only in 1989 carries the ominous title *Midlife Loss* (Kalish 1989). Its chapters have titles such as "Stress and Loss in Middle Age," "Divorce at Midlife," "Death of a Spouse," and "Job Loss in Middle Age." The subtitle of this book, however, is "Coping Strategies," and the chapters are written from what is described as a "developmental perspective." Rather than stoic endurance breaking down into depression, the key words are "challenge," "liberation," "growth," "development," "joy," "excitement."

Replacing Freud, the intellectual father figure among these current writers seems to be Jung. They quote Jung's argument that the second major phase of psychological development begins after forty years of age. Like Jung, they present the development of the maturing self as both work and moral obligation. They share his concern over the risks of stagnation, of clinging to the past. Describing the neuroses of midlife among women, Jung wrote: "They cling to the illusion of youth or to their children, hoping to salvage in this way a last scrap of youth. One sees it especially in mothers, who find their sole meaning in their children and imagine they will sink into a bottomless void when they have to give them up" (Jung 1954:114). Allowing oneself to stagnate is a sign of a lack of spiritual will. In its own way, the developmental approach to midlife is as much about virtue and the moral imperatives for women as any samurai code.

Rather than Jung, the new ideas about the woman in midlife might also be traced to the impact of the women's movement and feminist scholarship. The following quotation, for example, comes from an essay included in one of the collections of papers on women in midlife published in the 1980s:

> Although a woman may have enacted only her family roles to the exclusion of all others in early adulthood, at midlife as family demands slack off, she is capable of launching a delayed career in spheres other than the family. At this point in her life course, a woman may complete an education or begin one, train for a new job or seek promotion, join a volunteer association or found one. A midlife woman is much more than her familial roles, more than just a mother. (Long and Porter 1984:140)

The energetic, forceful, competent woman of this description is more attractive than the depressed and depressing homemaker. She is also very different from the Japanese image of the aging homemaker: idle, selfish, expressing her distress through "organ language." Appealing though she may be, the feminist version of the woman in midlife is equally a construct, an abstraction from the diverse realities of women's lives.

The Demography of Midlife

Our survey data reveal significant differences among Japanese or Canadian women at midlife, as well as cross-national variation or differences between them. The respondents vary in terms of marital status, reproductive history, family size, household structure, educational background, occupation, and class. Among Canadian women, there are also differences in ethnicity, language, national origins, and cultural identity.

The Japanese survey included three quite distinct groups: women living in the suburbs of Kobe (a mainly middle-class area), women employed as factory workers in and around Kyoto (working in large, modern plants or in small, traditional silkweaving enterprises), and women living and working in rural areas. This rural sample included women from the rich farming areas of Nagano and women from fishing villages in Shikoku. Finally, a few questionnaires were completed by women working in service and entertainment sectors in Kyoto. Questionnaires were distributed to 1,738 women; 1,328 were returned, giving a response rate of 76%; 1,316 were used to draw conclusions.

The Canadian study is based on a single sample selected from a listing of all Manitoban women, aged forty to fifty-nine, registered with the provincial health insurance system. (Coverage is almost universal for residents in Manitoba.) Completed questionnaires were received from 2,500 women, a response rate of 68%. For purposes of comparison with the Japanese survey, only the 1,326 women who were from forty-five to fifty-five are included.

The product of these two surveys is a long list of responses by Canadian and Japanese women to the same questions on health, medical care, menopause, medications, or other such matters. We have selected only very simple and standard demographic data for use in this chapter. Our purpose is not to set up any elaborate statistical comparisons; rather, we want to use these data initially as a series of clues, or stimuli, to thinking about the diversity among women at midlife, whether Japanese or Canadian.

Some direct comparisons can be made, such as the number of women who are married or have children. Measurement levels are often not the same, however. Educational data, for example, are not comparable; these same data are invaluable as a reminder of a critical difference among Japanese women and between them and Canadian women of the same age group. Reading the Japanese educational data reveals a sharp break in educational background between women born before and after 1933. This timing suggests that the split in these data is most probably a function of age at the beginning and end of World War II. The age band of the women included in the study is deceptively narrow. The assumption that they may be treated as a single cohort seems eminently reasonable. The educational data serve as a clue to a diversity born of the historical context of the lives of these women. Memories of the traditional household and the role of the traditional woman within that household will be vivid for the older of these women, but hearsay for those born too recently to remember the prewar years. The older women also remember much more clearly than the younger ones the hardships and poverty associated with the years of war and occupation.

The war had effects on the lives of Canadians, but without creating the same degree of discontinuity for the women born in Canada. The diversity among these women is less a matter of time than place, insofar as the latter is related to ethnicity, language, and cultural identities. Among the Canadian woman, while only 13% were born somewhere other than Canada, 51% said that their mothers and 66% that their fathers were not Canadian born. While 90% spoke English most of the time, 53% were in the habit of using a second language. The most common were Ukrainian (12%), German (11%), and French (5%), but the list includes twenty-two languages other than English. Admittedly, languages spoken and places of birth are crude, simplistic indicators; nevertheless, these data are corrective against any assumption of cultural homogeneity. There may be as many variations on what it is to be a woman in midlife as there are languages spoken.

Occupational data reflect the ways in which women in midlife spend their time, earn money, have access to a support group other than their family, have identities other than as wives or mothers, are powerless or have acquired some control in their lives. The same data also indicate something of the position of women within the macroeconomic and political structures of their society. The rapid increase since the sixties in the proportion of married women in the Canadian labor force is an economic statistic but the women who took part in the Canadian survey had lived this trend within their own lives. Women of their generation went into the labor force as their children started school, and most had remained there. In 1980–81, 55% of the respondents were currently employed. They worked in shops, offices, hospitals, schools, factories, banks, and universities. The occupations they listed were those standard for Canadian women: nurses, teachers, social workers, sales clerks, and clerical workers.

The single Canadian sample is a cross-section of women in midlife in the provincial population, but the three Japanese samples of women were selected from backgrounds chosen partly because of anticipated differences in occupation. In the Kyoto sample all respondents were factory workers. The Kobe sample was selected from a middle-class residential district, partly with the expectation that the majority of middle-class, middle-aged women would not work. The rural sample was chosen on the assumption that the majority of these wives of farmers and fishers would be engaged, much as the traditional Japanese woman, in working within and for the family as an economic unit.

By and large, the expectations about the occupational profile of these samples were confirmed, but not exactly. Only approximately a third of the women living in Kobe, for example, chose to describe themselves as *sengyō shufu,* a professional homemaker. Almost a quarter of the women from the farm and fishing communities, however, chose this term as their own designation. Another quarter of the rural women described themselves as working in a family business, as was expected, but so did slightly more than an eighth of the women living in Kobe. Other rural women said that they worked in manufacturing. While possibly a reference to the traditional processing of food or other products, small-scale modern factories do exist in the villages and do use women in their labor force.

Deciphering the occupational data is sometimes difficult, due partly to conventions of nomenclature, partly to issues of occupational law in Japan, and partly to the structure of the Japanese labor force and the position of women in that force. The use of the term *teacher* is a good example. A woman describing herself as a teacher might work in the formal school system or simply run a few classes in one of the traditional arts from within her own home. A question on the number of hours worked indicated that employment was often a matter of a handful of hours a week, particularly for the women from Kobe. Only slightly over a quarter of all the women in the study described themselves as working full-time outside the home, and almost half were in the sample of factory workers. But women in the factory sample also used part-time less as a descriptor of the number of hours they worked than of their legal status as workers. (Under Japanese labor law the rights and pay of part-time workers are much less than those of a full-time worker. Most women in blue-collar jobs are hired in the category of part-time worker, although they may be working more than forty hours a week [Cook and Hayashi 1980]).

At one level, the description of her work as part-time or freelance or piecework is simply information on how a particular woman divides her time between home and workplace. At another level, the cumulation of these data across all the women taking part in the survey is a source of insight into the relatively tenuous involvement of women in this age group within the Japanese labor force. Part-time and piecework is inherently more unstable than full-time employment and more subject to economic fluctuation. Another clue lies in relative absence of Japanese women working in the arenas that offer some degree of security, higher income, and career mobility to their Canadian counterparts. Using the Canadian occupational classification system, only 63 Japanese women relative to 225 Canadian could be classified as working in administration, teaching, social work, or the health professions. Like the educational or language data, occupational data are also crude and simplistic. Nevertheless, the overall impression of midlife women being marginalized to the fringes of the Japanese labor force economy is probably correct.

The proportion of married women is almost identical (85% in Canada and 86% in Japan) and the proportion of divorced and separated women is only marginally higher in Canada (6% relative to 3%). Canadian women are slightly more likely to have had children, but the proportion of childless women is marginal in both societies (5% relative to 9% among the Japanese women). The most striking difference between the Canadian and the Japanese data is in the number of children born by each woman. Among women with children, less than a third of the Canadians but approximately two-thirds of the Japanese women had one or two children. Approximately a tenth of these Canadian women had five or more children, but slightly less than a tenth of the Japanese women had four or more. The number of children in the Japanese survey ranged from one to seven, but from one to thirteen in the Canadian data. By the age of thirty-three, almost three-quarters of the Japanese women had given birth to their last child relative to approximately two-thirds of Canadian women.

If nothing else, these few statistics reflect a very critical difference in the relationship of these Japanese and Canadian women to the fertility and reproductive powers of their bodies. Yet, the difference in the number of children has only a relatively slight impact on the percentage of women who at this stage in their lives still have children living in the home. Only 30% of the women in the Japanese survey and 25% of the Canadian women live in homes without children. Apart from the presence of children, however, the structure of households is often quite different (see Table 1). Among the Canadian women, the majority (82%) live with only their husband, only their children, or with their husband and children; the corresponding figure for the Japanese is 59%. The difference lies not in the number of women who live in the same household as their parents (these figures are almost the same), but in the number who live with their parents-in-law: only 4 women in the Canadian survey, but 287 women in the Japanese data.

The purpose in presenting these data is partly to demonstrate the diversity of women's lives. Certainly, each study includes women who can be classified as middle-class urban homemakers who are not working, whose children have grown, and whose leisure has presumably increased. They seem more often content than depressed, but the demographic profile at least fits the portrait of the menopausal woman found in both medical literatures. There are also women in the Canadian sample who represent the new woman in midlife engaged in her career, active in political and community affairs, possibly liberated from an old marriage, certainly free from the daily care of young children.

Table 1 Household Structure for Canadian and Japanese Women (percentages)

	Household Structure	
	Canadian (n = 1,326)	Japanese (n = 1,316)
Woman living		
Alone	4.3	4.2
With husband only	27.3	14.3
With children only	6.3	5.2
Husband and children	50.3	39.5
Parent only	.8	.4
Parent and husband	.2	.6
Parent and children	.2	.4
Parent, husband, and children	.9	.8
Parent-in-law and husband	.1	2.7
Parent-in-law, husband, and children	.2	10.3
Other relative	.5	.2
Other relative and husband	1.3	2.0
Other relative and children	.7	.5
Other relative, husband, and children	3.0	3.7
Other relative and parent	.4	.9
Other relative, husband, and parent	.5	.4
Other relative, parent, and children	.1	.5
Other relative, parent, husband, and children	.8	.9
Parent-in-law only	0	.5
Parent-in-law and children	0	1.0
Parent-in-law and other relatives	0	.1
Parent-in-law, husband, and other relatives	0	1.3
Parent-in-law, children, and other relatives	0	.5
Parent-in-law, husband, children, and other relatives	0	5.5
Unknown	2.1	3.6

"Career women" are very rare in the Japanese sample. Most young Japanese women work, but more than 40% leave the work force permanently with the birth of their first child. There are important class differences, however. White-collar and professional women (those who might become career women in the North American sense) are under considerable pressure to comply with the customary withdrawal from the labor force, whereas women working in blue-collar occupations are sought after as a part-time, relatively cheap, source of labor. These women are invisible, however, when the woman in midlife is publicly discussed.

Talking with Japanese women of the middle class, it was clear that many believe that the work of running a household and raising children is of outstanding importance. Describing the punishing working routines endured by most Japanese men, many also said that they were not attracted by the idea of full-time employment, even when the choice was available. There are signs of change, however. The divorce rate among middle-aged women is rising. A few career women, again in the North American sense of that term, are emerging. There are other signs of unrest, including a small but active feminist movement.

The portraits of woman in midlife that are found in the medical literature of either society, while having their roots in the lives of real people, are simplified and decontextualized. The Japanese professional homemaker undoubtedly exists, although she is not necessarily depressed. She is also, however, a minority figure in the sense that whatever they may have thought of the popular model of woman as homemaker, the label was not chosen for themselves by the majority of women in either the Kobe, Kyoto, or the rural sample.

Profits, Loss, and Fear of the Old Woman

A cynical explanation for the new emphasis on menopause and hormones, the problems (physical and psychological) of the middle-aging body, the creation of middlescence, is that the medical marketplace senses a potential profit. Money is being made in North America (including Canada) by selling hormones, running exercise workshops, testing for osteoporosis. As the baby-boom generation ages, profits will increase. Obstetrician-gynecologists in both Canada and Japan find in the menopausal woman a convenient new source of patients. Their problem is to convince women that menopause requires the care of a physician. The barrage of propaganda presenting menopause as a disease in need of treatment can be interpreted as advertising, a promotion to attract new consumers.

While there is probably some element of truth to an explanation based on medical profit, it is not sufficient. Predictions based on the economic costs to society of the aging woman are more powerful and far more political in character. Fear of an aging population, more particularly fear of an aging population of women, is widespread in both Canada and Japan. Looking at the Canadian data, projections from Statistics Canada describe a demographic profile for the year 2000 in which there will be 134 women for every 100 men in the sixty-five to seventy-nine age group and 218 women for every 100 men in the eighty and over age group. In the year 2000 in Japan, there will be 136 women for every 100 men over the age of sixty-five (Japan Statistical Association 1987).

Describing what she terms as the crisis approach to aging, McDaniel writes: "The contemporary fear is that the growth in the older population will outrun the ability of society to provide pensions and health care" (1986:26). Canadian policymakers present a future image in which the health-care system is overburdened by sick, passive, dependent old women. The economic appeal of estrogen therapy and lifestyle modification lies in the promise that money will be saved by delaying or preventing high-cost conditions, such as hip fractures, by exercise, diet, hormone therapy. The message to women emphasizes individualism, responsibility, remaining autonomous, not being dependent on others.

Within the last five or six years, there is much talk in Canada—both formal academic talk published in journals and supported by research grants and informal talk between friends—about the problems of the caretaker generation, the women in midlife. Much of the official talk about women in midlife in Japan, however, deals with their neglect of obligations, their failure to serve as caretakers. At first sight, these two positions seem incompatible with the actual data. In this study at least, Japanese women are far more likely to be heavily involved in caretaking than Canadian women. The issue, of course, is not the numbers but their interpretation; a figure high from a North American perspective may be low from a Japanese viewpoint.

The explanation for an apparent discrepancy between the two societies can be tracked partly to differences in ideas about women and their place in the scheme of the political and moral order. The time Jung would have a woman spend on the development of self becomes idleness and a loss of self-discipline in the samurai code. But there is another explanation rooted in the place of women within the economic system: Canadian women are integrated into the economy of the workplace to a greater extent than the Japanese woman in midlife. Their labor power is essential to some sectors of the Canadian economy (the health-care system has long been propped up by the low wages of women workers), but so also is their earning capacity. The economy is set up on the assumption that most families will have two paychecks to buy not only their basic needs but also the array of unnecessary goods and services for sale. Canadian women have expressed the fear that the politicians may force them into a caretaking role for the old and the sick. They see this as another trap, akin to the trap of motherhood, into which they may fall. But as the population ages, it is doubtful that the economy could withstand the loss of too many women from the labor force, taking away their earning capacity and their capacity to pay taxes.

Faced with the same problem of an aging population, the alternative chosen in Japan is not to delay the burden on society but to deny that care of the old is a burden to be assumed by society. The shortage of nursing homes and ambulatory care facilities in Japan reflects this attitude on the part of government (Kiefer 1987). Rather than the government shifting resources from industrial to social services, the public message is that the care of the aged is a burden that should continue as the responsibility of women, just as it was in the years before the war. By this interpretation, the refusal to provide a meaningful place in the labor market to women ensures that they cannot escape the burden of caring for the old.

Menopause, Medicalization, and the Politics of Being an Aging Woman

Ironically, the attempt to medicalize menopause, sponsored by some members of the Japanese medical profession, is having a consciousness-raising effect among Japanese women. Meetings arranged to discuss the health problems of middle age may turn into "a forum for debate about family relationships, social roles, and even politics" (Lock 1988). To a greater extent than in Japan, the North American medical profession has inflated menopause into an event of critical medical significance. By the same process, however, the consciousness of women in midlife has also been heightened. A Canadian newsletter, focused initially on menopause, has broadened its mandate to encompass not only the health but other problems of women in midlife. Media discussion of the problems of menopause have fostered the emergence of support groups and the organization of information sessions for menopausal women. Such meetings shift easily from the discussion of estrogens and exercise into a critical exploration of the stereotype of the menopausal woman. Concern over osteoporosis may turn into a discussion of the economic pitfalls of aging or a questioning of the responsibilities of women toward their children, their husband, their parents. Shared identity as menopausal women may yet create an alliance among Japanese women and refusal to become sole caretakers of the old. They may demand more help, more sharing of the burden, more access for themselves and for the old to the resources of society. Canadian women may do the same, demanding not hormones, but the resources to maintain health in old age, including an adequate income, decent housing, security, and a health-care system responsive to their needs. In sum, consciousness of the menopausal body may lead into consciousness of the political self.

REFERENCES

Beyene, Yewoubar
  1989   From Menarche to Menopause. New York: State University of New
         York Press.
Cook, Alice H., and Hiroko Hayashi
  1980   Working Women in Japan: Discrimination, Resistance and Reform.
         Cornell International Industrial and Labor Relations Report, no. 10. Ithaca:
         New York State School of Industrial and Labor Relations.
Deutsch, Helene
  1945   The Psychology of Women. Vol. 2. New York: Grune and Stratton.
Ikemi, Yujiro, and Akira Ikemi
  1982   Some Psychosomatic Disorders in Japan in a Cultural Perspective.
         Journal of Psychotherapy and Psychosomatics 38:231–38.
Japan Statistical Association
  1987   Japan Statistical Yearbook. Tokyo: Japan Statistical Association.
Jung, Carl G.
  1954   On the Psychology of the Unconscious. *In* Two Essays on Analytical
         Psychology. Vol 7. R. F. C. Hull, trans. New York: Pantheon.
Kalish, Richard, ed.
  1989   Midlife Loss. Newbury Park, Calif.: Sage Publications.
Kiefer, Christie W.
  1987   Care of the Aged in Japan. *In* Health, Illness, and Medical Care in
         Japan: Cultural and Social Dimensions. E. Norbeck and M. Lock, eds.
         pp. 89–109. Honolulu: University of Hawaii Press.
Kyūtoku, S.
  1979   Bogenbyo. Tokyo: Sanmaku Shuppan.
Lebra, Takie Sugiyama
  1976   Japanese Patterns of Behavior. Honolulu: University of Hawaii Press.
  1984   Japanese Women: Constraint and Fulfillment. Honolulu: University of
         Hawaii Press.
Lock, Margaret
  1986a Ambiguities of Aging: Japanese Experience and Perceptions of Meno-
         pause. Culture, Medicine and Psychiatry 10:23–47.
  1986b Plea for Acceptance: School Refusal Syndrome in Japan. Social Sci-
         ence and Medicine 23:99–112.
  1988   New Japanese Mythologies: Faltering Discipline and the Ailing Housewife.
         American Ethnologist 15(1):43–61.
Lock, Margaret, Patricia A. Kaufert, and Penny Gilbert
  1988   Cultural Construction of the Menopausal Syndrome: The Japanese
         Case. Maturitas 10:317–22.
Long, Judy, and Karen L. Porter
  1984   Multiple Roles of Midlife Women: A Case for New Directions in
         Theory, Research and Policy. *In* Women in Midlife. G. Baruch and J.
         Brooks-Gunn, eds., pp. 109–59. New York: Plenum Press.

McDaniel, Susan A.
    1986   Canada's Aging Population. Toronto: Butterworths.
Roberts, Helen
    1984   Patient Patients: Women and Their Doctors. London: Pandora.
Roy, Manisha
    1985   Bengali Women. Chicago: University of Chicago Press.

15 Beyond Nurture: Developmental Perspectives on the Vital Older Woman

David Gutmann

As a developmental and clinical psychologist, I approach the cross-cultural laboratory with methods and questions quite different from those of anthropologists. Cultural anthropologists use their data to derive laws concerning the relations among the components and functions of a supraindividual entity: culture as such. Anthropologists' subjects are frequently old and they are used as informants not on their own lives but on aspects of cultural norms and usage. Developmental psychologists like myself are more likely to use our older respondents as informants on themselves—on their own history and circumstances. Nevertheless, we too are *required* to use the cross-cultural laboratory for the final and necessary test of our hypotheses and theories. In fact, *no* developmental hypothesis can be taken seriously until it has shown that the specified maturation has taken place, in predictable form and sequence, across a wide range of societies different from each other and from the culture in which the hypothesis was first conceived. In other words, we confirm a hypothesis of developmental import by demonstrating that some pattern of human growth—whether physical or psychological—is an aspect of *genotypic nature,* peremptory and predictable across widely varying conditions of social nurture. Through use of the cross-cultural, comparative method we randomize the influences of cultural nurture to bring out and identify the central thrust toward structural and functional maturation that is imposed by some intrinsic natural design.

This is not to argue a nature-nurture split. Sophisticated developmental theory holds that all adaptive growth of new executive structures requires a reciprocal and sponsoring environment and that the facilitating environment for psychological development is always social (though the versions of the social *other* may range from the mother's breast in infancy to the moral institutions and traditions of society in later life).

Nevertheless, while developmentalists and anthropologists might agree that an organized social life is necessary to development, we disagree as to the role that culture might play in shaping and guiding a developmental sequence. Thus the developmentalist would hold that the early stages of maturation are sui generis and guided by stimuli and programs that reflect evolutionary priorities, whereas the anthropologist is more likely to hold that culture is the independent variable and that the timing, direction, and sequences of development all reflect cultural priorities.[1] As we shall see, this dispute between nativist and culturalist understandings becomes particularly sharp when we turn to consider the fate of older women in various societies as documented by the various contributors to this volume.

The Staging of Development

To underline the source of our differences, and to prepare the ground for the later discussion of the older woman, I will first present my own generic model of development, one that has been greatly influenced by the ideas of Erik Erikson, a leading psychoanalyst.

Anthropologists are mainly interested in the extraindividual collective processes and institutions—rituals of passage, normative models of instruction, etc.—that surround some process of individual growth and they assume that such externalities fully account for the acquisition of new learning or new social statuses. By contrast, our model considers the intraindividual dynamisms that contribute to development and (particularly in the early maturational stages) gives these equal or greater status vis-à-vis extraindividual influence. Thus a full developmental sequence has at least three distinct phases, each keyed to a special form of psychosocial sponsorship and expression. Any significant developmental advance entails the transformation of inchoate strivings into formed, adapted executive capacities. As such, it begins with a *genotypic eruptive* phase (my term) in which "chemical" and biosocial events—e.g., weaning, the advent of siblings, the nutritive acts of a mother, etc.—lead to the emergence of raw, undifferentiated potentials. These diffuse energies are at the outset like the wings of fledgling birds: they have not yet tuned their beat, nor found their proper air.

Put more formally, the genotypic potentials have not yet entered into coordinated behavior or into consciousness, and they are mainly expressed in the relatively stereotyped metaphors of the unconscious, the imagery of dreams, and the preverbal communication of mood and involuntary gesture. At this juncture, behavior may be expressive in the idiosyncratic sense but it has not yet been set in the conventional symbols that make it socially communicative. Indeed, in this phase socially articulated behavior may serve to deny the eruptive potentials, rather than to directly express them: thus adolescents may deny burgeoning sexuality through displays of religious idealism; or older women, as we will see, might deny their emergent aggressivity by extravagant displays of depression and dependency. The contents of the eruptive phase can only be known indirectly and inferentially, through the eliciting of images and associations not under normative, conscious control: responses to projective tests, early memories, free associations to dreams, etc. Needless to say, anthropologists do not usually elicit or analyze such materials; accordingly, they are not likely to recognize the ultimate contribution to social development of this first, incoherent phase.

If the raw potentials of the eruptive phase meet congenial internal (psychological) and external (social) environments, if their first tentative and unfocused expressions are recognized and welcomed by important legitimators such as parents and teachers, then the developmental cycle will move into its second or *reciprocal* phase. At this stage, the social other no longer exists in syncretic unity with primitive drives as a releaser for instinctual discharge; instead, the other exists in his or her own right, as a counter player in the developmental drama. This other might be some adult who recognizes the possibilities inherent in the genotypic potentials and brings them into section with the most relevant symbol systems of the culture, so that they may become named and normalized, opened up for exploration and maturation along conventional lines. Again, this crucial period is studied through close observation of private rather than public domains: the often unspoken exchanges of gesture and feeling between parents and children and the private feelings, sensitivities, and fantasies that they bear toward each other (and will reveal only to a trusted investigator). Again, this kind of investigation—of the subjective side of social living—is not undertaken by most anthropologists.

If the role models of the reciprocal phase have done their job properly, mediating between eruptive potentials and their relevant social contexts, then development moves into the final *sculptured,* or phenotypic phase, in which potentials are solidly organized into personal skills and social resources, according to the idiom of a particular society. Thus, it is only in the final phase of a developmental sequence that culture as such becomes crucially relevant in shaping matured outcomes.

In sum, the raw energy that powers development is an aspect of the genotypic phase and has common origins and stereotypic (if unconscious) manifestations across cultures. Culture as such begins to infiltrate the intimate transactions of the reciprocal phase, dictating the persons involved in these exchanges, but not the idiosyncratic and subjective aspects of the relationship between the developing individual and the developmental sponsor. These relationships are shaped not only by role prescriptions but also by potent transference, reflections of early primary relationships that were even less under normative cultural control. It is only in the terminal, sculptured phase that culture plays a primary role in determining the conventional expressions, the personally useful and socially valued outcomes of the developmental potentials.[2]

Comparative Perspectives on the Older Female

The comparative data from cross-cultural sources point to a striking pattern: across a wide range of societies, particularly those characterized by stable, patrilocal extended families, postparental older women move toward a position of matriarchy, sometimes overt and formal, sometimes covert and implicit. This matriarchy, official or unofficial, of later life is so apparent that it has been recorded by many anthropologists. Thus Gold (1960) asked twenty-six ethnographers, varied as to their theoretical interests, to report on *any* age-related changes in sex role in the varied groups they had studied. Fourteen reported a shift toward greater female dominance in later life. The remaining twelve reported no change. But in no case was the balance seen to swing, with advancing age, toward greater male authority over women.

While the older woman may not always be found in a position of formal dominance, her social stance and behavior is notably ascendant and aggressive. Thus far I have identified, from a variety of ethnographic accounts, five distinct patterns and facilitators of later life matriarchy.

1. The aging husband gives up interest in secular power and in the management of the home. Losing his own powers, he becomes religious and links himself, through ritual means, to the power of the gods. The aging wife, often in concert with the oldest son, moves into the socket of power and dominion that the husband has abandoned. This pattern is reported for the traditional Chinese and rural Egyptians, among others.[3]

2. Another generic family pattern allows the aging wife to gain domestic power through her son. As he attains adult status through marriage, his mother acquires a potential rival in the daughter-in-law, but also a potential servant. If the mother retains some emotional hold over the son during this transitional time when his affections shift to a wife, then she and the son may share dominion over the family, with the mother becoming a senior adviser, an *éminence grise* who works her will through her son. The daughter-in-law then becomes something of a vassal to the mother-in-law, thereby enhancing the senior woman's scope and powers.

This pattern is reported for the traditional Japanese and for the traditional Moroccans, among others.

3. The older woman acquires power, particularly in religious circles, following menopause. The ending of her procreative period makes her acceptable in sacred places and rituals on two counts: she is less sexual, less likely to stir men to lustful thoughts when their minds should be on God, and she is no longer a danger to the ritual—she will not pollute the service with her menstrual blood. Accordingly, after menopause, women can join the circle of religious dancers or take on ritual tasks that are forbidden to fertile women. This motif is probably very common, and may be synergistic with other patterns, as noted above. However, we have specific reports for Lebanese Arab villagers and the North Piegan, among others.

4. Postmenopausal life may bring an endowment of destructive rather than sacred power to the older woman: as she ages, she becomes a witch rather than a priestess. In some instances, this occult transformation is based in family dynamics. Thus, the older woman does not always establish complete dominion, and there is chronic tension between her and those in her purview—the daughter-in-law or the husband. Under these conditions, the frustrated older women is often suspected of trying to have her way with the aid of supernatural allies, enlisted through witchcraft practices. This pattern has been noted for the Kikuyu and the Aranda, among others. But whether or not the above family dynamics are involved, the linking of the aging female with occult power is widespread.

5. Finally, the last transition, into death, can transform the older woman into a vessel of malign powers: unlike her milder spouse, in death she becomes an evil, retributive spirit, as reported for the Ainu, the Maori, the Tallensi, and the Yoruba, among others.

The above list refers mainly to folk-traditional societies; it is in these settings that the older woman's metamorphosis takes place via events and traditions that are explicit, culturally recognized, and even culturally sponsored. However, we have a number of reports from Western societies in which the same social and psychological transformations are noted (even though their manifestations are more subtle and less stereotyped). Again, the observers of Western societies report the usual outcome—the elevation of the older woman to new (but secular rather than supernatural) realms of influence—though usually without describing the transformative process. Thus later-life matriarchy may be facilitated by certain clear customs and usages of the traditional society, but it does not require them. These transformations occur, apparently with much the same regularity, in secular and nontraditional societies, including those in which elder-matriarchy is not sponsored by shared and rooted customs.

Primatological Studies of the Aging Female

Recent studies of aging among nonhuman primates indicate that the virilization of the older primate female may be general not only across human societies but across species as well.[4] Thus Hrdy (1981), who conducted field studies of the langur monkeys and of the very successful macaques (successful in the evolutionary sense: they are distributed across a wide range of varied habitats) finds that, like the majority of younger human mothers, a monkey mother is devoted almost exclusively to the care of the latest infant, the one still clinging to her fur. She is at the same time relatively inoffensive in her dealings with other adults; thus, during the period of intense parenting, she allies herself with dominant males and trades sexual access for their physical protection. However, in the postparental years a striking change occurs that parallels our cross-cultural observations among humans. Hrdy notes that the way in which older monkeys support younger animals "seems to vary with the sex of the animal and the situation of the group. Males generally bow out leaving older females to intervene actively in the fate of their descendants" (1981:75). In effect, female primates have two roles in regard to procreation: they provide physical as well as emotional security though—consistent with the exclusivity of these roles—they play them out sequentially rather than concurrently. As Hrdy reports: "When a troop of langurs is threatened by dogs or humans, or by encroachments upon its territory by other langurs, it is typically the adult male *or the oldest females* who leave the rest of the troop to charge and slap at the offenders" (1981:73, italics added). Similarly, courageous and persistent defense of younger relatives by older females has been documented for Japanese and rhesus macaques by Partch (1978), who recorded 572 separate instances of protection or defense of infants by postreproductive females, on occasions when breeding females did not take up defense of their own offspring.

Clearly, then, postreproductive female primates take up the defender's role that we had thought to be reserved for young and vigorous males. The breeding mothers are almost exclusively providers of emotional security, but, like males, the postreproductive female moves at times of danger not to the protected center of the troop but to its outer defense line.

Male View of the Older Woman

Not only cultural anthropologists and primatologists see the older woman as masculinized. Though they may, in their public behavior, deny her ascendance, across cultures older men represent the dominant woman in their more private fantasies and projections. I have gathered Thematic Apperception Test (TAT) data from younger and older men in urban areas in the United States and among the Navajo, Mexican Maya, and Druze, using stimuli that elicit covert conceptions of male-female relationships. The results are best summed up by the "heterosexual conflict" card of the standard TAT, which shows a young man half turned away from a young woman who reaches toward him in a restraining or pleading manner. Younger men—urban Americans, Maya, Navajo, or Druze—propose that the young man brushes aside a beseeching or timorous woman and forges out into a dangerous but exciting world of combat, carousal, and mistresses. Thus, for younger men, the sexes are sharply distinguished: the young man pushes toward some extradomestic periphery without much regard for consequences; inhibition and timidity are mainly located in the woman. But to the same stimulus older men propose more anergic, constricted, or "pregenital" themes. In their version the young woman tends to domineer or the male protagonist retreats back to her consolation and away from a world in which he has known danger and defeat. In either case, initiatives and strength have migrated away from the young man toward the young woman. Finally, for many older men, the male protagonist does not reject the nurturance offered by the young woman but instead dwells with her in contentment and harmony. Potential trouble comes from outside, not within the dyad, and menaces the young man and woman equally.

These age shifts appear to be developmental rather than secular in nature. Thus they appear with some predictability across a panel of disparate cultures, where the drift of generational, cultural change has been different in each case. Within cultures, these changes in sex-role perceptions show up in longitudinal as well as cross-sectional data— evidence that the original age × theme distributions of responses to this card were produced by psychological changes within individuals and not by intercohort differences having to do with generational changes in the various cultures. Thus, as they age, men are increasingly prone to assign dominance to the female figure and to see the younger man as her satellite; and this intraindividual change proceeds independently of culture.

This same sex-role turnover is dramatically captured by another card, used only among the Druze, which, for most subjects, elicits concerns around intergenerational and intermale relations and lines of authority. Almost invariably, Druze men below the age of sixty see the card as depicting relations between an executive or advisory older man and usually compliant boys or younger men. However, a number of men over sixty see the older man as a beggar, asking for food or money from a woman, who may or may not indulge him. Again, the tendency to turn a compliant young man into a dominant woman and to turn an authoritative old man into a beggar is not a cohort phenomenon, limited to a particular generation of Druze men. Longitudinal studies with this card reveal that nine Druze, all but one over sixty, who saw the older man as an authority at Time 1 see him as a beggar by Time 2.[5]

Engines of Later Growth

In sum, external observers of the older woman, whether these be anthropologists or the women's aging husbands, agree that they change drastically in the later years, showing aggressive and managerial powers that were only latent in their makeup before this postparental advance. In effect they become androgynous, sexually bimodal, a mixture, as many observers have put it, of mother and father. I would argue that these transformations, inasmuch as they fit the model of maturation set forth earlier, are *developmental* in nature and betoken a reliable pattern of growth for postparental women across a wide range of "average-expectable" human environments. Some cultural anthropologists would dispute such a developmental formulation. They would assert that such changes have an exogenous rather than an endogenous basis and are in each case a result of social opportunities that are made available to older women in the second half of life. The office has sought the candidate rather than the other way around.

Culturalist explanations, which lay stress on causes that are unique to each society, ignore an outcome that is found in all postparental female transitions. Whether old women become matriarchs or witches, a common factor underlies all these sundry transformations, namely, the general increase in their powers. Power always bears a double face. In most cases—as when they become matriarchs—older women acquire a new endowment of good power. In other cases—as when they are reputed to be witches—older women acquire bad power. But in all cases their potencies increase and give evidence of a surgent developmental event. Thus the transcultural variety in the older woman's role acquisitions registers the disparate effects of the local culture's parochial age norms and social opportunities, as these determine the phenotypic, *sculptured* developmental phase. By the same token, the generic increase in social and personal *power* registers the effects of the *genotypic,* or *eruptive* phase of development.

The fact that the older woman's postparental, liberated energies have been transmuted and sculpted into a wide array of structures by their impact with the larger social order does not negate either their reality or their developmental origins. Finally, it is this protean potency of the older woman, notable precisely because it invigorates so many disparate roles, that signals the presence of a unitary endogenous phenomenon, rather than many unrelated parochial and fortuitous social phenomena.[6]

I have contended that the phenotypic virility of the older woman is released when she emerges from the adult period of chronic emergency that we call parenting (Gutmann 1975, 1987). I have proposed that when her children show that they can maintain their own emotional security, the postparental woman can reclaim the aggression that, earlier on, would have put her children at risk. In effect, they take back into themselves the aggressive energy lived out vicariously during their parental years through identification with the prowess and exploits of the husband. Thus the postparental woman is energized to seek out, to take advantage of, and even to create the powerful roles that fit her expanded energies and new appetites. She is not merely reactive to expanded social opportunity but is also proactive in creating new leadership possibilities. Hence, just as the effects of the original "Big Bang" can still be traced in all the varied celestial phenomena of our universe, the energies of the eruptive phase, the energies originally released by the female exit from active parenting, can still be read in all the social activities, malign or beneficial, of the older woman.

Eruptive Energies: A Case Example

The reality of the eruptive phase can be inferred from the common features of the transcultural data—the reported energy that is ubiquitous across the older woman's role acquisitions. But the eruptive stage can also be studied more directly, via instruments that are available to the dynamically oriented psychologist but very rarely used by anthropologists. The Rorschach test, for example, presents unfamiliar, "strange" stimuli and thereby elicits interpretations metaphoric of the "stranger"—the unsocialized strivings within the personality. As such, the responses to standard psychological tests capture (if one accepts the logic of projection) tracings of the presocial eruptive phase as it shapes the response imagery. In short, the projectives provide "opportunity structures" for the respondent to externalize and review dangerous fantasies and images—the derivatives of surgent energies that have not yet been socially sculptured and normalized. Thus, as we can see in the following case study and Rorschach protocol, the projectives permit us to experience and *study* the derivatives of motives that not only cannot be expressed in public behavior, but that are specifically *denied* through such behavior.

The eruptive aggression of the older woman can lead to rivalry with men, and particularly with the husband; and this change in family politics can bring about a crisis of psychiatric proportions in older women, particularly if the older husband's health or fortunes are low enough to arouse a feeling of guilt in the wife. Thus, in our work at Northwestern Medical School, we find that many women come to psychiatric treatment for the first time in the postparental years, too often with a misdiagnosis of "depression." Such was the case with the fifty-three-year-old Polish-American woman whose Rorschach record is summarized below.

This patient comes to outpatient treatment in an anxious, weepy state and appears so needy that her novice therapist is reluctant to take her on, fearing that she will be "swallowed up." However, the Rorschach imagery is not consistent with the patient's weak, depressive presentation. Her first response visualizes two bulls in combat: "They're in battle, have hurt each other because there is blood spattering from them; both have collided or have been fighting, have locked horns or tusks." Her fourth response features "an eruption of some kind, with clouds and volcanic acid spewing over the sides." This is followed by "an eagle in flight." But the essential communication is contained in the seventh response, elicited by a stimulus area that normally provokes "phallic" imagery and associations: "It looks like an explosion of something—a coming up of creation. It looks like a butterfly, a beautiful butterfly, but like it broke loose. It's coming out of its cocoon. Out of eruption comes a work of nature. Looks like it would be all rainbow colors, like Niagara Falls. Out of eruption comes a spray of multicolors."

Clearly, this is not the imagery of a truly depressed woman. These are images given by a woman who is both fascinated and terrified by the powerful "masculine" and alien energies—represented by antlered deer, fighting bulls, eagles, and volcanoes—that are eruptive within her. These energies could lead on toward a rebirth (the butterfly emerging from a cocoon) in a more "phallic" masculine form; but rebirth necessarily entails the token death of the established, familiar self, as well as the possibility of combat and destruction (the deer that guard their territory, the bulls that collide and fight). Like anthropologists, psychiatrists are prone to view the older woman in externalized terms, and they typically blame this patient's kind of pain on outward and imposed losses: of beauty, of procreative capacity, of the "mothering role," or of the husband. However, when we explore her unconscious fantasies, we find evidence of eruptive energies that are not consistent with such passive victimization and that are at the same time responsible for the symptoms leading to the glibly rendered diagnosis of "depression."

In this instance, the patient was literally poisoned, in the psychological sense, by her own potential strengths. She treated them as though they were foreign invaders and developed psychological antibodies that—just as physical antigens produce fever—in her case produced agitated, weepy depression. Because of her early life in a family of orientation that taught her to fear aggression and because of her marriage to a husband who needs a submissive wife, her crescent energies could not move beyond the eruptive phase, and her shackled aggression turned inward, taking the form of self-punishing symptoms. It was only when she found the reciprocator and facilitator, in the person of the psychotherapist, that her aggression could find a more alloplasmic expression and become available for "sculpting" into more personally and socially useful forms. In effect, the therapist took over and performed a self-function that the patient lacked—that of recognizing and welcoming her own assertiveness— and the therapist demonstrated that function, until the patient could take over and exercise the function for herself.

Conclusion: Development or Victimization?

This example from the ranks of the stricken teaches us that late-onset, postparental female psychopathology can have a base in development rather than depletion and that the causes are often reversible rather than (as is commonly proposed) irreversible. By supplying the missing facilitator, the practice of psychotherapy can return the patient to the main sequence of female maturation in later life.

Cases like this teach us that the energies driving later-life female development exist apart from and can be studied apart from the social roles and stations into which they are finally articulated. To repeat, the clear and obvious advance of most postparental women across the most varied social settings is a culture-free phenomenon, one that can generate psychopathology as well as useful role adoptions. And while the culture-centered view can help us to understand socially normal outcomes of development, it is not useful in helping us to understand the abnormal outcomes that result when phenotypic energies do not achieve the sculptured phase and are sidetracked into pathology. In addition, a view of the older woman that ignores her developmental potentials has its own pathogenic effect: when the more hopeful, growth-centered possibilities of the older woman are ignored by social scientists, the "depletion" view, the denigrating view of the older woman as perpetual victim, becomes paramount.

NOTES

1. Speaking as an outsider, it seems to me that having such a limited, exclusive focus on cultural variables has a stultifying effect. Anthropology is potentially the most creative and enlightening of the social sciences, and we are all losers when it locks itself into a discipline-centered, defensive parochialism.

2. The dialectic relationship between the surgent and the socializing aspects of development shapes two major advances: the formation of self-boundaries and the acquisition of language—both equally vital to individual growth and social

continuity. Thus culture may dictate, for the child, the qualities and properties of the social *other;* but the readiness on the child's part to create self-other distinctions, to recognize the social other whatever her or his properties, constitutes a psychosocial and developmental advance of vast consequence, one that *must* take place in all viable cultures. By the same token, culture dictates the content and syntax of language but it does not dictate the child's developmentally given readiness to actively *seek out* language and to turn parents into language providers.

3. For additional examples for each of the patterns and for the ethnographic sources, the reader is advised to contact the author (also see Gutmann 1987).

4. Certain crucial similarities among primates allow us to make what are more than accidental interspecies comparisons. Most significantly, human and nonhuman primates have in common the long dependency and vulnerability of infancy and childhood. In both nonhuman and human primates, the infant may have—as we are beginning to discover—some developed communicative and social skills, but it is almost completely lacking in the skills that ensure physical security: it cannot move in any coherent fashion, it cannot remove itself from danger, and it can barely secure its own milk. Among the lower primates, the infant has, at best, the guaranteed capacity to cling, during the first months of life, to its mother's fur. Of necessity then, adult primates—whether human or otherwise—have in common an intense concern with parenting.

5. By the same token, the age distribution of "beggarly man, authoritative woman" themes does not reflect the influence of Druze age-graded prescriptions. The Druze are a fiercely independent people, and it is not proper for a man to beg—particularly from a woman—at any age.

6. Like other behavioral scientists (including developmental psychologists), anthropologists make imperial claims for the cultural variables that they "own"; and they will claim that these are the independent variables that ultimately account for all major patterns of human behavior. By definition, the sculpted phase involves the final fitting in and adaptation of the individual to prior role formats; and the anthropologist who has not observed the connections between the eruptive and sculptured phases can always claim that the latter outcome was "created" by prior social opportunity rather than by prior, intrinsic development. However, such ad hoc, culture-based interpretations become less plausible and more cumbersome with each fresh observation from another culture and another independent observer.

REFERENCES

Gold, Sue Schlenker
    1960   A Cross-cultural Comparison of Changes with Aging in Husband-Wife
           Roles. Student Journal of Human Development (University of Chicago)
           1:11–15.
Gutmann, David
    1975   Parenthood: A Key to the Comparative Study of the Life Cycle. *In* Life

Span Developmental Psychology: Normative Life Crises. N. Datan and L. Ginsberg, eds. pp. 167–84. New York: Academic Press.

1987　Reclaimed Powers: Toward a New Psychology of Men and Women in Later Life. New York: Basic Books.

Hrdy, Sarah Blaffer

1981　"Nepotists" and "Altruists": The Behavior of Old Females among Macaques and Langur Monkeys. *In* Other Ways of Growing Old: Anthropological Perspectives. P. Amoss and S. Harrell, eds., pp. 59–76. Stanford, Calif.: Stanford University Press.

Partch, Jennifer

1978　The Socializing Role of Post-reproductive Rhesus Macaque Females. Paper presented at the Forty-seventh Annual Meeting of the American Association of Physical Anthropologists. Toronto.

Notes on Contributors

AARON ANTONOVSKY received his Ph.D. in sociology from Yale University in 1955. He is Kunin-Lunefeld Professor of Medical Sociology in the Faculty of Health Sciences, Ben-Gurion University of the Negev, Beersheba, Israel. His most recent book is *Unraveling the Mystery of Health*. He is currently conducting a longitudinal study on stress, coping, and health in the retirement transition.

JANICE BODDY received her Ph.D. in anthropology from the University of British Columbia in 1982. She is currently assistant professor of anthropology at the University of Toronto. Her research interests include gender roles and constructs, the Middle East and North Africa, and feminist theory in the postmodern context. She is the author of *Wombs and Alien Spirits: Women, Men, and the Zār Cult in Northern Sudan*.

JUDITH K. BROWN earned an Ed.D. in human development from Harvard University in 1962 and is currently professor of anthropology at Oakland University. Her research interests have had a "life course of their own," beginning with a thesis on initiation rites for girls, moving on to the study of women's economic roles and their relationship to child rearing, and finally to the lives of middle-aged women. Her most recent research centers on wife beating and wife battering, and she is a co-editor of *Sanctions and Sanctuary: Cultural Perspectives on Violence against Women*.

DOROTHY AYERS COUNTS is professor and chair of the Department of Anthropology at the University of Waterloo. She received her Ph.D. in 1968 from Southern Illinois University and has conducted periodic field research in West New Britain Province, Papua New Guinea, since 1966. She has published papers and books on a range of topics, including political change and development, the analysis of myth, and aging in the Pacific. Several publications on female suicide and on domestic violence are forthcoming. She is a co-editor of *Sanctions and Sanctuary: Cultural Perspectives on Violence against Women.*

The late NANCY DATAN received her Ph.D. in human development from the University of Chicago in 1971. She taught at West Virginia University (1973–84) and at the University of Wisconsin, Green Bay (1984–87), and published numerous articles on adult development. She was a co-author of *A Time to Reap: The Middle Age of Women in Five Israeli Subcultures.*

DAVID GUTMANN received his Ph.D. from the University of Chicago and is now professor of psychiatry and education, as well as director of the Older Adult Program at Northwestern University. He has published articles on the psychology of later life and is the author of a recent book, *Reclaimed Powers: Toward a New Psychology of Men and Women in Later Life.*

PATRICIA A. KAUFERT earned a Ph.D. in sociology from the University of Birmingham in 1976 and is currently an associate professor in the Department of Community Health Sciences at the University of Manitoba. She has published extensively on the topics of childbirth and menopause. Her most recent article is "The Politics of Obstetric Care: The Inuit Experience" (with J. O'Neill).

VIRGINIA KERNS received her Ph.D. in anthropology from the University of Illinois in 1977 and is now professor and chair of the Department of Anthropology at the College of William and Mary. She is the author of *Women and the Ancestors: Black Carib Kinship and Ritual* and a former associate editor of the *American Ethnologist.* Her research interests center on gender and the life course.

BARBARA J. KING is a biological anthropologist who specializes in the study of primate behavior. She received her Ph.D. in anthropology from the University of Oklahoma in 1989 and is currently assistant professor of anthropology at the College of William and Mary. She has published a number of papers on primate cognition. The topic of her current research and writing is social information transfer by monkeys, apes, and hominids.

MICHAEL LAMBEK earned his Ph.D. in anthropology from the University of Michigan in 1978 and is associate professor of anthropology at the University of Toronto. His major research interests include ethnomedicine, spirit possession, ritual, kinship, and gender. He is the author of *Human Spirits: A Cultural Account of Trance in Mayotte* and numerous articles, the most recent being "Certain Knowledge, Contestable Authority: Power and Practice on the Islamic Periphery."

JANE B. LANCASTER, professor of anthropology at the University of New Mexico, earned her Ph.D. in anthropology from the University of California, Berkeley, in 1967. She is the author or co-editor of several books, including *Parenting across the Lifespan: Biosocial Dimensions* and *Offspring Abuse and Neglect: Biosocial Dimensions.* Her research interests center on human reproduction, parental investment strategies, and the evolution of human behavior. She currently serves as scientific editor of *Human Nature.*

RICHARD B. LEE is professor of anthropology at the University of Toronto. He received his Ph.D. in anthropology from the University of California, Berkeley, in 1965. His publications include many articles on the !Kung and several books: *The !Kung San: Men, Women, and Work in a Foraging Society, The Dobe !Kung,* and *Politics and History in Band Societies* (coeditor, with Eleanor Leacock).

MARGARET LOCK, professor of medical anthropology at McGill University, received her Ph.D. in anthropology from the University of California, Berkeley, in 1976. She is the author of numerous articles and the author or editor of several books, including *East Asian Medicine in Urban Japan: Varieties of Medical Experience, Biomedicine Examined* (with Deborah Gordon), and *Health, Illness and Medical Care in Japan: Cultural and Social Dimensions* (coeditor, with Edward Norbeck). Her major research interests are the anthropology of the body, life-cycle transitions, and culture and technomedicine.

BENJAMIN MAOZ trained in psychiatry at Ben-Gurion University of the Negev and is currently head of the Psychiatric Department at the Soroca Medical Center in Israel. His research interests center on psychiatry and family medicine. He is a co-author of *A Time to Reap: The Middle Age of Women in Five Israeli Subcultures.*

DOUGLAS RAYBECK received his Ph.D. in anthropology from Cornell University and is now professor of anthropology at Hamilton College. His major research interests are deviance, cognitive systems, nonverbal communication, and psycholinguistics. Based on his fieldwork in West Malaysia, he has published extensively on the cognitive strategies employed by Kelantanese Malays in managing their cultural and social situations.

KAREN BRODKIN SACKS is director of the Women's Studies Program and a member of the Department of Anthropology at UCLA. She is the author of *Sisters and Wives: The Past and Future of Sexual Equality, My Troubles Are Going to Have Trouble with Me: Everyday Trials and Triumphs of Working Women* (with Dorothy Remy), and *Caring by the Hour*.

KAREN P. SINCLAIR is professor of anthropology at Eastern Michigan University and former head of Women's Studies. She received her Ph.D. in anthropology from Brown University in 1976. Her research interests include Maori (New Zealand) religion, gender ideology, and the cultural construction of identity. Her publications include articles on these topics as well as several chapters in *The Cross-cultural Study of Women*. She is currently writing a book about Maori prophesy and the cultural construction of history.

JACQUELINE S. SOLWAY is assistant professor of women's studies at the University of Toronto. She received a Ph.D. in anthropology from the University of Toronto in 1987. Her most recent publication (co-authored with Richard B. Lee) is "Foragers, Genuine or Spurious?: Situating the Kalahari San in History." She is currently writing a book on the political economy of the region in Botswana where she conducted fieldwork.

SYLVIA VATUK received her Ph.D. in anthropology from Harvard University in 1970 and is now professor of anthropology at the University of Illinois at Chicago. Her research interests include family, kinship, and gender roles in India and South Asia, and she has published extensively on these topics. At present she is working on an ethnographic and historical study of a Muslim family in southern India over a period of two hundred years. The focus of this research is the changing lives of women.

BEATRICE BLYTH WHITING is distinguished scholar at the Henry A. Murray Research Center for the Study of Lives, Radcliffe College, and professor emeritus of anthropology and education at the Harvard Graduate School of Education. She earned a Ph.D. in anthropology from Yale University in 1942. Her most recent publication is *Children of Different Worlds: The Formation of Social Behavior* (with Carolyn P. Edwards).

Index

Adoption. *See* Fosterage
Adultery. *See* Infidelity
Africa. *See* Bakgalagadi; Hazda; !Kung San;
    Mayotte; Sudan; Tuareg
Age. *See* Seniority
Age groups: among Bakgalagadi, 50–51; in
    Mayotte, 79–80, 87, 91n3
Agnatic descent. *See* Kinship
Ahern, Emily, 184
Alexander, Richard, 17
Amoss, Pamela, 17.
Antonovsky, Aaron, 4, 191, 193
Arabs. *See* Israel; Sudan
Asia. *See* Bengali; China; India; Japan;
    Malays; Sri Lanka; Taiwan; Tamil
Asmat, 70
Australian Aborigines, 43
Autonomy: 2, 49, 51, 52, 62, 67, 83, 87, 90,
    98, 103, 107, 108n10, 146, 147, 148,
    149

Babb, Lawrence A., 166.
Bakgalagadi, 3, 31, 49–56
Barnett, Rosalind C., 17, 27n3
Baruch, Grace K., 17, 27n3
Bart, Pauline, 17
Batswana, 50
Belize, 98
Bella Coola, 42
Bengali, 25, 161, 203

Beyene, Yewoubdar, 12
Biesele, Megan, 36
Bilateral kinship. *See* Kinship
Birth control. *See* Contraception
Black Carib. *See* Garífuna
Boddy, Janice, 5, 139
Botswana, 35, 53
Breastfeeding. *See* Lactation
Bridewealth. *See* Marriage payments
Brown, Judith K., 1, 2, 6, 61, 91,
    108n4, 113, 150, 155, 156, 173, 182,
    183
Buddhism, 162–63, 178

Canada. *See* North America
Carstairs, G. Morris, 161
Catholicism, 123, 124, 130
Celibacy, 97, 101, 160, 165–66
Childbirth, 11, 52, 100, 104, 152. *See also*
    Pregnancy
Child care, 19, 24, 37–38, 85, 86, 113, 122.
    See also Fosterage
Childlessness, 79, 96, 102, 108n8, 145, 147,
    149
Children: marriage of, 39; preference for
    female, 175; preference for male, 145,
    179, 183; sexuality of, 38; value of, 66,
    86, 98, 175, 179. *See also* Child care;
    Female infanticide; Fosterage; Mortality
China, 5, 25, 173–74, 178–84, 224

Christianity. *See* Catholicism
Climacterium. *See* Menopause
Clitoridectomy. *See* Pharaonic circumcision
Colonialism, 78, 115, 122–23, 126
Comoro Islands. *See* Mayotte
Confucianism, 173, 178–79, 205
Contraception: absence or avoidance of, 38, 64, 103, 119; and the state, 96; use of, 197
Counts, Dorothy Ayers, 3, 31

Datan, Nancy, 4, 191, 194
David, Kenneth, 156, 164
Depression: absence or infrequency at menopause, 4, 64, 198, 213; misdiagnosis of, 230; mentioned, 193, 195, 207, 208, 209
Descent. *See* Kinship
Deutsch, Helene, 207
Division of labor. *See* Men; Gender segregation; Work, women's
Divorce or separation: in China, 180; among Garífuna, 99, 104; grounds for, 69, 82, 83, 85, 99, 104, 145–46, 180; initiated by women, 39, 69–70, 81, 85, 149, 177; among Lusi, 69–70; among Kelantan Malays, 175, 176, 177; among !Kung San, 39; in Mayotte, 81, 82, 83; in northern Sudan, 144, 145–46, 148, 149, 150. *See also* Remarriage
DNA fingerprinting, 102, 109n15
Domestic violence: 66, 117, 131. *See also* Wife beating
Dowry. *See* Marriage payments
Draper, Patricia, 36
Druze, 227, 228
Dupré, G., 43

Economic roles. *See* Men; Work, women's
Education, 51, 54, 90, 133n2, 206, 210. *See also* Literacy
Edwards, Carolyn, 133n5
Employment. *See* Labor Migration; Men; Wage Labor, Work, women's
Europeans: as colonizers, 78, 98, 114, 115, 116, 117; as immigrants, 193–98 passim, 211
Extramarital relations. *See* Infidelity

Family honor, 107, 145, 152n6, 155, 156, 160
Family structure. *See* Household structure; Kinship; Residence (postmarital)
Fathers, 31, 52, 63, 65, 71, 104, 105, 108, 109n18, 180, 181. *See also* Paternal certainty
Female infanticide, 179
Female life course: continuity in, 71–72, 78, 80, 91, 113, 125, 178; transitions in, 35, 43, 51, 56, 78, 79, 95–96, 145, 147. *See also* Middle age in women; Middle-aged women; Menopause; Old age
Female sexuality: conflict about, 39, 44; cultural construction of, 5, 97, 100–103, 156–58, 160–67; after menopause, 44, 101, 156–57, 161–67; social control of, 63, 65, 95–97, 103–6, 108, 159. *See also* Celibacy; Fertility; Infidelity; Menopause; Menstruation; Pharaonic circumcision; Purdah; Surveillance; Virginity
Feminism, 1, 209, 215
Fertility: cessation of, 7, 10, 11, 78, 96, 103, 106, 107–8n3, 207; and completed family size, 37, 119, 197, 213; control of women's, 95, 106, 144, 145; dysfunction, 101–2, 145–46; loss of welcomed, 64, 92, 163–64, 191, 197, 198. *See also* Contraception; Infertility; Menopause; Reproductive span
Firth, Rosemary, 177
Flinn, Mark, 108
Flint, Marcha, 12, 17
Forster, J., 115
Fortes, Meyer, 51
Fosterage: among Garífuna, 98; among Lusi, 66, 72; among Maori, 122; in Mayotte, 84–85, 86; mentioned, 18
Freud, Sigmund, 207, 208, 209
Friedl, Ernestine, 183
Fry, Christine, 17

Garífuna, 1, 3, 5, 31, 75, 95–107
Gaulin, S. J. C., 17, 26
Gender ideology, 32, 44, 50, 63, 90, 97, 117–19, 127, 132, 173, 175, 178–79, 205–6
Gender segregation, 24, 51, 56n2, 105, 118, 119–22, 144, 152n6, 157–58

Gerontocracy, 43
Gilligan, Carol, 27
Gold, Sue Schlenker, 224
Gosden, R. G., 10, 107–8n3
Grandmothers: age of, 52, 79; relations with grandchildren, 79, 122, 166, 185–86; in ritual, 163; mentioned, 8, 64, 120, 145
Griffen, Joyce, 17, 113
Gutmann, David, 6, 178, 182

Hames, Raymond, 8
Harper, Edward B., 161, 166–7
Harrell, Stevan, 17
Hart, G. L., 161
Hawkes, Kristen, 8
Hayes, Rose Oldfield, 147
Hazda, 8
Health, women's, 131–32, 133n3, 134n12, 184, 193, 197, 201–17 passim. *See also* Medical models
Hershman, Paul, 156
Heuer, Berys, 118
Hinduism, 158–60, 162–63
Ho Ping-ti, 179
Household headship, 52, 53, 181, 182
Household structure, 24–26, 50, 52, 62, 80, 90, 141, 207, 213, 214. *See also* Residence (postmarital)
House ownership. *See* Property ownership
Howell, Nancy, 12, 36, 37
Hrdy, Sarah Blaffer, 226
Hunter, Monica, 1

Illegitimacy, 99, 155
Impotence, 161
Inclusive fitness, 7–8
India, 5, 12, 139, 155–67
Indians. *See* Native Americans
Infanticide. *See* Female infanticide
Infant mortality. *See* Mortality
Infertility: at adolescence, 39, 100; perceived causes of, 101–2, 104; mentioned, 79, 107–8n3, 149. *See also* Childlessness; Fertility; Lactational amenorrhea; Menopause
Infidelity: by middle-aged women, 41, 64, 106; and paternal certainty, 96–97, 104, 109; and violence, 40, 44, 69, 108n9; mentioned, 70, 99, 101, 103, 104, 105

Inheritance: nonpatrilineal, 5, 81; patrilineal, 50, 179; of property by women, 54, 81, 144, 149, 150, 175; mentioned, 151n1, 152n2
Involutional psychosis. *See* Depression
Iroquois, 27
Islam, 4, 25, 78, 89, 90, 141, 150, 152n7, 175, 177, 185, 186, 195
Israel, 4, 17, 191, 193–98. *See also* Druze

Jacobson, Doranne, 161
Japan, 4, 191, 201–7, 209–17, 225
Johnson, Virginia, 101
Judaism, 195
Jung, Carl G., 6, 22, 209, 216

Kakar, Sudhir, 161, 162
Kaufert, Patricia A., 4, 17, 191
Kehoe, Alice, 113
Kelantan. *See* Malays
Kemper, Steven, 163
Kerns, Virginia, 1, 2, 3, 17, 27n2, 75
King, Barbara J., 1
Kinsey, Alfred C., 109n14
Kinship: bilateral, 26, 84, 98, 175; matrilineal, 26; patrilineal, 3, 5, 26, 50, 62, 71, 142, 178; women's knowledge of, 40–41, 43, 52, 86, 148–49
Kung San, 5, 8, 11, 12, 31, 32, 35–44

Labor migration, 35, 50, 54, 99, 116, 141, 145, 185
Lactation, 12, 38, 64, 197
Lactational amenorrhea, 12, 38, 64
Lambek, Michael, 4, 75
Lancaster, Chet S., 9
Lancaster, Jane, 1, 9
Language, 35, 50, 62, 77–78, 98, 122, 126, 129, 141, 156, 211
Lee, Richard B., 3, 31, 32
Life course. *See* Female life course; Male life course
Life expectancy, 10, 11, 36, 131, 133n2
Life span, 8, 36, 131
Literacy, 195
Lock, Margaret, 4, 191
Lusi, 5, 31, 61–72

McDaniel, Susan A., 215–16
McGilvray, D. B., 162

Madagascar, 77, 78

Malays, 3, 4, 5, 139, 173–78, 182–86

Male life course, 43, 52, 56, 80, 114, 119, 120, 158–59

Male sexuality: beliefs about, 101, 159–60; control of, 159. *See also* Celibacy; Impotence; Infidelity

Maori, 3, 4, 75, 113–32, 225

Maoz, Benjamin, 4, 191, 193, 194

Marital status. *See* Divorce or separation; Marriage; Remarriage; Single Women; Widows

Marriage: age at, 25, 39, 119, 145, 195; among Bakgalagadi, 50; among Chinese, 179–81, 183; among Garífuna, 98, 99; in India, 158, 159, 163, 165–66; among Kelantan Malays, 175, 176, 177, 183, 186; among Lusi, 62, 63, 65; among Maoris, 119; in Mayotte, 78, 80–83; in northern Sudan, 141–42, 143–46, 152n6. *See also* Divorce or separation; Fertility; Infidelity; Marriage payments; Polygyny; Remarriage; Residence (post-marital); Widows; Wife beating

Marriage payments: bridewealth, 50, 55, 56n4, 65, 144, 176; dowry, 81, 92n5, 176, 179

Marshall, Lorna, 36, 39

Masters, William, 101

Matrilineal descent. *See* Kinship

Matrilocal residence. *See* Residence (postmarital)

Maya, 203, 227

Mayer, Peter J., 7, 8, 17

Mayotte (Comoro Islands), 4, 75, 77–91

Mead, Hirini Moko, 128

Medical models: 100–103 passim, 159–61, 162, 193, 203–17 passim

Meillassoux, Claude, 6, 22, 43

Men: and interethnic relations, 122, 126; at middle age, 43, 44, 52, 53, 55, 63, 69, 79, 82, 114, 120, 227; work roles of, 36–37, 51, 52, 54, 67, 81, 83, 99, 105, 125, 130, 133n2, 141, 215; *See also* Fathers; Gender ideology; Gender segregation; Male life course; Male sexuality

Menarche: age at, 11, 37, 100; mentioned, 78, 147. *See also* Menstruation

Menopause: age at, 7, 11, 12, 102–3, 146; anthropological research on, 17, 201–3; attitudes of women toward, 12, 63, 64, 71, 92n8, 162, 163, 191, 194, 198; cultural significance of, 42–43, 62, 71, 78, 162–63, 197; defined as deficiency or disease, 208, 215; evolution of, 1, 7–11; historic changes in, 11–12; and hormone replacement therapy, 205, 207, 208, 215; medical models of, 203–17 passim; in nonhuman primates, 9–10; psychological views of, 198, 207–8; and sexuality, 5, 44, 101, 155–57, 160, 161–62; and stereotypes, 207; symptoms of, 11, 12, 64, 163, 203–4; mentioned, 22, 61, 64, 66, 107, 147, 150, 197, 225. *See also* Depression; Middle age in women

Menstruation: beliefs about, 21, 63–64, 118, 155, 160, 225; infrequency of, 12, 64; mentioned, 39, 61, 100, 103, 104, 152n5, 195. *See also* Lactational amenorrhea; Menarche; Menopause; Pollution

Middle-aged men. *See* Men

Middle-aged women: arrangement of marriages by, 3, 20, 31, 41, 65, 86, 142, 150, 181; as assertive or aggressive, 40, 178, 181–82, 228, 229, 230–31; authority and power of, 2, 3, 19–20, 43, 51, 67, 72, 90, 107, 115, 142, 152n9, 166–67, 224, 225, 228; autonomy of, 2, 51, 62; as caretakers of children, 66, 84, 85, 98, 122, 186; as caretakers of elderly, 85–86, 216–17; delegation of work by, 3, 19–20, 23, 24, 52, 56; dress of, 19, 40–41, 164–65; as entrepreneurs, 83, 84, 92, 150, 177, 186; financial position of, 55, 82–83, 92, 147–48, 149–50, 184, 186; as heads of compounds, 52, 53, 56; as healers, 20, 87, 90, 115, 124; health of, 163, 184, 197, 208; as household heads, 53, 181, 182; and infidelity, 41, 64, 106; knowledge and skills of, 40–41, 43, 52, 100, 102, 114–15, 122, 124, 129–30; men's perceptions of, 162, 226–27; as midwives, 4, 20, 90, 149; mobility of, 3, 19, 31, 56, 82, 105, 106, 124, 130, 150, 176; as mothers-in-law, 24, 25, 51, 65–66, 72, 180, 181, 182, 224; as nonchildbearing adults, 95, 107n2; in politics and public life, 4, 43, 53, 75, 87, 89, 91, 121–22,

Middle-aged women (*continued*) 126, 128, 132, 177–78, 213; relations with adult children, 8, 20, 21, 24, 25, 43, 52, 85, 98, 122, 131, 156, 166, 181, 182, 183, 184, 224; relations with husbands, 20, 41, 61, 70, 161, 166, 181, 186; religious or ritual roles of, 20, 39, 69, 89, 90, 97, 115, 121, 124, 149, 150, 162–63, 177, 181, 225; responsibility of, 22, 31, 53, 61–62, 71, 72, 78, 113, 114; restrictions imposed on, 164–66, 167; restrictions removed for, 3, 18–19, 32, 41–42, 61, 96, 103–4, 106, 113, 122, 125, 142, 155, 156, 165, 225; sexuality of, 5, 31, 41, 44, 64, 95, 101, 103, 106, 108, 155–67 passim; sexual joking by, 35, 42, 165; single (divorced or widowed), 86–87, 98, 147–48, 149–50, 177, 182; as social control agents, 25, 26, 75, 97, 104–7 passim, 133n4; and stress, 184, 193, 198; suicide by, 184; as witches, 184, 225, 228; and work, 8, 19–20, 23, 31, 37, 41, 55, 69, 83, 84, 85, 86, 98, 177, 178, 183–84, 186, 213–15. *See also* Grandmothers; Seniority; Widows

Middle age in women: cultural perceptions or definitions of, 108, 120, 150, 174; defined transculturally, 2, 18, 95–96, 142, 147; not a culturally marked life stage, 50–51, 77, 78, 178; psychological perspectives on, 22, 161, 162, 193, 194, 207, 208, 209, 221–31. *See also* Middle-aged women

Middle East. *See* Druze; Israel

Midwives, 4, 20, 21, 90, 149

Mobility: increased at middle age, 3, 19, 31, 56, 82, 105, 106, 124, 150, 177; of young women restricted, 19, 83, 104, 105, 144, 155, 156, 175, 176, 179; mentioned, 84, 85, 147, 149

Modesty. *See* Restrictions

Mortality: infant and child, 36, 133n2; rates, 131, 134n13

Motherhood: culturally valued, 52, 79, 86, 97, 163–64; social and legal eligibility for, 98, 145. *See also* Children; Fosterage

Mothers-in-law, 24, 25, 51, 52, 65–66, 72, 166, 180, 181

Mundurucú, 23

Murphy, Robert, 23, 42

Muslims. *See* Islam

Myerhoff, Barbara, 80

Mythology, portrayal of women in, 66, 71, 73n3, 118, 162

Namibia, 35

Native Americans, 12. *See also* Garífuna; Iroquois; Maya; Mundurucú; Navaho

Navaho, 227

Neandertals, 8

Neolocal residence. *See* Residence (postmarital)

New Guinea. *See* Lusi

New Zealand: interethnic relations in, 115–17, 129, 131; population statistics for, 116, 131, 133n2. *See also* Maori

North America: Canada, 4, 17, 191, 201–3, 207–17; United States, 7, 12, 21–22, 24, 26, 27n3, 227

Old age: attitudes toward, 43, 71, 78, 79, 85, 120; care and support in, 66, 85, 86, 175, 216–17; sex ratio in, 36, 37, 215; women in, 36, 62–63, 64, 70, 71, 72, 79, 120, 156, 166–67, 215–16; mentioned, 208. *See also* Gerontocracy

Olson, R. L., 42

Pacific. *See* Asmat; Lusi; Maori

Papua New Guinea. *See* Lusi

Parental investment, 7, 9, 11

Parenthood. *See* Fathers; Motherhood; Parental investment; Paternal certainty

Partch, Jennifer, 226

Paternal certainty, 26, 97, 99, 102, 104, 106, 107. *See also* DNA fingerprinting; Illegitimacy

Patrilineal descent. *See* Kinship

Patrilocal residence. *See* Residence (postmarital)

Pharaonic circumcision, 144, 147, 152n5

Politics and public life. *See* Men; Middle-aged women

Pollution, 63–64, 104, 118–19, 125, 155, 164, 184, 225

Polygyny, 70, 82, 83, 92, 146, 152n7

Pregnancy, 92, 100, 103, 104, 118, 145, 147, 155, 156, 166, 195. *See also* Childbirth

Premenstrual syndrome, 101

Primates (nonhuman), 9, 10, 226

Property ownership: by women, 55, 67, 80, 81, 144, 149–50, 176; mentioned, 70. *See also* Inheritance

Purdah, 25, 96, 106, 144, 149, 150, 156, 157–58

Quinn, Naomi, 65, 70

Ramsay, P., 115

Rapp, Rayna, 108n6

Raybeck, Douglas, 3, 4, 5, 139

Religion and ritual: exclusion of men from, 39; exclusion of women from, 21, 62–63, 72, 90, 118, 162–63, 177, 225; participation of women in, 20, 39, 68, 69, 89, 90, 97, 115, 118, 119, 120, 121, 123–25, 150, 162–63, 177, 181, 225. *See also* Buddhism; Catholicism; Confucianism; Hinduism; Islam; Spirit possession

Remarriage: avoided by women, 92n7, 146, 149, 177, 182; initiated by women, 147, 148, 177; leviritic, 146, 149; mentioned, 36, 41

Reproductive span: 7, 10, 11, 37, 73n2, 96, 103, 107–8n3, 195, 213. *See also* Fertility; Menarche; Menopause

Residence (postmarital): bilocal, 145, 176; matrilocal (uxorilocal), 25, 39, 80, 176; neolocal, 26; patrilocal (virilocal), 19, 24–25, 26, 50, 51, 62, 72, 145, 165, 178

Responsibility, 22, 31, 53, 61–62, 71, 72, 78, 113, 114

Restrictions: imposed at middle age, 164–66, 167; imposed on young women, 40, 51–52, 62–63, 95, 96, 97, 103–7, 118–19, 142, 155, 156, 175, 179; removed at middle age, 3, 18–19, 32, 41–42, 61, 96, 103–4, 106, 113, 122, 125, 142, 155, 156, 165, 225; removed in old age, 62–63, 72, 156. *See also* Mobility; Purdah

Rey, P., 43

Ritchie, James, 116, 134n12

Ritchie, Jane, 134n12

Rohrschach test, 229–30

Rose, Frederick G. G., 43

Ross, Ellen, 108n6

Roy, Manisha, 25, 161

Sacks, Karen B., 183

Salmond, Anne, 119, 133n4

Sanday, Peggy, 183

Schapera, Isaac, 50

Seclusion. *See* Purdah

Seniority, 67, 78–79, 87, 108n4, 180

Sexual abstinence. *See* Celibacy

Sexuality: attitudes toward, 39, 64, 100, 157–61; of children, 38; in old age, 41–42, 64, 103. *See also* Female sexuality; Male sexuality

Short, R. V., 12

Shostak, Marjorie, 36, 38, 40

Simić, Andrei, 27n6, 80

Sinclair, Karen P., 4, 75

Single women, 53, 92n7, 146, 147–48, 149–50, 177, 182. *See also* Divorce or separation; Widows

Solway, Jacqueline S., 3, 31

South Asia. *See* India; Sri Lanka

Spirit possession, 85, 90, 149

Sri Lanka, 156, 160, 163

Sterility. *See* Infertility

Strange, Heather, 174, 176, 178

Stress, 131, 133n3, 184, 193, 198

Sudan, 5, 139, 141–51

Suicide, 5, 66, 70, 184

Surveillance, 96, 97, 105, 107. *See also* Female sexuality

Taiwan, 174, 182. *See also* China

Tamil, 156, 160

Thematic Apperception Test (TAT), 226–28

Thompson, D. D., 8

Trinkhaus, Eric, 8

Tuareg, 42

United States. *See* North America

Uxorilocal residence. *See* Residence (postmarital)

Van Arsdale, Peter, 70

Vatuk, Sylvia, 3, 5, 139

Violence against women, 66, 70, 97, 145, 180. *See also* Domestic violence

Virginity: culturally valued, 145, 147; not culturally valued, 39, 106; mentioned, 95, 163

Virilocal residence. *See* Residence (postmarital)

Wage labor, 24, 35, 51, 54, 75, 78, 91n1, 99, 125, 130, 174, 185. *See also* Labor migration
Walsh, A. C., 116
West Indies, 98, 108n13
Whiting, Beatrice B., 1, 133n5
Widows: 36, 41, 55, 66, 72, 73n3, 86, 146, 149, 150, 162–63, 164, 166–67, 173, 182
Wiessner, Pauline, 36
Wife beating, 40, 63, 69–70, 72–73n1, 108
Wilson, Peter, 174
Witches, 167, 184, 225
Wolf, Arthur, 179, 182
Wolf, Margery, 179, 180, 181, 182, 184
Women: American, 7, 21–22, 24, 26, 27n3, 230–31; Asmat, 70; Bakgalagadi, 3, 31, 49–56; Bella Coola, 42; Canadian, 4, 17, 191, 201–3, 207, 217; Chinese, 5, 25, 173–74, 178–84; European immigrant, 193–98 passim, 211; Garífuna, 3, 5, 31, 75, 95–107; Greek, 203; Hazda, 8; in India, 5, 12, 25, 31, 139, 155–67;

Iroquois, 27; in Israel, 4, 191, 193–98; Japanese, 4, 191, 201–7, 209–17; Jewish, 193–98 passim; Kelantan Malay, 3, 4, 5, 139, 173–78, 182–86; !Kung San, 3, 8, 11, 31, 32, 35–44; Lusi, 5, 31, 61–73; Maori, 113–32, 225; Maya, 203; in Mayotte, 77–91; Moroccan, 25; Mundurucú, 23; Muslim, 25, 77–91, 141–51, 173–78, 182–86, 193–98 passim, 225; Sinhalese, 163; in Sri Lanka, 156, 160, 163; Sudanese, 5, 139, 141–51; Taiwanese, 174, 182; Tamil, 156.
Work, women's: in agriculture, 20, 23, 51, 56, 67, 81, 86, 105, 176; as entrepreneurs, 83, 84, 92n7, 150, 177, 186; in food processing, 20, 23; as foragers, 8, 36, 37; as full-time homemakers, 142, 205–6, 212, 214–15; in trade and marketing, 31, 41, 42, 55, 67, 68, 84, 86, 150, 176; as wage earners, 24, 54, 84, 130, 149, 186, 210–13, 214; mentioned, 52, 69, 71, 81, 98, 105, 120, 121. *See also* Child Care; Inheritance; Property ownership